Econ... ...werful

Economists and the Powerful

Convenient Theories, Distorted Facts, Ample Rewards

Norbert Häring and Niall Douglas

ANTHEM PRESS
LONDON · NEW YORK · DELHI

Anthem Press
An imprint of Wimbledon Publishing Company
www.anthempress.com

This edition first published in UK and USA 2012
by ANTHEM PRESS
75-76 Blackfriars Road, London SE1 8HA, UK
or PO Box 9779, London SW19 7ZG, UK
and
244 Madison Ave. #116, New York, NY 10016, USA

British Library Cataloguing-in-Publication Data
A catalogue record for this book is available from the British Library.

Library of Congress Cataloging-in-Publication Data
Häring, Norbert.
Economists and the powerful : convenient theories, distorted facts,
ample rewards / Norbert Häring and Niall Douglas.
p. cm.
Includes bibliographical references and index.
ISBN 978-0-85728-546-1 (alk. paper) – ISBN 978-0-85728-459-4 (pbk. :
alk. paper)
1. Economics. 2. Power (Social sciences) 3. Executives. I.
Douglas, Niall. II. Title.
HB71.H395 2012
330–dc23
2012016685

ISBN-13: 978 0 85728 546 1 (Hbk)
ISBN-10: 0 85728 546 7 (Hbk)

ISBN-13: 978 0 85728 459 4 (Pbk)
ISBN-10: 0 85728 459 2 (Pbk)

This title is also available as an eBook.

CONTENTS

INTRODUCTION

> Whether you can observe a thing or not depends on the theory which you use. It is the theory which decides what can be observed.
> —*Albert Einstein, 1926*

Americans often feel exasperated with the economic intransigence of their continental European cousins. To a typical American, the typical non-English speaking European often seems obsessed with big government, large welfare systems and making it hard to do business by interfering with capitalism. In fact, despite much rhetoric to the contrary, even Anglo-Saxon Britain is right in the middle of big-government, large-welfare European countries. The scale to which Europeans have directed economic resources toward this goal is staggering: between 2004–2009, Europe was a "lifestyle superpower" that expended €2.6 trillion (US$3.42 trillion) per annum on social protection, equal to 58 percent of the global spend, which for the rich European countries was around one-fifth of each member country's gross domestic product (GDP) (Gill and Raiser 2012). As a comparator, in 2010 the US achieved its military superpower status through 43 percent of the global military spend, more than the next 15 largest spenders combined, but costing "just" US$689 billion (Gill and Raiser 2012).

There is, of course, a rationale behind the European pattern of expenditure. Nowhere else in the developed or developing world, apart from Japan, are disability-adjusted life expectancies so high, income and educational inequalities so low, old age provision so generous, fossil fuel efficiency so high, nor regional economic convergence so typical (Gill and Raiser 2012). Despite the apparent emphasis on the equality of outcome (rather than on opportunity), every known empirical measure shows the equality of opportunity in continental Europe to be among the best in the world – and much better than in the United States, despite Americans' enduring and irrational belief to the contrary. There is ample empirical evidence suggesting that the European approach is much better economically than is typically thought by the Anglo-Saxon economic discourse. By reading this book you will gain a good introduction to this evidence from a European perspective. The wide disparity in approach to social protection by European countries is not frequently realized outside European discourse, despite the very similar net expenditure levels as a percentage of national GDP. In truth, rather than being as economically intransigent as they usually seem to non-Europeans, European countries have in fact been *experimenting* for 50 years with a variety of different forms of capitalism.

Although Asians and Latin Americans admire US economic power, as a result of the ever-increasing empirical evidence they rarely choose to use their new wealth to copy the US social model. Almost always, they choose as Europe has: tax personal income and consumption heavily but personal investment and company income lightly. They ensure that the well-to-do receive welfare entitlements just as the poor do. They ameliorate the cost of government bureaucracy by automating and streamlining it, rather than pretending to eliminate it in showy gestures while actually building an even bigger state. Over the past 15 years, European governments have been actively and successfully shrinking themselves – unlike the US government which has grown in proportion to the economy. They try to eliminate the "free rider" problem by mandating participation in endeavors beneficial to society, and they try to diffuse professions such as doctors, lawyers and especially bankers from using their *power* to extract unfair, outsized economic rents from society. This is smart, evidence-based, practical government, rather than large or small ideological government. Yet you will not hear about any of this in the conventional US economic discourse. This is because of the *power* of the vested interests who want to distract you from realizing the extent to which they have captured government and economic opportunity for themselves. They tax the middle class, destroy their job security, steal from their pensions and divert those monies into capital gains, tax breaks, perks and freebies for themselves. What is being done to the American middle class is an exercise of *power* by a ruling elite just as morally corrupt and tyrannical as the European monarchies of old.

Power. It is ubiquitous, yet mainstream economics – despite having been made into a Cold War weapon by the US – is highly limited and one-sided in how it models power relations. Monopolists and unions are always bad. Consumption and competition are always good. Taxes are always bad. More money is always good. Government is held to be coercive, so it is generally bad. Markets are held to mean freedom, so they are generally good.

As you will discover from reading this book, economics has been molded typically to benefit the wealthy and the interests of the elite of the United States. Just as with the US political system, economics has been captured by the powerful and they are not in the mood for fairness. They are not even in the mood for discussion: you will not find academic articles about fairness in the top economics journals. Only through having been caught so blatantly with their noses in the troughs (e.g. the 2011 Academy Award–winning documentary *Inside Job*) has the American Economic Association finally been forced to adopt an ethical code, and that code is weak and incomplete compared with other disciplines. Increasingly, and especially during the past ten years, there is evidence that the US is beginning to doctor the numbers for measures such as productivity and GDP to make itself look stronger and more powerful than it actually is. In this it is copying its forebear, the British Empire, which increasingly began to tell itself lies as it failed to arrest its relative economic decline after the recession of 1873–79, until the Second World War bankrupted and broke up its global hegemony.

Economics is supposed to be about revealing truth such that society learns to become better than it was before. In this, it is supposed to be like physics or medicine. It is not supposed to be another tool for the powerful to enrich themselves at the expense of others. And it is most certainly not supposed to be a weapon for achieving US hegemony at the cost of everything else – including the long-term sustainability of the United States itself.

This book is not about Europeans telling others to be more European. There is plenty of evidence showing that the European policy mix is far from ideal, what with its endemic youth underemployment and denial of opportunity to anyone without political power (especially immigrants and gypsies), or indeed ongoing euro currency breakup or country bankruptcy problems. However, on the whole, during the decades since the Second World War, European experimentation with capitalism has been rather successful, which is why emerging economies are taking the European and not US social model as inspiration (Gill and Raiser 2012). There are plenty of empirically proven practical ideas for countries to consider. All you need to do is to ignore economic orthodoxy and especially those economists being paid to deceive you. Look instead at what has been proved. Follow the evidence, not the paid-for rhetoric.

The global financial crisis that started in 2007 made it obvious to many that there is something amiss in mainstream neoclassical economics as propagated by the leading Anglo-Saxon economists and their epigones. Few people still agree that what happens in the economy has everything to do with market forces, and nothing to do with power in its various guises. These include the power to abuse informational advantage, the power to give or withhold credit, the power to charge customers more than it costs you to produce, and the power to change the institutional setting to your advantage. There is the power of the corporate elite to manipulate their own pay and to cook the books, the power of rating agencies to issue self-fulfilling prophecies, the power of governments to manipulate the yardsticks that voters are offered to judge their economic policies. All these types of power, which were important in bringing about the global financial crisis, are defined away by standard assumptions of most mainstream economic models. These models feature perfect competition, efficient financial markets, full information and eternal equilibrium. People are modeled as being perfectly substitutable for one another, which stands in stark contrast to the championing of the individual that has long been a mainstay of mainstream economics. In particular, defining away imperfect and asymmetric information – and not talking about it – goes a long way in tacitly taking power out of economics.

Power has been made taboo and thus acquired a negative connotation. However, most firms and corporations would not function without it. Without functioning corporations, there would be no basis for the high wages that they pay. Thus the exercise of power can be good for society (Bowles and Gintis 2008). As power is a fact of life, it is far more important to account for it than to judge it. If powers are distributed and used in unfair ways, the important thing is to make the real power structure visible. Informed voters can demand redress. Only uninformed voters can be fooled into electing politicians who collude with the economically powerful. This is why the widespread failure of economists – arguably the most influential social scientists by far – to deal with power issues is so damaging to those at the receiving end of power relationships. The less power is talked about and analyzed, the more easily it is abused for personal gain to the detriment of others.

The Structure of this Book

The structure of this book follows the idea that there is a hierarchy of power, with power cascading downward starting from the cultural totem of money itself, through the loan market or financial market in general, to the market for managers and to the market for normal employees (Bowles and Gintis 2008). A single illustration may suffice. Both the CEOs of General Motors and Chrysler were bailed out by the government during the financial crisis and had to step down in the spring of 2009. Vikram Pandit, CEO of Citigroup, the commercial bank that received the most federal rescue money, remained in office, as did most of his bailed-out colleagues in the other Wall Street institutions. Some of the latter even moved on to become highly respected government consultants; one even became treasury secretary. Ordinary workers and taxpayers bore the brunt of the adjustment after the subprime crisis.

To set the stage, Chapter 1 looks at the history of economic doctrine and shows how the definition of economics, its methods and its assumptions were reformed in several steps, eliminating considerations of power in the process. The historical and social context can explain why these dogmatic revolutions took place and why they were successful. The United States as the leading global power had a decisive influence on the development of modern economic doctrine. It was also successful in promoting international statistical standards for measuring economic success that conform to the ideological underpinnings of mainstream economics. Using GDP as the dominant measure of success makes the US seem more successful than it really is, and it makes it easy to discredit sensible alternative ideas of good economic policy as inimical to economic growth.

Chapter 2 examines the financial sector, which over recent centuries and especially recent decades has come to occupy the top of the power hierarchy. This is the longest chapter, and not by coincidence. Financial institutions have something which is always in short supply – money and credit – and they can direct the flow not only of their own money but also of other people's money. This is why they get away with so much, and have become so morally corrupt in the process. The idea that financial markets are efficient, which was propagated by US economists, has helped the financial sector conceal its power and escape regulation. An impressive list of rigorous empirical economic studies shows that fraud and strategic misinformation of customers are endemic in the financial industry, proving that the efficient market–rational consumer idea is wrong. Bankers and financiers have lived in a symbiotic relationship with government for centuries. They have obtained important privileges in the process, many of which we can hardly recognize as such any longer. Chief among them is the right to create money out of thin air, coupled with free taxpayer-funded liquidity insurance against any mistakes or outright fraud if it is done on large enough a scale.

On the next level is the small world of the corporate elite, the managers of large corporations. Their powers are the subject of Chapter 3. In theory, they decide for the firm on behalf of the owners or of stakeholders in general. However, examples and systematic studies show that managers have abundant leeway to further their own interests instead. Recognizing this problem, economists have developed pay schemes that enabled managers to inflate their paychecks tremendously, under the pretext that this would make them do what shareholders want. This conveniently happened just as communism was considered defeated, thereby removing the last substantial objection against an elite taking all the opportunity and wealth for itself.

Chapter 4 deals with the power of producers to determine the prices that their customers have to pay, and the wages that their workers receive. It will become evident that the textbook assumption (called "perfect competition") that producers sell their products for what it costs to produce one more unit of them is false, theoretically and empirically. Most real markets are very far from being perfectly competitive. The profits possible due to imperfect competition are distributed among capital owners, management and workers according to their respective bargaining power. It is exactly because much of what goes on in an economy is about distributing economic rents, rather than maximizing allocative efficiency, that the European social model has been much more successful than it would have been if perfect competition had any semblance to reality.

At the bottom of the power hierarchy are the workers (Chapter 5). Workers do not exist in most neoclassical models of the labor market. There is only *labor* in those markets – labor that consumers sell if the price is right and do not sell if the price is too low. In reality, the firm employs *workers*, not their labor. The presence of market power, established in Chapter 4, implies that the law of one price for labor does not hold. The result is a dichotomy of good jobs and bad jobs for similar workers. Thus luck is very important for earnings and careers, rather than individual merit. Labor market institutions, and legal restrictions on voluntary trade, work very differently on such a real labor market than in the fairy-tale labor market that textbooks like to use.

The final chapter deals with the thorny question of who can deal with economic power if the spheres of economic power and political power are connected. Economic elites can capture the government and use government power to their benefit. Powerful politicians can use their office to acquire economic power. It may be naïve to suggest government regulation for redressing problems of unequal power, if economic elites can capture the government. However, we will see that such skepticism is based on cynical and unrealistic assumptions about the nature of the political process that mainstream economics has propagated. An economic model of the political process starting from more realistic assumptions is more constructive and optimistic. It allows the conclusion that governments will do what is in the interest of the citizenry if voters are well informed and there is a culture of political participation. Equally, if voters are deliberately misinformed and political participation means choosing from a carefully controlled, narrow range of options preselected by the ruling elite, it is hard to see how any political process can have the citizenry's best interests in mind.

We have deliberately avoided our own original research in this work. It seemed to us more important to report on the present state of the field in economics, as the number of people who remain ignorant of any kind of economics outside what is taught in introductory economics classes continues to amaze us. If you want to discover a lot more about what economics can do, look into the journals of the World Economics Association that can be found via Google, Facebook and LinkedIn.

Finally, if you enjoy this book, please like it on Facebook and/or Google+ and feel free to post a message to the book's wall. We may not be able to reply to everything personally, but we will read anything posted.

Norbert Häring, Frankfurt am Main, Germany
Niall Douglas, Cork, Ireland
February 2012

Chapter 1

THE ECONOMICS OF THE POWERFUL

All professions are conspiracies against the laity.
—*George Bernard Shaw, 1906*

The lack of explicit consideration of power in modern mainstream economics is odd. Mainstream economics is built around the theme that people impersonally use their resources to achieve their goals. No one seriously denies that power is an important goal for many people, so why then would the theory of the acquisition and use of power not be a core part of economic theory, especially given that power relations and hegemonics are a core part of most other social sciences? A look at the history of economic doctrine reveals that power was not always absent. It dropped from the radar screen at some point; or rather, it was erased.

This chapter will examine how we got from an economic science that treated relative economic power as an important variable and regarded the resulting income distribution as a core issue of the discipline, to a science that de-emphasizes power and does not want explicitly to deal with distributional issues. The reader should not expect a history of economic thought in general from this chapter. Rather, it is concerned with the dogmatic shifts that led to the current mainstream, which dominates textbooks and policy advice.

Three developments were particularly important. The first was the triumph of marginalism in the second half of the nineteenth century, which allowed economists to appear to have the power to predict the future using numbers just as a hard science like physics might. The second was the so-called "ordinalist challenge" – a dogma imposed starting in the 1930s that forbade the comparison of preferences or utilities between different people. Finally, there was the rational choice movement, which gained prominence in the 1950s and served to discredit any kind of group action or even religious faith as being irrational and destabilizing. Each of these dogmatic revolutions had a sociopolitical or geopolitical role to play. One of these roles was the intellectual defense of the capitalist system against the threat of communism. As this confrontation morphed into the Cold War between the capitalist West and the communist East, economic science became a tool in the geopolitical arsenal of the dominant nation of the West, the United States.

The problem with using economic science as a weapon in an ideological war is that as a result it has become driven further away from helping society better understand itself. Since the end of the Second World War, the US has been able to control the way in which economic success is measured and to promote an economic science that makes the economic model of the United States appear better than any other. This, especially in the past decade, is beginning to look like self-deceit: the relative power of the United States within the world has begun to wane, but the methods by which the numbers are calculated have been modified since the 1990s to show less of a decline than under previous calculation methods. One must wonder if it is wise for the United States to pretend that its decline is not as substantial.

In Search of Power Lost – A Brief History of Economic Doctrine

> Facts do not enter the world in which our convictions live, they
> have not caused them, and they cannot destroy them.
> —*Marcel Proust*

Pre-classical economists from the fifteenth to the seventeenth century had a viewpoint very different from the current individualist bent. The perspective and interests of the state and of the emerging merchant class dominated. Early protagonists of this statist school of thought, the Bullionists, were concerned with maximizing the amount of gold and silver coins circulating in the national economy, as they considered this the basis for a high tax base and profit base. They wanted to keep imports down and promote exports. At the time, all economists were aware that gold was an important means to achieve wealth and power, and that wars were won with gold (Screpanti and Zamagni 1993; Reinert 2007). Later, a more refined and generalized form of mercantilism emerged, which distinguished between *kinds* of goods. Raw materials and unprocessed food were to be imported freely, as these could be used to produce industrial goods with high added value.

Exports of raw materials were discouraged or prohibited, with the twin goals of making industrialization harder for competing countries and of promoting usage of these raw materials in local industries. High tariffs on imports of industrial goods served to protect the domestic industry against foreign competition. These policies were widely pursued in Europe in the late sixteenth and seventeenth century, including, most notably, England (Screpanti and Zamagni 1993; Reinert 2007). And if such an export-orientated policy sounds familiar today, it is because China and Germany (in the guise of the EU) have recently been using similar policies to gain advantage against all others in industrial production with great success.

How power was purged from international economics

However, after Britain had obtained the position of industrial world leader, classical British economist David Hume (1711–1776) fiercely criticized mercantilist theories and politics as unreasonable. He and his famous compatriots Adam Smith (1723–1790) and David Ricardo (1772–1823) became champions of global free trade. They agitated against continental European attempts to grab market share from the leading economy using the same mercantilist policies that Britain had so successfully employed before. Even so, it was not easy to convince other countries that it was best for them to continue exporting raw materials to Britain and importing industrial goods back from Britain. Thus England often used her supreme military power to back up the message of the economists. England explicitly prohibited colonies from engaging in manufacturing. Their negotiation strategy with weaker countries was to adopt treaties that forced the weaker country to deliver raw materials for English industry and to provide open markets for industrial goods from England, thus ensuring that the native industries of the weaker country were put out of business. One of many examples is the Methuen Treaty of 1703–1860 with Portugal (Reinert 2007). This treaty granted a one-third reduced tariff import of Portuguese wine into Britain in exchange for tariff-free import of British cloth into Portugal. This placed the Portuguese cloth industry in direct competition with Britain's vastly larger cloth industry, which was technologically more advanced and had significant economies of scale, and thus could produce cloth at much lower prices. In exchange, Portugal gained free access to British ports throughout the world, which was a boon for its traders, who were able to resell British manufactured goods with a much better profit margin than their French or Spanish counterparts (and Britain did not try to seize Portugal's Brazilian colonies, unlike those of Spain or France). Ricardo would later use this treaty as his famous example to illustrate the mutual benefits of comparative advantage (Ricardo 1817); however Portugal to this day still lives with an unusually global-trade-dependant economy as a legacy of that treaty (Almodovar and Cardoso 1998).

The birth of marginalism

While the classical economists touted the virtues of free international trade and took issues of power out of international economics, they still left some room to discuss power in the national context, notably on the labor market. When Adam Smith wrote his famous *Inquiry into the Wealth of Nations* in 1776, large parts of the British population hardly had enough income to feed their children adequately and provide decent housing. For Smith, it was clear that wages were determined by the relative bargaining powers of industrialists and workers:

> What are the common wages of labour, depends everywhere upon the contract usually made between those two parties... The workmen desire to get as much, the masters to give as little as possible... It is not, however, difficult to foresee which of the two parties must, upon all ordinary occasions, have the advantage in the dispute, and force the other into a compliance with their terms. The masters, being fewer in number, can combine much more easily, and the law, besides, authorizes, or at least does not prohibit their combinations, while it prohibits those of the workmen... In all such disputes the masters can hold out much longer... Though they did not employ a single workman, [they] could generally live a year or two upon the stocks which they have already acquired. Many workmen could not subsist a week. (Smith 1776/2007)

The introduction of marginalism in the second half of the nineteenth century helped to take discussion of power out of domestic economics. An important ingredient was marginal utility theory, which German statistician Hermann Gossen (1810–1858) first presented in 1854. His main theorem says that the more we consume of a particular good, the less additional or *marginal* utility we derive from any additional unit of the good. Gossen's work was not well received and very few copies were sold (Screpanti and Zamagni 1993).

It was only in the 1870s that William Stanley Jevons, Alfred Marshall, Carl Menger and Leon Walras triggered the marginal revolution in earnest. A self-confident and wealthy class of industrialists could make good use of a theory defending the virtues of a free capitalist market economy against Marxist assaults and socialist tendencies. Karl Marx had just published *Das Kapital* in 1867, and the Marxian labor theory of value, which built on classical value theory (that value comes from *production*, i.e. natural resources and the labor which transforms them into products), made the claim that capitalists exploited laborers. To combat Marxian theory and its followers, industrialists had to argue against the classical theory of value. This was quite urgent for all those interested in preserving the status quo against revolutionary impetus. The International Workingmen's Association, also called the First International, was inaugurated in London in 1864 and held important congresses in European capitals between 1866 and 1872. In 1889, the Second International, strongly influenced by Marxism, was founded in Paris. There were violent repressions in Britain, Germany, the US and Italy in the 1870s (Screpanti and Zamagni 1993). Those who owned the capital were extremely aware of the potential threat.

The theory of marginal utility could challenge the theoretical foundations of socialism without being openly ideological, and therefore have the appearance of being "scientific" and value-free. While classical economists had explained prices with the costs of production, the marginalists switched the focus to a *consumer* perspective. This new approach explained prices and quantities by utility or usefulness for consumers (Screpanti and Zamagni 1993). This was an odd switch at an odd time, given that it occurred during the Industrial Revolution, when production technologies were changing dramatically. One would have expected that the production sphere would become increasingly central to theories explaining what was going on in the economy.

At the center of the Marginal Revolution was the notion that available goods are allocated to the uses and users with the greatest marginal utility. At the same time as the early marginalists de-emphasized the production side, they also eliminated the element of social interaction as best they could. Their examples featured self-reliant people like Robinson Crusoe, who had to decide how to use a given stock of goods, like an allotment of grain. If they produced, they were the producer and consumer all in one, not opening up any possible discussion of how the proceeds from production were shared. Thus economists began to divorce themselves from the pressing socioeconomic problems of the era. They took the focus away from social phenomena and put it instead on the individuals as the "atoms" of society (Screpanti and Zamagni 1993).

Within this artificially simplified framework, and with a number of auxiliary assumptions, the marginalists showed that the allocation of goods and means of production would be optimal in a free market economy. All prices and quantities would be such that the economy was in equilibrium, and workers would receive the fair value of what they produced with any additional hour of work. This result was the core of the neoclassical defense of capitalism against the Marxist charge of exploitation (Screpanti and Zamagni 1993).

In the US, the principal protagonist of this line of thought was John Bates Clark (1847–1938). When Clark derived his theory of distribution, he was urgently aware of its political implications, as can be seen from the following quote from his influential book *The Distribution of Wealth: A Theory of Wages, Interest and Profits*, published in 1899:

> Workmen, it is said, are regularly robbed of what they produce. This is done by the natural working of competition. If this charge were proved, every right-minded man should become a socialist.

This quote may explain why his new theory was met with such enthusiastic support and had such lasting impact, despite a few rather fundamental shortcomings and contradictions that we will further explore in Chapter 4. His theory says that the workings of the market make sure that workers and capital are paid exactly what they contribute to the value of the product at the margin, i.e. by what they contribute to the last unit of the good that can gainfully be produced (Clark 1899/2001).

Finding market-clearing prices for goods, labor and capital is tricky both in theory and reality. They have to be found not only for each market separately, but for all markets at the same time. Leon Walras (1834–1910) was the first to tackle this problem. He formulated a large number of equations describing the whole economy. He was able to show that the system *could* have an equilibrium. However, he had to realize that there was no guarantee that any equilibrium would be unique and stable. This has remained the rather unsatisfactory state of affairs, even though the equilibrium-loving economic mainstream has been rather successful at concealing or ignoring it (for example, examination questions given to economics students always assume that there are known and stable points of equilibria, and the only problem to be solved is how best to move an economy from one known point to another known point) (Screpanti and Zamagni 1993).

What Walras offered instead was a theoretical method for finding the equilibrium if it existed. It was a process of trial and error by a hypothetical research firm, which he called the auctioneer. The auctioneer would poll people about how much of the various goods they would demand and supply at particular prices, without actually trading at these prices. Whenever demand exceeded supply at a particular price, the auctioneer would raise that price a bit and run all equations again until he found the equilibrium. This is only a theoretical solution, though. In reality, the market will not necessarily find this equilibrium because there is always trading going on at the wrong prices. This trading at off-equilibrium prices can take the economy away from the equilibrium and there is no guarantee that equilibrium will be reached or that it will be optimal in some sense (Screpanti and Zamagni 1993).

Nobel Memorial Prize winners Kenneth Arrow and Gerard Debreu later were able to prove that under certain conditions a unique equilibrium did exist (Arrow and Debreu 1954), with these conditions later taking the unwieldy moniker of the "Sonnenschein–Mantel–Debreu theorem" better known to postgraduate students as the "SMD conditions." However, this proof of equilibrium should rather have been recorded as proof of its non-existence because the conditions are extremely demanding and hardly ever fulfilled in reality. Moreover, how they view human beings and the free market says much about the field of economics in general. For example, all consumers have identical tastes and preferences (i.e. are identical clones), each is perfectly selfish and rational (i.e. is a robot), and each has perfect knowledge of all possible future market prices (i.e. is substantially omniscient), while all firms produce identical goods and services and make zero profit, and there are no transportation or transaction costs. Perhaps coincidentally, much of how globalization has been implemented and justified by economists during the past decades seems to assume that just such a worldview is true.

Even from purely within the perspective of economics, the SMD assumptions exclude the possibility of increasing returns to scale. That is, mass production cannot be cheaper per unit than producing few units of the same good, which if true would make mass production uneconomical. Despite the absurdity of such an assumption given the reality of two centuries of mass production, it remains customary to assume that the SMD conditions for equilibrium hold. There is nothing in reality that justifies this, but it is essential for the equilibrium-oriented economic analysis, devoid of history and power, that has become the economic mainstream, particularly because the mathematical models fail to produce stable equilibria if mass production is permitted. It is also the scientific basis for the laissez-faire bent of orthodox economic doctrine (Screpanti and Zamagni 1993). And best of all, due to the detailed consideration of the SMD conditions being considered as doctoral-study-level material, hardly anyone outside the inner circle of PhD-level economists will understand how far removed from anything in the real world an axiomatic economic analysis is. It is rarely even mentioned in academic papers that the SMD conditions are assumed to hold – rather, it is brought up when they are *not* being assumed to hold in some way.

The rigorous analysis and clear, apparently predictive results that neoclassical economics offered helped it to overtake rival schools in importance. This mathematical precision stood in sharp contrast to the often vague and context-dependent – what we would now call "qualitative" – results that its main contender had to offer. That contender was the "historical school" from Germany and its Anglo-Saxon knockoff called Institutionalism. Economists belonging to this school believed that economic arrangements are specific to cultures and institutions and therefore cannot be generalized over space and time.

How institutionalism was pushed out of economics in the US

> Transactions intervene between the labor of the classic economists and the pleasures of the hedonic economists, simply because it is society that controls access to the forces of nature, and transactions are, not the "exchange of commodities," but the alienation and acquisition, between individuals, of the rights of property and liberty created by society, which must therefore be negotiated between the parties concerned before labor can produce, or consumers can consume, or commodities be physically exchanged.
>
> —*John R. Commons, 1931*

Looking back on the past century with the benefit of hindsight, it is strange to think that the great post–Second World War qualitative, sociological push back against the mechanistic, quantitative, dehumanizing worldview of society (that has since become known as the poststructuralist movement) actually had one of its roots in economics, beginning with a 1919 *American Economic Review* article by Walton H. Hamilton.

Institutionalism is taught as part of the core undergraduate curriculum in Law, Politics and especially International Relations, yet it is totally absent from core modules in any economics course. A large part of the reason is that the leading figures of the institutional school in the US came under pressure because of alleged socialist leanings. They included John R. Commons, Richard T. Ely, Edward Ross and Edward Bemis. They were accused around the turn of the twentieth century of poisoning the minds of their students with ideas hostile to corporate interests and private wealth (Bernstein 2001). It is important that we briefly tell their stories, because how wealthy benefactors applied pressure to what was considered acceptable discourse within US universities had important consequences to developments in economics from the 1930s onwards.

Commons' crime was to publish in 1893 a book called *The Distribution of Wealth*, in which he integrated economic theory with a theory of law. He argued that wealth distribution is the result of state policy, notably state regulation and legal rules, which protect and define property rights. He detailed the role that legal rules play in shaping the distribution of negotiation power and the distribution of income. Commons' argument was that state-created entitlements like monopolies, patent, copyright and franchises enable their owners to restrict supply and raise the price of the goods they sell. Since the state is one of the most important determinants of the relative values of goods, Commons argued, the state is implicated in income distribution and should intervene to improve the bargaining power of the weaker groups. The idea that monopolists could raise prices by restricting supply, today standard textbook knowledge, was considered outrageous at the time. Commons' book was banished from economics bibliographies and reading lists. Commons was let go from his teaching position at Indiana University. He went to Syracuse University in New York, but within a few years he was fired from there as well. According to Commons, the Syracuse chancellor, James Day, told him that several potential contributors were disturbed by Commons' "radicalism" and refused to contribute as long as he was employed at the university. Day also told him that he should not bother to look for another academic position because college presidents had agreed that no person of radical tendencies would be employed. For five years, from 1899 to 1904, Commons would not find an academic position. In 1904, Richard Ely, who had his own experiences with political inquisition, invited him to take a position at the University of Wisconsin (Stone 2009).

While Commons took a while to stay clear of contentious issues and resurrect his academic career, John Bates Clark abandoned his pro-labor views early on, after Yale economist Arthur Hadley berated him for spreading socialist fallacies. Others needed more prodding. Henry Carter Adams was fired from his position at Cornell and only employed at Michigan after he repudiated his former advocacy of state control of productive resources. Richard T. Ely was forced to resign as president of the American Economic Association (AEA) in 1892. Two years later, the Wisconsin superintendent of education publically accused him of using his university position to preach socialism and to promote strikes. In a formal trial at the university, Ely just managed to escape the allegations. He stopped writing about labor matters and his work became much more conservative, sufficiently conservative for him to be appointed president of the AEA again and to praise "the beneficence of competition" in his presidential address (Stone 2009; Bernstein 2001).

Edward Bemis was fired from Chicago in 1895, and Edward Ross was forced to resign from Stanford in 1900. The AEA established a committee to investigate the implications of Ross' forced resignation for the freedom of science, as it was a very obvious attack on academic freedom. Ross had repeatedly criticized the historical labor practices of the Stanford's railroad company, and the still-living Stanford family representative on the executive board had used their influence to ensure that every pressure was brought to bear on Ross' position. However, aware of the general threat to the funding of higher education in the United States, the committee was sufficiently afraid of alienating wealthy benefactors of economics faculties that no formal report was ever issued and the AEA never even admitted to the existence of this committee (Bernstein 2001). Ross, having been permanently excluded from the field of economics, moved into sociology and went on to become one of the most important early figures in the new field of criminology.

Clark moved over to the neoclassical movement and earned a lot of praise and honors in this new line of thought. He strove to develop a theory that would rationalize capitalism as a better system than Marxism. However, he and other early neoclassicals were far from being right-wingers. Most early neoclassicals were what contemporary commentators Robert Cooter and Peter Rappoport call "welfarists." Francis. Y. Edgeworth, Alfred Marshall, Irving Fisher, Arthur C. Pigou and Clark shared the prevailing consensus among economists of the time. They regarded distribution of income as a major issue in economics and were convinced that redistribution from the rich to the poor was the right thing to do because it increased overall welfare (Cooter and Rappoport 1984).

Based on introspection and empirical evidence, the early neoclassicals reasoned, in the utilitarian tradition of Jeremy Bentham, that if a dollar was taken away from rich people and given to the poor, the rich might hardly notice and it would enable poor people to better feed themselves and their children. Therefore, if basic human needs can be met by an absolutist reallocation of money from rich to poor, the overall welfare of the society increases, and this line of thinking was the welfarist consensus of the time. It was not meant to be true in every individual case, but in statistically observable groups of people, like *the poor* and *the rich*, it seemed a reasonable set of assumptions to make. Some early neoclassicals did empirical research on these assumptions. Irving Fisher and his followers, for example, deduced marginal utilities of income from observing the consumption structure of communities at different income levels. This research generally supported welfarist conclusions (Colander 2007; Adler 2009).

The early neoclassical economists were concerned with material welfare as opposed to the sole focus on preferences, which would become the norm later. This is hard to grasp for today's economists who have been brought up thinking exclusively in terms of preferences. It means that economists cared more about (objective) *needs* for goods near the bottom of the pyramid of needs, like food and shelter. They felt less secure about – and cared less about – the *preferences* for goods near the top of the pyramid, like operas versus jewelry (Cooter and Rappoport 1984).

Thou shalt not compare – The ordinalist challenge

> Economic ideas are always and intimately a product of their own time and place; they cannot be seen apart from the world they interpret.
>
> —*John Kenneth Galbraith, 1987*

The 1930s had a profound effect on the field of economics in two particular ways. The first effect was on the economics itself as economists tried to make sense of the Great Depression, and of course the focal point of the field of economics in the English language was moving away from declining Britain and towards the ascending United States. The second – and equally important, as we shall shortly see – effect was on how the field of economics was perceived, promoted, and particularly funded within American society, which was and still is very different from European societies including Britain.

The changes to economics

Interestingly, the major theoretical changes to economics that came about from the crisis of confidence in economics of the 1930s were generally incomplete imports of theories from Continental Economics into the English discourse. It is worth explaining exactly how these came about, for they introduced the depersonalization of economics such that we no longer consider the rich and the poor as the British economists of the nineteenth century did: now we aim to maximize output, measured in a rather particular but seemingly objective way, above all else. Power and accolades flow to those who can think of any way of increasing output still further – whether or not it is feasible, or for that matter wise.

The story begins with the Italian economist Vilfredo Pareto who, after an exhaustive empirical study of individual rich and poor families, attacked the notion that one could compare and sum up individual utilities to arrive at a judgment about societal welfare. He argued that rich people and poor people might have such fundamentally different tastes that it would be impossible to compare their utilities. According to Pareto, you could only say that one alternative was socially preferable to another if it made at least one person better off and no other person worse off (Pareto 1906/1971). These ideas did not have much impact during his lifetime, but the criterion would become famous as the Pareto criterion after the Paretian revival of the 1930s.

The British economist Lionel Robbins spearheaded the ultimately successful assault in the 1930s on the redistribution friendly theories of the early neoclassicists. In his *Essay on the Nature and Significance of Economic Science*, Robbins (1932/1935) proposed an apolitical definition of welfare centered on *scarcity*. It made the demand and supply of opera tickets just as worthy a subject for economic study as the demand for and the supply of food and housing, and therefore appeared on the surface to have a more powerful explanatory capacity. "Economics is the science which studies human behavior as a relationship between ends and scarce means which have alternative uses," he postulated, referring to similar definitions suggested by Austrian economists Carl Menger and Ludwig von Mises (Robbins 1932/1935), but in truth this interpretation of welfare was actually a drastic simplification of Friedrich von Wieser's value and alternative cost theory (von Wieser 1914) – and Robbins was well known at the time for being the leading interpreter within the English language of Continental Economic thought.

However, note carefully what happens when economists focus on scarcity rather than allocation: economics stopped looking at the fairness or wisdom or sanity of general patterns of allocation in society on the basis that no one can reliably compare *individual* differences of preference. Instead, it now focuses all resources upon maximizing the efficiency of the economic machine, on the basis that a rising tide lifts all boats. In short, it depersonalized economics for the very first time, making the wellbeing of the economic machine the priority above all else, including long-term sustainability or the human beings inside that machine.

This was hardly the first time that the drastic simplification of a foreign economist's arguments when entering into the local economic discourse caused the incorporation of something very different from what the foreign economist had intended, and it certainly wouldn't be the last, as we will see later. Economics, just like any other intellectual field, tends to pick out bits of theory from new works and incorporate those into the orthodox mainstream. The trouble here was that Robbins' interpretation did not distinguish between needs and desires, calling both "utility" on the basis that both have the same effects on demand, as is still the norm today. As Pareto had done, he insisted that there was no reliable way to measure and compare the satisfaction of desires of two people and that anything involving such comparisons was unscientific and irrational. To discredit the earlier neoclassical approach, Robbins' examples featured named individuals who were not necessarily far apart in their material wellbeing, rather than groups of people like *the rich* and *the poor*. As a result of this change, any paper referring to anything involving the wisdom of allocation, such as Yale economist Irving Fisher's 1927 piece, "A Statistical Method for Measuring 'Marginal Utility' and Testing the Justice of a Progressive Income Tax," simply ceased to be publishable in any leading journal.

The next change in how value was perceived was when John Hicks and R. G. D. Allen (1934) introduced a new theory that did away altogether with the notion of marginal utility of consumption. Rather than saying that the hungry derive more utility from eating their first piece of bread than from eating their fifth piece, they would now say that they would be willing to give up more of some other good to obtain the first apple than they would to obtain the fifth apple (proponents of this theory generally prefer the apple example, because apples arguably do not carry the inconvenient connotation of existential need that bread does). If that other good is the generic good money, this new concept (called the marginal rate of substitution) looks very similar to the concept of marginal utility. However, there is one very important difference: if the problem is framed like that, one will no longer be inclined to conclude that the apple is worth more to a poor person than to a rich person, thus implying that a poor and hungry person is not necessarily more likely to give up more money to obtain an apple than a rich and well-fed person is. This clearly ignores the fact that the poor will not only need the apple more than the rich, they will also need the money more, assuming they have any. There is therefore no reason to assume that the marginal rate of substitution is different in a specific and important way between rich and poor people. As economics ultimately focused almost entirely on the concept of marginal rates of substitution, distributional concerns were pushed to the periphery of economics. They had no room in the new welfare economics.

Much later, after a series of devastating attacks on its internal logical consistency, enthusiasm for Paretian welfare economics faded. Even Hicks (1983) deserted the movement he had helped to establish. He argued that economists should not "overplay their hands" and limit themselves to estimating "the gains and losses that are likely to accrue, to various classes or sections of the population, from the proposed action." However, the new mainstream was already firmly established. Nobody paid any more attention to the deep cracks in its methodological foundations after an elaborate house of ideas had already been built over them.

To get around (or to hide) the fact that Paretian welfare economics was not able to pass judgment about anything important, it became standard practice in applied economics to take refuge in the representative individual, a.k.a. averages. This "representative agent" populates nearly all macroeconomic models. As mentioned in the SMD assumptions earlier, it amounts to assuming that all consumers and producers have identical needs and preferences. By definition, distributional issues disappear if everybody is the same. The popular notion that the maximization of GDP is *the* goal of economic policy goes back to this shortcut. For all practical purposes, it is equivalent to assuming that a dollar is worth the same in everybody's hands, be they very poor or exceedingly rich.

"In effect, more than a generation of economists was trained to believe that economic science treats a dollar as equally valuable to everyone, whereas a non-scientific approach treats a dollar as more valuable to the poor than to the rich," write Daniel Cooter and Peter Rappoport

(1984). To this day, most economists think that only laypeople and incompetent economists fail to treat a dollar as having the same value for a rich and a poor person, without ever asking themselves where their curious distributional judgment stems from.

Changes to how the field of economics was promoted and funded

> This is an age of mass production. In the mass production of materials a broad technique has been developed and applied to their distribution. In this age, too, there must be a technique for the mass distribution of ideas.
>
> —*Edward Bernays, 1928*

The success of new welfare economics in permanently changing the discourse permitted in economics away from distributional concerns did not come about by chance, especially given its deep methodological problems. In fact, much of its form and content can be attributed directly to campaigns undertaken by the new field of public relations in the United States.

It is a testament to the success of public relations throughout the twentieth century that very few know what it actually did during that time. Public relations – in its modern business-sponsored, rather than politically sponsored, guise – probably began with the 1906 coal miners' strike where a man called Ivy Lee was employed by the coal mining bosses to ensure that newspapermen would tell their side of the story rather than relentlessly focusing on the newsworthy abuses told by the miners. Ivy Lee – nicknamed "Poison Ivy" – would later make the gravest error in PR by "becoming the story" when he was hauled in front of a Congressional Inquiry to explain how he had widely disseminated a 1914 smear campaign for the Rockefellers using plausible-sounding lies about strikers. However, such a lack of finesse was already outdated, for one of the greatest PR men of all time was just coming into his prime.

Edward Bernays, nephew of the famous Sigmund Freud, spent the First World War sitting on the US Committee on Public Information. He was worried by what he saw, feeling that the stupidity and ignorance of the average member of public led inevitably to violence. Growing increasingly convinced that the public's democratic judgment was not to be relied upon, he decided that they had to be guided from above lest they make the wrong choices and he was the man to make a living from doing so – what his daughter Anne later called an ideology of "enlightened despotism" (BBC 2002). He was not – at that time – particularly concerned with what they were guided towards, as long as it was something non-violent, and therefore saw no problem in hiring out his services to the highest bidder. In 1919, he opened an office in New York; in 1923, he inaugurated the first university course in public relations, which he taught. He was a prodigious writer of books, with his 1923 book *Crystallizing Public Opinion*, his 1928 book *Propaganda* and his 1947 book *The Engineering of Consent* considered his most important works.

Bernays was a master of the "tie-in," where multiple, typically disparate, venues were holistically employed to deliver the same marketing message from multiple sources over a sustained period of time. This technique effectively bombards the consumer with encouragement to believe a given myth that would in turn have the irrational or rational psychological effect of the consumer wishing to behave in a way beneficial to the campaign's sponsors (typically, both rational and irrational motivations were simultaneously employed). A typical Bernays' campaign would meld together stage, screen and sports celebrities, respected professionals such as doctors and politicians, department stores, film and radio placements, and of course newspapers and radio. As a typical example, when contracted by General Motors (GM) to arrest a net sales decline of 46.6 percent in 1932 alone, Bernays employed a multiple, simultaneous approach that incorporated luncheons held by GM's CEO which were attended by distinguished US economists. They attended despite the fact that economics wasn't discussed, and there was no particular reason for any economist to be there, except of course for the legitimacy and prestige that they conferred upon the proceedings.

This use of distinguished economists for the purposes of promotion was of course not new. The great British founder of neoclassicism, Alfred Marshall, was the undisputed leader in economics from the death of Jevons in 1882 until his own death in 1924, and was famous for his evenhandedness and avoidance of controversy. But even he got involved in media campaigning against imperial initiatives, such as the 1903 tariff reform movement that aimed to turn the British Empire into a single free trade zone in order to inhibit the rise of the United States and Germany. The big change, however, was that Bernays was merely having distinguished economists put in appearances at media events *completely unconnected* with economics. This, over time, caused the American public to begin to see distinguished economists as a type of celebrity, especially as Bernays found that the typically male experts of that time were particularly likely to put in appearances at events where famous actresses would be present. This in turn changed how the field of economics was perceived in the US until it resembled the fields of medicine and engineering: they become totems of rational, numbers-driven, scientific opinion. This perception remains to this day: psychologists, sociologists and educators might have interesting qualitative things to say, but for the big decisions one always turns to a quantitative expert such as a doctor, an engineer, or an economist for advice (Alonso and Starr 1987; Rose 1991). Indeed, for just this reason the famous book *How to Lie with Statistics* is the best-selling statistical text of the past 50 years (Steele 2005).

The American economists of the ordinalist challenge regularly attended Bernay's PR junkets. We have no knowledge of who was paid what honorariums and likely never will, much as the 2011 attempt to get the American Economic Association to adopt an ethical disclosure of potential conflicts of interest when writing articles has been met with a stony silence (e.g. in an interview with the New York Times published on December 31, 2010, Nobel Memorial Prize laureate Professor Lucas of the University of Chicago objected: "What disciplines economics, like any science, is whether your work can be replicated. It either stands up or it doesn't. Your motivations and whatnot are secondary."). What we do know, however, is that those employing the PR men were desperate to use every available measure to stimulate demand, and were willing to sponsor with significant monies radical ways of achieving it. Paul Mazur, the third non-family man to join Lehman Brothers after its creation, and broker and financier for consumer goods firms and consultant for Roosevelt's New Deal, famously wrote in the *Harvard Business Review* of 1927, "We must shift America, from a needs to a desires culture. People must be trained to desire, to want new things even before the old have been entirely consumed." In a statement that should pre-empt the theoretical "advance" of the ordinalist challenge, he added, "We must shape a new mentality in America. Man's desires must overshadow his needs." Not only did American consumers do just that, but so did Lionel Robbins and his followers. Economists decided to simply forget about needs and care only for desires.

Mazur's was one of many articles along similar lines in the *Harvard Business Review* at the time. While there is no evidence proving that the leading American economists of the 1930s were encouraged directly by those championing this shift from needs to desires, there is absolutely no doubt that in the surrounding economics field, multiple articles in the *Harvard Business Review*, all the major corporations and of course the Roosevelt government were all agitating strongly for any justification and/or method for stimulating demand. American universities were and still are very much dependent on donations from wealthy benefactors for much of their running costs, and we saw how Edward Ross was pushed out by the Stanford family due to his criticism of that family's historical labor practices (a fate he shared with many others who refused to conform). Of course, controlling the higher education system is symptomatic with the exercise of power: in Europe universities were funded by the church until the twentieth century, after which governments took on the role of the church. In Europe, to this day, there is no tradition of universities seeking substantial operations funding from anyone except the state, and there is ample legislation from the nineteenth century onwards to ensure that government always retains a veto over what universities can do, which ensures the continuation of the European state's monopoly of power over what is taught at the highest levels.

Nevertheless, the point is that the types of discourse promoted within economics are strongly related to how the US funds, perceives and promotes its academics. When wealthy industrialists control the discourse, topics that threaten wealthy industrialists are stifled, just the same as when governments control the discourse, topics that threaten governments are similarly stifled. The question is not which of the two options is better, and the debate about higher education in the US in recent decades has sadly stagnated into this binary choice (Docampo 2007). Rather, what we should be asking is who can make best use of this power over economics now that the Cold War is over?

Cold War economics

If we are to succeed in the war of ideologies and to win over the decent element in the enemy countries we must first of all regain the belief in the traditional values [of individual freedom, truth, and democracy]…

—*Friedrich August von Hayek, 1944*

While in the early 1930s there was a great worry that capitalism might collapse due to lack of demand, as the Second World War approached the worry became that capitalism might simply be replaced outright. There was a pervasive sense of dismay and defeat among the intellectuals of the West. Support for communism grew and it was considered a very acute challenge for the Western economic model even among leading economists (Amadae 2003).

Joseph Schumpeter (1943/2003), famous for describing entrepreneurship as a process of creative destruction, expressed his conviction that "a socialist form of government will inevitably emerge from an equally inevitable decomposition of capitalist society."

Frank Knight of the Chicago School, which later became famous for its uncompromising support of free markets, also expressed serious doubts. "Economics and politics based on competitive mass selling is bankrupt and it is only the question of a successor to bid in the effects of the defunct at a nominal figure," he wrote in 1933 and argued that elites under communism might be well suited to provide the government control that markets needed (Amadae 2003).

The enemies of capitalism attacked its perceived weakness in bringing about an equitable distribution of income and promised that intervention by a benevolent socialist government would achieve better results. An economics emphasizing efficiency and de-emphasizing distributional issues helped reframe the question in a way that was very favorable to capitalism. Questioning the possibility to judge the welfare effects of redistribution defined away the perceived strong point of socialism (Amadae 2003).

The Second World War and the preparations for it greatly helped the ascent of the new interpretation of economics as a science concerned mostly with the allocation of scarce resources. The exclusive focus of the new welfare economics on efficiency of resource utilization suited the priorities of warring governments. During those years, the best contribution economists could provide for their nations was helping to make sure that scarce resources were used to the maximum effect in the war effort. Unsurprisingly, during that time the majority of all research funding came from the military (Mirowski 2002).

After Germany and its allies were defeated, the ideological battle between capitalism and socialism erupted again. Economic doctrine and teaching was regarded as an important weapon in the Cold War of ideologies. Thus, military and quasi-military units like the Office of Naval Research, the Atomic Energy Commission, the National Advisory Committee for Aeronautics, the Office of Strategic Services (or the OSS, which later became the CIA), the Weapons System Evaluation Group and the Joint Chiefs of Staff constituted the primary source of research funding in the years after the Second World War. According to some estimates, the Office of Naval Research alone funded 40 percent of US research contracts (Mirowski 2002). Still, the full extent of the military's involvement in funding and steering postwar science has not been unearthed, and will probably never be, as archival collections have been purged of military evidence. Many resumes omit military reports and publications. Correspondence with military funders was destroyed or sequestered (Mirowski 2002).

How important economic doctrine was to the military can also be gleaned from the fact that a headquarters of a camp for German prisoners of war in Kansas distributed the *American Economic Review* to inmates and obtained the right to translate it into German to make sure every inmate had a chance to understand it. Development of economic curricula was not left to chance. Security related agencies were in close contact with the AEA and with university deans. The OSS recruited many of the most eminent professors, including five former presidents of the AEA and one future Nobel Memorial Prize winner. Later it would be common for AEA officials and deans to help recruit the best economics graduate students for work in the CIA (Bernstein 2001).

Herbert Giersch, a young German officer who had just taken his examinations in economics, was generously provided with Anglo-Saxon economic literature while he was a prisoner of war in England. After he returned to Germany, he had a stellar career. He was invited to the London School of Economics immediately upon obtaining his PhD, got a job at the Organisation for Economic Co-operation and Development (OECD) and soon became Germany's most influential economist of the second half of the twentieth century.

During the war, the Department of War and the Navy insisted on changes in the economics curriculum that the AEA felt obliged to institute. The association reformed economics education from college-level to PhD degree, enshrining the new interpretation of economics. The AEA also became involved in rebuilding and reshaping economics education in the devastated areas overseas. The US contributed free books and copies of the *American Economic Review* along with lists of recommended texts and cash donations to scholarly libraries in Europe and East Asia. The association was charged with revising curricula and rehabilitating and vetting faculties in the defeated nations (Bernstein 2001).

On the other hand, pursuing research that had unsanctioned political implications was not at all conducive to a successful academic career at that time, for neither the faculty involved nor their students.

In the late 1940s and during the McCarthyism of the early 1950s, economists who advocated Keynesianism or socioeconomic planning in the Institutionalist tradition were at risk from university administrators, local state governments and research institute trustees who sought to purge their faculties of reds and pinks even if the economist in question was right wing politically (Morgan 2001). As an example, historian Michael Bernstein (2001) reports how under Raymond Saulnier, who was president of the Council of Economic Advisors from 1956 to 1961, there were thorough security checks on new staff of the council. He wanted to avoid hiring researchers, even at the lowest level, who "might have worked for people who are under a cloud" (Bernstein 2001).

Only in rare cases did the purging of economic faculties of unorthodox elements involve outright harassment or worse. Such crude interference was not necessary. In a social science like economics, it is hard to separate your scholarly work from your own convictions. Deviant economists could be denied promotion and tenure and their papers rejected by editorial boards, all on the grounds that their work did not meet scientific standards of excellence (Bernstein 2001). While everyone is well aware of the repression and censure of new ideas in Soviet Russia during the same time period, it is not widely realized just how similar in effect destroying the credibility of those who engage in free speech can be: where in Soviet academia everyone knew what not to do, in the United States it was much less clear what would be fatal for your career. Such uncertainty can be remarkably stifling.

The rational choice movement and negative freedom

Becoming a weapon in the Cold War had profound effects on economic doctrine. The economic mainstream of today, which is often equated with neoclassical economics, is actually neoclassical economics reformed by the ordinalist challenge and combined with rational choice liberalism. The latter is an ideology developed and presented as a definition of objective science during the Cold War. History scholar Sonia Amadae, who has written a book about the geopolitical background of rational choice liberalism, calls it "the linchpin of the triumphant West's ideological victory over Soviet communism" (Amadae 2003). It succeeded by discrediting what the other side claimed as its strength and by focusing the debate instead on the strengths of the Western capitalist model. Following the lead of Pareto, Robbins and Hicks, it purported to show by means of scientific discourse that the concepts of "the public" and "public interest" or "general welfare" were arbitrary and meaningless (Amadae 2003).

The Research and Development Corporation (RAND) was a Cold War institution at the centre of the development of the rational choice school. It started out more as an engineering institution, but by the end of the 1950s economists had become the dominant profession. In 1948 RAND became an independent non-profit organization. H. Rowan Gaither Jr., whose family owned the Pacific National Bank, arranged for a start-up loan. He obtained generous funding from the Ford Foundation (Amadae 2003). The Ford Foundation was the richest foundation at the time and had close ties to the CIA (Saunder 1999; Weiner 2007).

RAND and the Ford Foundation would become tightly linked and Gaither would assume important roles in both. Under his leadership, the movement worked to define policy formation as a highly technical and quantitative process, predicated on the authority of scientific expertise instead of politics (Amadae 2003). The rational choice movement was so successful at this that president Dwight Eisenhower would famously coin the phrase "military–industrial complex" in his farewell address to the nation in 1961 and express his fear that in the future "public policy could become the captive of a scientific-technological elite." (Bernstein 2001). Economists who could convince the conservative Gaither of the merits of their work and be invited to RAND, or one of its sister institutions, were in for the privilege of working for a high salary in a campus-style atmosphere but with no teaching burden at all (Amadae 2003).

It is hard to overestimate RAND's impact on the modern economic mainstream let alone modern society. As a quick indicator, to date, some 32 recipients of the Nobel (Memorial) Prize, primarily in the fields of economics and physics, have been involved or associated with RAND at some point in their career. Among other things, it had a big role in de-emphasizing empirical real-world oriented research in favor of axiomatic, mathematical deduction across the fields it touched. RAND was an important source of funds for the Cowles Commission in the 1950s. The Cowles Commission, funded by the businessman of the same name, would be the most important driver of the advanced mathematical formalization of the neoclassical mainstream after the war. In 1951, it received almost a third of its funds from RAND and another quarter from the Office of Naval Research. According to Mirowski (2002), it was RAND who pushed the Commission to abandon (unsuccessful) efforts to find empirical evidence for neoclassical theory in favor of an abstract axiomatic approach pursued by RAND scholar and later Nobel Memorial Prize laureate Kenneth Arrow, against substantial resistance from its members. In 1953, Oskar Morgenstern proposed in a letter that it should be a requirement for membership in the Econometric Society (Econometrics is the statistical study of economic behavior) that a researcher had come "in one way or another in actual contact with data." This proposal was defeated by procedural maneuvers despite its widespread support in the Society (Mirowski 2002).

The other major influence of RAND on economic doctrine was through its support of the rational choice movement from the very beginning, which laid the foundation for the strictly individualistic approach of the modern economic mainstream. Several of the canonical works of the rational choice approach to economics and politics were devised either at RAND or in close association with its researchers. The most notable one is Kenneth Arrow's *Social Choice and Individual Values* (1951), containing his famous impossibility theorem. It is one of the most often cited modern texts in economics. Other examples are *An Economic Theory of Democracy* (1957) by Arrow's student Anthony Downs and Mancur Olson's *The Logic of Collective Action* (1965). The link to RAND is somewhat more tenuous but still existent for Nobel Memorial Prize laureate James Buchanan and his *Calculus of Consent* (1962), written together with Gordon Tullock (Amadae 2003).

Arrow's impossibility consisted of the elegant logical proof that if certain conditions were met no "rational" collective decisions could be stably achieved. "Rational" in Arrow's sense are transitive preference orderings. That means that if alternative A is considered better than B and B better than C, then A must be considered better than C. The result was not entirely new and not surprising, as critics soon pointed out. The theorem was a rediscovery of an idea presented in a simpler way by the French mathematician, philosopher and politician Marquis de Condorcet (1743–1794): the Condorcet paradox. He had shown that pairwise voting on (at least) three alternatives by (at least) three voters can result in rotating majorities, depending on the order in which the alternatives are presented. The overwhelming success of Arrow's work might have less to do with originality and more with how he and his followers exploited it as a source of arguments to counter the Cold War enemies' philosophical basis.

An important condition for Arrow's impossibility theorem to hold is the assumption that intensities of preferences cannot be compared. We will see in the last chapter that there is no justification for such an assumption in the context of collective decision making. However, Arrow received the Nobel Memorial Prize for successfully preventing all "serious" economists from entering into a discussion about collective welfare on the grounds that such reasoning could not pass the test of analytical rigor. Ironically, Arrow himself made explicit that his negative verdict held true for *any* mechanism to select or rank social states; not only democratic decision making, but also markets. Therefore, there was no way of saying on a scientific basis that free market exchange would maximize social welfare. However, this part of the result was never given much attention. The impossibility theorem was only used to discredit any arguments in favor of big or strong government (Amadae 2003).

James Buchanan, who worked as a resident researcher at RAND in 1954 and did consultant work for RAND until 1958, built on Arrow's influential article. He drove the primacy of the individual even further, forbidding the discussion of the rationality of group decision making on the grounds that social groups had no "organic existence" apart from that of their individual parts. In *The Calculus of Consent*, this theme is central. The notion of the public does not have meaning if individuals' private goals and values are to be preserved. Any group decision binding individuals comes across as an evil. Together with his co-author Gordon Tullock, Buchanan in 1967 founded the Public Choice Society, which would be extremely successful in promoting and spreading these views in the profession (Amadae 2003). In part one of the BBC's 2007 documentary *The Trap: What Happened to Our Dream of Freedom*, in an interview Buchanan is extremely clear: he considers "the public interest" as being in fact the disguised self-interest of governing bureaucrats, and that anyone motivated by anything other than rational self-interest – such as job satisfaction, a sense of public duty, or faith in God – is a zealot and to be feared as destabilizing and dangerous to society.

In *The Logic of Collective Action*, Mancur Olson opposes any theory that works with the assumption that groups work together to further the group's interests. While earlier theorists had deemed such behavior among group members rational, Olson insisted that it was the opposite. To him, it is rational for individuals to pursue their own narrow self-interest, rather than their interest as group members. "Rational" individuals would let the other group members work to further the group interest and coast on the others' effort, with the result that nobody exerts an effort, at least not without coercion. Thus, any group activity, be it by grassroots movements, charitable work, the government, unions or even religious work, needs an element of coercion. This framing gave all forms of social action an authoritarian undertone, putting them in suspicious proximity to socialist command economies (Amadae 2003). The anti-organizational attitude of many mainstream economists owes a lot to the extremely influential public choice and rational choice movements and their generous supporters, and it stands in stark contrast to the economic theories of sociologists such as the extremely influential (outside of economics) Pierre Bourdieu, much of whose work concerns the patterns in how powerful professions such as doctors, lawyers and teachers continually reassert their self-organizing power.

To be fair to economics, it was hardly the only science or social science that was heavily manipulated for the purpose of winning the Cold War. The fields of politics and political science received the brunt of the rational choice movement, so much so that one of the dominant liberal scholars of the twentieth century, Isaiah Berlin, coined in a 1958 lecture the term "negative liberty" for this new conceptualization (Berlin 1958). The West was so afraid of destruction by communism – whether ideologically or via the atom bomb – that the concept of liberty, especially in the United States, became redefined as "freedom from interference by other people" (negative freedom) rather than its historical definition, "freedom to act to fulfill one's potential" (positive freedom). Some readers may not see much difference between these two types of freedom: negative freedom requires that people not reduce the freedom of others, which when applied in aggregate and taken to its logical conclusion prevents anybody from even talking to anybody else. Positive freedom, on the other hand, explicitly assumes that the opinion and worldview of a few will come to dominate and subjugate the opinions and worldviews of the many. The latter, clearly, can lead to Hitlers, Stalins, and communism and therefore was repressed within the West and especially in the United States. Of course, the possibility of new religions like Christianity and many other good things born the same way is also eliminated. The status quo becomes sacrosanct.

In summary, one can say that it was not an improvement of knowledge or tools that led to the shift from classical and institutional economics to today's "antigovernment–neoclassical–rational choice" mainstream. It was the result of a redefinition of what economics should be concerned with – from a fair to an efficient allocation of resources – an effort that was generously funded by businessmen and the military in the name of cementing the power and legitimacy of their selves and their beliefs within society in a post–1929 Depression ideological Cold War world. It has become time, especially in light of the 2008/2009 financial crisis and the fact that the West won the Cold War two decades ago, to reacquire the power to substantially change how we perceive our economic behavior, and in so doing to reacquire the power to behave better in the future than we have until now.

Heresy is for the Lesser Journals

What we have seen up until now is how funding, fame, Nobel Memorial Prizes and resources were allocated to those who have generated the economic theories that most furthered the aims of the scientific-technological elite. A very important part of the mechanisms used was to control what information and research is held to be reliable and what is to be excluded as at best unorthodox "fringe theories." It is worth looking more deeply at how information is controlled in the name of maintaining the authority of orthodoxy.

What is and isn't good research is decided by the editors and referees of the leading scholarly journals. Three of the most important ones, the *American Economic Review,* published by the AEA since 1911, the *Quarterly Journal of Economics*, published at Harvard, and the *Journal of Political Economy,* published at the University of Chicago, are US-based. The leading journals accept less than ten percent of submitted articles. It is not easy for scholars challenging the orthodoxy to find a leading journal that will publish their articles. The editors of the journals are economists who have made their name within the orthodoxy. They are not likely to consider a paper that fundamentally challenges the theories upon which they have built their careers, especially if it attacks a theory that they themselves helped develop. Even if they do send it on to a reviewer, the reviewer will most likely also be wedded to the mainstream. As the economic mainstream is dominant almost to the point of monopoly, chances are slim that a dissenting economist would be paired with a sympathetic referee.

It is also true that editors and reviewers do not always disregard the societal repercussions of certain theories they are supposed to judge. When the mainstream had yet to be established, decisions along such lines were made with full consciousness. Michael Bernstein's account of the history of American economic thought cites letters that were exchanged when the first editor of the *American Economic Review,* Davis Dewey, had to decide whether or not to publish an article on "Capital and Profits." He received two referee reports, a favorable one and an unfavorable one, both of which based their arguments mainly on political considerations. One wrote that "in view of the rapid growth of socialist views and sentiment it is of the very highest importance that this question 'Is interest earned?' is threshed out fully and completely." He was enthusiastic that the reviewed paper answered the question in the affirmative. The other reviewer wrote that the paper was unacceptable because the argumentation was potentially inflammatory, providing "grist to the mill of trade unionists and radical agitators" (Bernstein 2001).

Early in the life of the AEA journal, it was also rather common to have economists who worked as representatives of industry associations act as referees on papers like "Wage Disputes and Profiteering." Unsurprisingly, the director of the National Industrial Federation of Clothing Manufacturers recommended rejecting a paper with that title. Anything with political implications outside of the increasingly exclusionary mainstream had a very hard time entering the leading journals during the Cold War (Bernstein 2001).

Exporting the American way of thinking

After the war, the US could virtually reconstitute from scratch the economics departments in many parts of Europe and Asia. The US did not let go of that influence. Furthermore, Washington has long recognized that having universities that are global leaders in higher economics education and have curricula supporting the American economic policy agenda are valuable tools for exerting soft power. A 1957 Bureau of the Budget study into the controllability of multilateral organizations explicitly recognizes the benefits derived from the foreign staff of such organizations receiving a US education (McKeown 2009). In the case of the International Monetary Fund (IMF) and the World Bank, the US harvests these benefits by de facto requiring graduate economics training from Ivy League US universities (the London School of Economics being the only fig leaf exception) in order to be considered for an entry-level position.

The proportion of foreign students is very high in top graduate programs in the US. Thus, their curricula are important in shaping the socialization not only of American students, but also of foreign students and their peers back home who form the elite of their home countries (McKeown 2009). Inviting many members of the Latin American elite to study economics at the market-fundamentalist University of Chicago with money from the Ford Foundation was only the most visible of the initiatives that strove to systematically expand that influence (Weiner 2007).

Grants and support by RAND or similar institutions were used to enlist leading economists in the effort to win the ideological Cold War. Now, the global predominance of US economics journals ensures that only developments that fit into the research agenda of the dominant nation have a chance of becoming influential. Likewise, it ensures that researchers occupy themselves predominantly with questions that are of interest to industrialized countries in general and the US in particular (Das and Qui-Toan 2009), and that they do so from a viewpoint that is not unfriendly to the interests of the US.

It is common for foreign-based scholars to complain that they do not have a fair chance to be published in the top journals. This complaint is well grounded in fact. Das and Qui-Toan (2009), two economists at the World Bank, found that in the 20 years prior to 2004, the five top journals printed a mere 39 papers on India and 65 on China, while at the same time publishing 2,383 on the US economy. Examination of 76,000 country-specific papers in a wider roster of 202 journals showed that roughly 50 percent concerned the US. Of all the studies concerning US data that were published in this wider roster of journals, 6.5 percent made it into the top journals. Of the studies about other countries, the top journals accepted only 1.5 percent. Even after the researchers include a generous higher-quality factor for studies done by US faculties, these are still almost three times as likely to make it into a top journal as similar quality papers about a non-US country.

The power to choose the measure of success

The successful campaign to eliminate distributional issues from the core of the economic discipline has its mirror image in the popularity of GDP as *the* measure of economic success of a nation. While the pioneer of national accounting (ie. GDP), Simon Kusnetz, explicitly said that GDP should not be used as a measure of welfare, and few economists would explicitly advocate such use, it is also true that economists as a group have done precious little to counter the popular opinion that growth, in the sense of maximization of GDP, should be the main goal of economic policy.

GDP is the money value of final goods and services that an economy produces in a quarter or a year (i.e. not including those goods and services used as inputs in the production of other goods and services). This definition makes it is a reasonable yardstick of how much money moved around in a quarter or a year, and therefore captures to some extent how much economic activity in *money* terms there was in that period.

It is a poor measure of actual activity in absolute terms due to using money rather than physically measuring human activity or indicators of human activity (e.g. how many tons of material were moving around in a year, or how many bits of information were exchanged in a year). Some activity that commands a large premium in money terms for institutional reasons, like investment banking, even if it is only one powerful person doing a moderate amount of work, will count the same as the activities of hundreds of factory workers and much more than the activity of millions of housewives. Societal changes like providing more institutional childcare or reigning in the market power of investment banks can make a huge difference in terms of measured GDP, without significantly changing the actual activities performed. Because of this reliance on using money valuations, GDP has severe issues with accurately measuring technological progress.

This method of measuring economic activity has two things going for it. It makes the mathematics a lot easier than measuring in a sensible way. And it conforms with the implicit assumption of mainstream economics that an extra dollar is worth the same to a poor person than it is to a rich person, just as it makes no differentiation between types of activity, for instance whether they are good (i.e. charitable work) or bad (i.e. criminal activity). If a hedge fund manager makes five billion dollars in a good year, as John Paulson reportedly did in 2010 (Burton and Kishan 2011), this is just as good in GDP terms as 13.7 million people living on a dollar a day doubling their incomes.

Policies that treat human beings as social creatures and try to reach the best results in the most important dimensions of human goals cannot flag their successes with equally prominent and simple statistical measures like a single number where higher is "better." The rich and wealthy benefit most from this way of measuring the economic success of a nation, since it de-emphasizes the gains of the mass of low-income people relative to those of a minority of rich people. As far as nations are concerned, it benefits nations that champion the policies favored by this approach, with the US being foremost among these. If you leave out city-states like Luxembourg and small oil-rich countries like Norway, then the US is first in terms of GDP (purchasing power parity adjusted, i.e. for costs of living) per citizen or per worker. This is a beneficial status, as a large and consistently fast-growing economy attracts large sums of international capital. It enables the receiving nation to consume more than it produces and to receive credit at very favorable interest rates, especially when that country's currency is also the world's reserve currency. Additionally, other nations will take the growth leader as a role model, providing a valuable source of soft power. Since the 1990s, the status of the US as a growth leader has enticed Europe to try to emulate this apparent success by becoming more like its role model.

The early neoclassicals, being concerned with the living conditions of the masses, would have found the American economy trailing behind much of Europe and even some "developing" nations. Although the US spends more money per person on health than any other large nation (which provides for a very strong contribution of the health sector to GDP, despite the obvious problems with the ways in which sickness expenditures contribute to actual welfare), tens of millions consider easily curable chronic illnesses to be normal and as a result the US suffers from *60 percent* more years lost due to disabling ill health than Japan, 20–35 percent more than continental European countries, and 12.5 percent more than the next worst member of the OECD, Portugal (World Health Organization Disability Adjusted Life Year statistics 2004). In a comparative assessment of child wellbeing in 21 industrial nations, the US ranked 21st and last in terms of child health and safety, far behind much poorer nations like Greece, Hungary or the Czech Republic (UNICEF 2007). A higher proportion of the population lives in absolute poverty than in many European countries and in Canada – absolute poverty being defined for all countries as 40 percent of the median income of a US citizen (Smeeding 2005). The prisoner to population ratio in the US is five to ten times as high as it is in Europe. A staggering 2.3 percent of the male working age population was in jail in 2004 (Schmitt and Zipperer 2006). Until 2008, the numbers kept going up (PEW Center on the States 2008).

Due to the lack of prominence given to that sort of statistics, which stand deep in the shadow of GDP, modern conventional economists on both sides of the Atlantic can sell the US as the great example to be emulated, despite its shortcomings. It was not coincidence or luck that led to statistical practices so favorable to the world's leading nation. Rather, the United States used its influence as the dominant power of the West to steer international statistics standards in the right direction when they were developed after the Second World War. There is not much written about this. It is not a subject for polite conversation. However, a book by British statistician Michael Ward, whom the United Nations charged with exploring the history of international economic statistics under UN auspices, contains a number of interesting hints. The language of *Quantifying the World* is rather diplomatic. Where it becomes juicy, Ward

(2004) often chooses vague, noncommittal formulations like "this was not politically feasible." However, between the lines he makes clear who had the most influence:

> Behind the façade of internationalism, the US government began to assume an influential role in defining the course of the UN. In this early period, what the US did and said as a leading world power and as a recognized statistical authority exerted a marked impact on UN data policy. The concepts of value added, growth, gross domestic product and gross national product became soon the hallmarks of economic progress.

At the same time, Ward notes, there was resistance against "social measures" and everything that was supposed to measure equity or social progress. To fend these off, the US used their influence on the statistical office of the UN as well as on the Washington-based and firmly US-controlled international financial organizations World Bank and IMF, who in turn helped form statistical standards.

It was not hard to steer the development of statistical standards. A handful of UN technocrats made the key decisions in some back rooms, hardly noticed by the public. Documentation on how and why the relevant decision-making bodies rejected certain statistical initiatives or put them on the back burner to be forgotten is rudimentary. According to Ward, "Certain US politicians believed that capitalism could be undermined and that the American way of life could be threatened, if ideas were espoused that extolled the merits of adding a social dimension to policy."

Lies, damned lies and growth statistics

It is not easy to understand how the United States can be so rich and still have so many people living in poverty; many more, relative to population size, than most Western European countries. The traditional explanation is the unusually unequal distribution of income. There is something more to it, though. The US might be less rich than official statistics make us believe. The leading nation has not only influenced the choice of the measuring stick for economic success, it has also used its power to fix how exactly it applies this measuring stick to its economy. After all, measuring GDP is an art as much as a science. What is usually portrayed as a straightforward act of objective measurement involves value judgments and much guesswork. For reasons which are not hard to see, the way these issues are dealt with and the way measuring techniques are reformed have almost always resulted in higher recorded growth, lower recorded inflation and have almost always benefited the US relative to other large nations.

The status of the US as a role model of economic success during the past 20 years owes a lot to a strong increase of GDP per hour worked (defined as "productivity") from the second half of the 1990s, after a long period of stagnation in productivity growth that started in 1973. This recent status stands in stark contrast to European productivity that had been improving since the 1970s, but began to stagnate from around the second half of the 1990s. From 1983 to 1995, output per worker hour in non-farm US businesses rose by 1.4 percent annually, whereas from 1995 to 2007 US productivity increased by 2.5 percent per year (Feenstra et al. 2009). The Zurich-based economist Jochen Hartwig has shown that the opening of the productivity gap between the US and Europe in the 1990s coincided with a number of statistical innovations in the US, while Europe has emulated these changes only partly and with large delays. Hartwig's analysis of these changes shows that the larger part of the productivity advantage of the US is a "statistical artifact." Measuring with the same methods as before would result in a much smaller advantage for the US, with as much as one-fifth being knocked off the official Bureau of Labor Statistics growth figures since 1998 (Hartwig 2006). This matters a lot, as it reduces the advantage of US productivity growth over Europe by about 60 percent.

As the most important economic and political power by far, the US has been able to make sure that measurement methods help cast the US economy in a favorable light. "The US [is] not in the habit of coordinating any statistical innovations internationally. They make their changes and inform the rest of us afterwards, at best," said Norbert Räth, who is responsible for economic accounting in the German statistical office, upon request by the authors. After the US has made changes, the rest of the world convenes in international statistical committees to decide when and how the new methods shall become international standard, according to Räth (Häring 2010).

In the latest example of this strategy, the US has long been insisting on classifying their large and quickly increasing outlays for weapon systems as investments rather than government consumption. Those who set standards at the UN decided in 2009, over protests from Europe, that this treatment shall become the norm internationally. This standard will be introduced in Europe in 2014. Until then, weapon systems are classified as government consumption in Europe and as investments in the US. The latter classification raises GDP because the *gross* in *gross domestic product* leads to double counting of investments. A naval destroyer, for example, counts into GDP once in the year the government buys it. In the following years, until the end of its economic life, the service that it provides (call it enhanced national security) counts again in the form of depreciation. The double counting results from the fact that depreciation of the stock of investment goods is not detracted from GDP. Even after the rest of the world has switched to the same method, this way of classifying weapons will continue to favor the US since it spends much more money on weaponry than any other sizeable country.

If you remember the earlier statement that technological progress causes significant problems in GDP measurements, you will be glad to hear that the solution adopted by the US is to "adjust" GDP to "more accurately" reflect the "obvious" economic proceeds of technological improvement. This has been done in an arbitrary way that reduces the reported rate of inflation and takes two forms: (i) quadratic weighting in inflation measurement and (ii) the "hedonic method" in inflation measurement.

Quadratic weighting

Quadratic weighting is a mathematical method that ensures that goods that increase more in price than others automatically get a smaller weight when average inflation is calculated. This is done for similar kinds of products, like various kinds of apples or breads. The practice is justified on the grounds that consumers are likely to shift their purchases away from the brands that have increased in price and toward those which have had smaller price increases. No attempt was ever made to empirically validate this assumption. One can equally plausibly argue that goods that happen to become more popular have steeper price increases because producers of these goods take advantage of the increasing demand. According to the calculations of the Bureau of Labor Statistics (BLS), an agency of the labor ministry, quadratic weighting lowers inflation by 0.3 percentage points per year compared to traditional methods (Greenlees and McClelland 2008). If inflation is lowered, the *real* or *inflation-adjusted* GDP will be higher. Economic growth is generally reported in inflation-adjusted terms. Many countries, including Germany, do not use this trick. All else being equal, for this reason their inflation rate will be reported 0.3 percent higher and their growth rate about 0.3 percent lower.

The hedonic method

The most important innovation that the US has introduced since 1997 is quality adjustment according to the "hedonic method" in inflation measurement. This is particularly important for goods with fast changes in product characteristics, like computers and other information technology (IT) goods. Hedonic adjustment involves calculating what attributes determine the price of different kinds of computers at any given time. If models change over time and the new models have more memory and faster processors than the old ones, statisticians calculate what a computer with the attributes of the current model would have cost a year ago. Then, the actual price is compared with this hypothetical price and the difference is recorded as (negative) inflation.

Hedonic adjustment is a large part of what made it possible for US statistics to record an increase in labor productivity (i.e. production volume per hour worked) from 1990 to 2000 in the computer-producing industry of 1,500 percent and of 1,000 percent in the semiconductor-producing industry (Houseman 2007). Since information technology and consumer electronics account for a higher share of the US economy than in most other nations, this massive statistical blowup of IT production benefits the US even as methods of measuring are harmonized.

For this statistical blowup of production volumes of the US economy to occur, it is necessary that the hedonic method is not used as much on imports. Government policy has ensured this. The steep increase in productivity of the US economy coincided with an equally steep increase in the global engagement of the US IT industry after 1995. US firms have offshored a very large proportion of their production of computers, software, semiconductors and consumer electronics to developing countries. They import intermediate goods and production services such as programming from China, India and other countries. What is left in the US is often only marketing and distribution activities. The US imports a lot more IT products than it exports. In 2008, the trade deficit of this sector was a spectacular US$104 billion (Feenstra et al. 2009). Imports are subtracted from final domestic production value. Thus in principle the hedonic increase in production values should be counterbalanced by a hedonic increase of the same order of magnitude of the volume of these imported intermediate goods and services.

However, in reality they are not. The International Prices Program at the BLS, which is responsible for recording import prices, is one of the programs that has experienced the largest budget cuts in recent years, according to a spokesman for the BLS (Häring 2010). In spite of the huge difficulties and gaps in measurement of import prices, and in spite of a huge increase in import volumes, the BLS had to shed a significant proportion of their personnel in this area. In contrast, the program that is responsible for the personnel-intensive hedonic quality adjustment of domestic prices was exempt from these budget cuts.

The BLS is thus unable to hedonically inflate these imports just as with the sales of the final product. If Microsoft sells a new version of its operating system, hedonic quality adjustments vastly increase the value of these sales when being recorded for GDP purposes. However, the gain in product quality that goes back to the work of Indian programmers is treated as though it were done entirely in the US. The same happens whenever Apple sells a new gadget assembled in China.

On top of that, statistics expert Susan Houseman has assembled evidence that the import statistics of the US do not cover many imported products and do not adequately take into account price declines of imported products (Houseman 2007). Both inadequacies artificially increase measured GDP and productivity. Feenstra et al. (2009) have recently calculated that about a fifth of the apparent increase in productivity of the US economy was due to miscalculation of import prices in the IT sector. Their calculation uses potentially problematic official import price data, which the BLS obtains from importing firms. It does not deal with the issue of hedonic adjustment, thus leaving out two important sources of bias which would likely account for even more of the apparent productivity increase.

While the asymmetrical application of hedonic price adjustment to local production versus imports is clearly wrong and misleading, one can argue that many of the statistical reforms of recent decades that have invariably raised measured GDP have indeed been improvements in measurement. However, a strong bias still results from the selectivity with which possible improvements of statistical methods are pursued. It is more likely that those which lead to higher growth and lower inflation will be pursued rather than those which would lead to the opposite result. While the statisticians in the US, directed by their government, put a lot of effort into the quality adjustment of the domestic prices of goods that are subject to strong technical progress, quality changes of other goods and services are blatantly left out. This can lead to absurd results. One example is quality of hospital care. Statisticians used to equate output in the health sector with a measure of its inputs, such as the number of nights spent in hospital beds and the number of doctors and nurses caring for the occupants. Now they measure output "directly," for instance the treatment of a patient with a stomach ulcer or a birth. This sounds reasonable in principle. The strange thing, however, is that there is no attempt at quality adjustment. Under pressure from insurers, hospitals today send patients home much earlier than before, often allegedly before they are fully cured. Official statistics record such practices as steep increases in production and productivity. If a hospital sends a woman home two days after childbirth, when they used to keep new mothers in the hospital for seven days, they can perform about three births for what was previously the cost of one. The fact that mothers get much less care is not taken into account. The hospital can increase its measured output and productivity threefold, according to the official statistics. Ironically, US statisticians made this change in 1997, at exactly the same time when government directed them to put more effort into the quality adjustment of IT prices. Other countries followed. In the education sector the same has happened: now, if fewer teachers teach more students in larger classes, this is recorded as a productivity increase. No attempt at quality adjustment is made.

With these biases in mind, it is less surprising that there are so many people depending on welfare payments and food stamps in such a rich country. If recorded income increases consist largely of hedonically inflated bits and bytes and similar statistical artifacts, a poor American family cannot have derived much benefit. They cannot survive on bits and bytes. If the American government continues to simply inflate numbers rather than actually doing something to improve livelihoods, then it cannot be long before the average American family will need the support of soup kitchens while GDP and incomes continue to "rise." Perhaps not coincidentally, the clientele of soup kitchens has increased tremendously in recent years.

Lastly, as to why there is such effort to reduce the reported rate of inflation in the US, consider that US social security payments, including pensions, must be raised annually at the rate of inflation, as is required by law. The Boskin Commission which came up with many of the described statistical "improvements" had been explicitly charged by Congress to counter the problem of overpayment of social security arising from an alleged overstatement of official inflation. Also, the required payment on US debt is reduced when inflation is declared to be lower.

Economics' self-fulfilling prophecies

> Social science theories can influence reality in profound ways, by influencing how we think about ourselves and how we act.
> —*Ferraro, Pfeffer and Sutton, 2003*

An influential social science like economics can shape reality. Assumptions that were false at the onset can become true if people believe distorted analyses and act upon this belief. If the science is shaped in the interest of the mighty and rich, it not only shapes beliefs in the interest of this group, but also reality.

A plethora of studies have found that economists have different values than people on average. Maxwell and Ames (1981) conducted a series of experiments with public goods games. In such games, experimenters ask subjects to provide some of their own resources for the benefit of the group as a whole. The experimenter puts in an additional percentage, say 50 percent of what is in the pot, before the money is distributed back equally to all group members. Thus, the more money people put in the joint pot the better off is the group as a whole. However, participants have the opportunity for a free ride on the contributions of others. Pure self-interest would dictate that participants choose to take the free ride. In spite of this incentive to do so, the researchers found that people would contribute significantly, counting on others to do the same. The only exceptions were those participants who were graduate students in economics. They were far more likely to free ride than any other group of participants. After the experiments, the researchers asked their subjects follow-up questions: One was, "What is a fair investment in the public good?" About three-quarters of the non-economists considered "half or more" of the endowment as a fair contribution and one-quarter answered "all." A second question was, "Are you concerned about fairness in making your investment decision?" Almost all non-economists answered "yes." The corresponding responses of the economics graduate students were too difficult to summarize. More than one-third of them refused to answer the question on what was a fair share or gave complex responses that couldn't be coded. Most of those who did respond said that little or no contribution was "fair."

Cadsby and Maynes (1998) found a similarly striking result using a variant of the public goods game. Economics and business students tended toward the free riding equilibrium in which nobody contributed and the group as a whole fared relatively badly. Nurses were much more likely to achieve the more attractive cooperating equilibrium.

A "prisoner's dilemma" game played by economics majors and other students yielded the same general pattern. This is also a game where a pair of participants does best if both cooperate, but individuals can always improve their situation by acting selfishly. Only 40 percent of the economists cooperated, while 60 percent of students of other disciplines did (Frank, Gilovich and Regan 1993).

Thus do economic theories influence social norms of accepted behavior and become self-fulfilling. In his book *The Vote Motive*, the economist Gordon Tullock writes that "the average human being is about 95 percent selfish in the narrow sense of the term" (Tullock 1976). Such convictions, propagated by an influential science like economics, shape the public's feeling of what constitutes normal behavior. The tendency of neoclassical economics to equate non-selfish behavior with irrational behavior seems to have made inroads into the feelings of the public. Many people seem to feel a need to justify themselves if they contradict it. In experimental research where participants could donate some of their rewards for specific causes, people were hesitant to promote publicly a cause in which they had no stake. They were less hesitant to support it in an anonymous way. Apparently, they dreaded being considered irrational if they were seen acting in somebody else's interest. Consistent with this finding, opinion surveys have shown that Americans regard selfishness as increasingly prevalent, i.e. normal (Miller and Ratner 1998).

Even the terms and concepts used by the economic mainstream seem to shape people's preferences and actions. The vocabulary of economists focuses on norms of market exchange between strictly selfish people. This vocabulary provides the framework in which people think about economic issues. Experiments with American college students and Israeli pilots have shown how semantics can influence people's behavior. The participants played a prisoner's dilemma game. The game was introduced as the "Wall Street Game" to half of the participants, while to the other half it was introduced as the "Community Game." Cooperation was the norm if the game was called the Community Game. Mutual defection was the norm if it was called the Wall Street Game (Liberman, Samuels and Ross 2004).

American "exceptionalism" and the false belief in a just world

To the degree that the peculiar attitude and language of economists has a disproportional influence on political decision makers and the public, it can cause feedback loops which make this influence self-reinforcing and permanent. The famous and highly cited 1998 paper "The Paradox of Redistribution" by Korpi and Palme showed that from ample empirical evidence, *not* targeting the poor with redistribution, but rather letting social policies be universal, reduces the total net cost of redistribution to society and is far better at achieving equality of opportunity (in terms of the number of people who do better than their parents each year) and reduction of poverty. How can this be the case? It turns out that this counterintuitive result is due to those just above the poverty level being most opposed to enforcing equality of opportunity through targeting the poor. Thus, the more targeted income redistribution policies are, the more resistance there is and the smaller the redistribution budget will be. In fact, earnings-related benefits like misfortune insurance and social security pensions (where the benefit received *rises* with your income) were found to have by far the best effects in practice on reducing poverty and improving equality of opportunity. Yet economists freely dismiss such an outcome as being economically impossible: mainstream economic theory is extremely clear that subsidies "tend to create serious distortions in market mechanisms, reduce work incentives and thereby reduce economic efficiency and growth" (Korpi and Palme 1998). This is despite the fact that no empirical study has ever found any empirical evidence for this assumption, as Korpi and Palme point out.

Of all the rich countries in the world, singling out the poor for intervention is by far the most popular in the United States. There, economists have popularized the calculation of "target efficiency" which is defined in terms of the proportion of expenditures going exclusively to the poor – thus the greater the targeting, the better the program. This is despite this approach having exactly the opposite empirical effects from its stated intent, which is to provide succor to the unfortunate, and to help create fairness in society.

Why therefore do US policymakers persist with ever more targeted assistance? Americans are exceptional in their widespread belief in a just world in which everyone who tries hard enough will make it, and that people generally get what they deserve and deserve what they get. This stands in contrast to those in most other Western countries who tell their children that the world is not fair, and that no matter how hard they will try they will not earn their fair share (Benabou and Tirole 2006). This is strange, because equality of opportunity in terms of the number of people who do better than their parents each year is lowest by far in the United States, and this has been the case since the late 1970s.

If you live in a state with a well-designed set of welfare incentives that intelligently equalize opportunity (and even most South American countries have intelligent and well-funded welfare systems relative to the size of their economies by US standards), you can afford to admit to yourself and your children that life is not fair without doing them much harm. In the US, to end up relying on welfare supports is very unattractive, so parents have an incentive to instill into their children an ethic and a belief system that entices them to do their utmost to avoid that outcome. This could explain why Americans insist on believing – against all empirical evidence – that their society is one in which everybody can make it, and one in which your family background determines your economic fate much less than in other countries. This is a belief that defiantly ignores the facts. Three international comparisons of the correlation of income between fathers and sons had the US come out highest or among the highest in the respective sample of countries at values around 0.5. This means that half the income advantage or disadvantage of a father would on average be transferred to his son. In a country with a correlation coefficient around 0.2, like Germany or Denmark, descendants of poor families are likely to reach the average income within two generations. In countries like the US, it takes 75 to 100 years for this to become likely (Schmitt and Zipperer 2006).

This feedback loop hypothesis can help explain why Europe and the US, though they have very similar populations, can go in such different directions with their equality of opportunity policies. Researchers from the London School of Economics tested the theory empirically. They analyzed the answers to British opinion polls regarding questions of fairness and responsibility for one's own fate and found evidence that people's attitudes do indeed change with alterations in income inequality the way Benabou and Tirole hypothesized. After the reforms under Margaret Thatcher, the demand for state enforcement of minimum incomes as stated in opinion polls collapsed. Britons became on average more and more convinced that generous benefits for the poor and unemployed would make those who received them lazy and that large income differentials were required to motivate people to study and work hard (Georgiadis and Manning 2007).

Thus the thesis that only individual selfishness is rational and that it is irrational or even dangerous to act in the interest of the group is not an innocent assumption or an inconsequential exercise in semantics. That the most influential social science works with this definition of rationality has made it harder to promote group interests. This hurt those groups which are relatively large and hard to organize and that are dependent on a widespread feeling of group solidarity the most. Measures to ensure equality of opportunity, faith-based solidarity movements or unions are prime examples.

As food for thought and an example of creating equality of opportunity in a society without giving no-strings-attached money to the poor: while the minimum personal income guarantee in Britain is a small fraction of the EU15 average and by far the lowest in the EU15 apart from Greece (just US$5100 as compared to an EU15 average of US$18,200 according to the OECD Benefits and Wages database), Britain is much more generous than the EU15 in non-monetary low-income benefits. For example, those on welfare support get free full-time and distance university tuition and an additional stipend for attending university worth around US$40,000 across three years, and cost of living expenses such as public transport tickets and even movie theater admission are substantially reduced in price for anyone on welfare support, including the old and disabled. There are also additional free services such as free dental care, free glasses, free medicines and even free wigs in addition to the free healthcare everyone in Britain is entitled to, which in aggregate cost the British state about as much per person as it does for Germany despite the fact that Germany is more than three times as generous in minimum income guarantees (Eurostat 2011).

The previous discussion shows how the typically polarized and emotionally charged debate about the welfare system in the US achieves little but a colossal waste of money: what matters is to achieve equality of opportunity for the least net cost such that society is more meritocratic and fair, not whether one form or another is morally wrong or theoretically wrong according to the "economics." Whether this is done via generous minimum income guarantees, subsidies of expensive investments in self-improvement such as qualifications in new skills, or even an "escalator" system where payments are tied to society-benefiting behavior such as in the highly successful Bolsa Família program in Brazil, the lesson is that it doesn't matter which you choose as long as you choose something which is empirically known to deliver results.

He who pays the piper calls the tune

The Member of Parliament, who supports every proposal for strengthening this monopoly, is sure to acquire not only the reputation of understanding trade, but great popularity and influence with an order of men, whose numbers and wealth render them of great importance.

—*Adam Smith, 1784*

What Adam Smith said in the above quote from the second edition of his *Wealth of Nations* regarding parliamentarians and their incentives to please powerful economic interests holds true for economists as well, and still does to this day. The modern mainstream conception of economics is attractive to all those who do well under the status quo and who would do even better with less grassroots and collective action. Its focus on voluntary exchange protects those who have become rich and powerful against any deterioration of their situation from group action. Its antigovernment and anti-grassroots spirit delivers arguments to roll back whatever public action there is, whether it be activists from the Tea Party or anti–Wall Street movements.

Christian Arnsperger and Yanis Varoufakis (2006) describe the mixture of dogma and self-censorship that shields the dominant paradigm of economics:

> When an inquisitive graduate student, or academic, who has mastered neoclassical technique, but has started developing doubts, starts questioning the meta-axioms, she is effectively questioning the hegemony of her profession. Publishing in the 'good' journals is hard enough. Publishing articles, which question the meta-axioms, is even harder. It takes a foolhardy young soul to jeopardise a hard-earned career path in pursuit of the truth-status of one or more of the meta-axioms.

They also suggest an explanation for why there is not more dissent that might eventually swamp the dogma. The status quo is highly favorable to mainstream economists. Their influence is much bigger than that of any other social scientists. Research funding is vast compared to what other social sciences get, employment in the field after graduation is the highest of all social sciences, and the average pay is substantially higher (Payscale 2012). Being able to give simple and clear answers that do not offend the people holding the purse strings is certainly more conducive to being influential and obtaining public and private research funding than engaging in fundamental methodological discourse. Taking power out of the equations helps to avoid any alienation of sponsors.

In the context of the subprime crisis, University of Pennsylvania economist Devesh Kapur (2009) made one of the rare mentions of the powerful incentives that steer economics in certain directions. He notes that many of the intellectual underpinnings of the causes of this crisis – financial innovation, financial deregulation, capital account liberalization and the promotion of stock options – have come from researchers at the leading economics and finance departments of the US. He draws attention to the fact that these economists have benefited very handsomely from the developments they promoted. As the financial sector grew enormously and hauled in huge profits, some of these profits went to them and their institutions as research grants and speaker fees. Many of them have strong business interests ranging from partnerships or consulting in hedge funds to board directorships in financial institutions. "There would be little chance of being invited to give a lucrative talk at Citicorp if one were in favor of sovereign debt forgiveness in the 1980s, against capital account liberalization in the 1990s or against stock options in the 2000s," Kapur notes. One may add that if you held any of these views during these time periods while looking for a good job in academia, you were not likely to land one. In a similar way, most public finance chairs have become tax avoidance chairs. Their brightest students will pursue careers in investment banks and law firms. Their job will be to help these companies reduce their tax burdens. They want to be trained for such jobs. There is much less money and career prospects in researching ways to implement an efficient and fair tax system without loopholes.

According to Kapur, economics is falling behind other sciences, like biology, which have recently made efforts to ensure greater transparency about conflicts of interest. It hardly created a stir when it was first exposed in 2009 that Frederic Mishkin, Columbia professor and governor of the Federal Reserve from 2006 to 2008, had taken US\$124,000 from the Icelandic Chamber of Commerce for a report called "Financial Stability in Iceland." In this report, published in 2006 when Iceland started to face mistrust from market participants over its severely overextended banking industry, Mishkin and his co-author Tryggvi Herbertsson praise strong prudential supervision in Iceland and call a meltdown very unlikely (Herbertsson and Mishkin 2006). In a videotaped interview for the film *Inside Job*, Mishkin later calls this a mistake. Asked on what kind of research he had based his conclusions, he mentions a general attitude at the time and his strong faith in the Icelandic central bank. Presented with a copy of his CV in which the name of the study had changed to

"Financial Instability in Iceland," he calls this a typo (Alloway 2010). In the meantime, the "typo" has been corrected on Mishkin's website.

Not before the run-up to the annual meeting of the AEA in January 2011 did the subject of professional ethics and conflicts of interests of economists receive some attention. The AEA was pushed into action by a damning research report into the systematic concealment of conflicts of interest by top financial economists and by a letter from three hundred economists who urged the association to come up with a code of ethics. Epstein and Carrick-Hagenbarth (2010) have shown that many highly influential financial economists in the US hold roles in the private financial sector, from serving on boards to owning the respective companies. Many of these have written on financial regulation in the media or in scholarly papers. Very rarely have they disclosed their affiliations to the financial industry in their writing or in their testimony in front of Congress, thus concealing a potential conflict of interest. If financial economists argue against pay limits for managers of financial firms as, for example, the so-called Squam Lake Group did, a well-informed public could not help wonder if the fact that the majority of members held well-paid positions in the financial sector might have influenced the findings. The report of the Squam Lake Group, which comprised the *crème de la crème* of financial economists, was taken very seriously; it was presented in the presence of Federal Reserve chairman Ben Bernanke (Chan 2010). Potential conflicts of interest were never mentioned in the process.

Another rare case where these incentives have come to the light is the controversy around the Friedman Institute at the University of Chicago. After the Nobel Memorial Prize winner had died, the university wanted to establish an independent Friedman Institute on campus. A large number of non-economist faculty members signed a petition against this name choice because they considered the name Friedman to be associated with a biased social agenda. They feared the Institute's agenda would exclude views not in keeping with its namesake. In October 2008, after months of fierce discussion, Nobel Memorial Prize winner James Heckman, a member of the faculty committee, expressed some sympathy for the idea of changing the name. In an interview with the student newspaper of the university, the *Chicago Maroon*, he described the most important counterargument quite frankly: much more external money would likely flow into the institute if it were associated with the agenda of Friedman. Asked about the notion that seeking donors with particular opinions and naming the Institute for a figure who espoused those opinions could influence the Institute's research he said, "Yes, it's true for any institute. You state a mission, attract funders. They expect the mission to be fulfilled. Very rarely do people fund pure knowledge" (Heckman 2008).

The way in which economic theories are weeded out, left to wilt or hatched and promoted means that nobody has to do biased research intentionally to create a profoundly biased science. Most of the bright and successful mainstream economists who are honestly convinced that their approach is the right one will never realize that their success is aided by a very uneven playing field. They are justified in their pride of being the best among many, but it never crosses their minds that they would not be half as successful if they had the misfortune of holding a worldview different from that of their sponsors.

Conclusion

In this chapter, we have seen how the power of economic science and discourse, in shaping the way people think about society and the economy, have exposed scholars to subtle pressure and incentives. While there is not much in economic theory or even in neoclassical theory that would bar economists from including issues of economic power into their analysis, these external influences have, over the decades and centuries, created a science that is strongly biased in favor of negative viewpoints regarding issues like creating equality of opportunity or the role of government and society versus the individual. An important element of this has been neglecting or even denying the influence of power and the tendency of market economies toward the concentration of wealth, power and opportunity in a minority.

This does not mean that economics is forever doomed to have a big blind spot. Such blind spots will always be explored by particularly independent, honest, naïve or adventurous minds. This is what made this book possible. Alas, this is also why the problem is ongoing. The rich and powerful continue to hold the purse strings and wield inordinate influence over those who decide what is good and important research, and what is not.

This bias in favor of the powerful is present on the level of social class as much as on the level of countries. Countries who achieve global economic, military and political dominance tend to also achieve dominance in economic science and can create biases in their own favor. This was true for Britain during her Empire, where mainstream economic opinion switched from promoting protectionist industrial policy to free trade after Britain had achieved dominance. The same happened in the US after the country obtained the status of economic superpower. US-dominated economics increasingly emphasized the strong points of free market economics over Soviet-style central planning and became increasingly critical of government and of any form of grassroots action. This was useful for the West in the Cold War and, within the West, it made the American model of capitalism appear superior to all others.

These biases in economic theory have their counterpart in measurement of economic success. Measures which illuminate the living conditions of the poor or the majority of the population are neglected in favor of income averages, which treat a billion dollars earned by a hedge fund manager as equal to a billion-dollar increase in the combined incomes of the poor and destitute. Choices in statistical methods have consistently favored alternatives that present the results of governments' economic policies in a more favorable light. Reforms of statistical methods in the last decades have also consistently resulted in a better measured relative performance of the dominant nation.

In the next chapter, we will examine how a particularly powerful set of economic agents, those controlling the financial industry, have always used and still use their power to extract high profits to the detriment of ordinary citizens and of industries further down the hierarchy, while a biased economic mainstream pretended it was free competitive forces at work.

Chapter 2

MONEY IS POWER

An open, competitive, and liberalized financial market can effectively allocate scarce resources in a manner that promotes stability and prosperity far better than governmental intervention.
—*Hank Paulson, 2007*

Market fundamentalism has served well the interests of the owners and the managers of financial capital… Deregulation of financial transactions also served the interests of the managers of financial capital. The financial industry grew to a point there it represented 25 percent of the stock market capitalization of the United States.
—*George Soros, 2009*

Shortly before the subprime crisis, US treasury secretary Hank Paulson insisted that it is best to leave the financial sector alone to do its work. This is not a surprising statement for a former CEO of investment bank Goldman Sachs, whom we would expect to have the interests of the financial industry close to his heart. However, the statement also embodies the prevailing view espoused by textbook economics and economists giving policy advice. According to this view, competition among financial service providers, issuers of securities and investors will ensure that prices of financial instruments reflect their value at all times and that scarce financial resources are allocated to their best uses. It also holds that financial markets tend toward equilibrium and accurately reflect all available information about the future.

The laissez-faire attitude of mainstream economics stands in contrast to popular wisdom. "Money is Power" goes the saying. Those who have a lot of money tend to have commensurate power. There is nobody with more money at their disposal than financial conglomerates who are charged with managing vast amounts of other people's money.

Other people's money is an important source of power, because the sums involved can be enormous and because you do not have to take quite as much care when you are making decisions about other people's money. After all, it is not your money. You can sacrifice some of the return or incur some extra risk if it's to your own advantage.

Other people's money is, however, only the lever for the power of banks and other financial institutions. The ultimate source of their power is the fact that money is always scarce and financing hard to come by. According to the efficient market view, anybody who needs financing and can afford to borrow will get credit. In truth, the credit markets are among the least perfect markets. Credit rationing is the norm, and those who have money to lend or the power to steer other people's money have commensurate power.

Anybody with a sense of history would know that the flow of money has always shaped the development of economies. However, for economics textbooks and many leading mainstream models, the financial sector hardly exists. It is just greasing the wheels of the economy in the background, unselfishly making sure that capital goes to its most productive uses.

A lot has been written on the financial industry in recent years, and very little of it is new or surprising to anyone versed in economic history. Rather than reiterate the well-documented problems with the theories and practices of modern day finance, we will firstly explain why finance is a very special kind of industry with unusual characteristics and conflicts of interest, most of which are generated by the superior information advantage financial institutions hold over everybody else. Secondly, we will explain the economic history that gave birth to the modern relationship between finance and government. For many centuries it has been a highly incestuous relationship, and much of why finance, banking and government are the way they are derives from that history of precedent and convention irrespective of whether it is sustainable in the long term, wise or even sane – particularly the unique privilege conferred on banks to create money out of nothing that has been the root cause of the majority of the 124 systemic banking crises that economists of the IMF have counted between 1970 and 2007 (Laeven and Valencia 2008). Thirdly, throughout the chapter we present proposals suggesting how to diffuse the financial sector's ability to abuse customers and investors and its penchant for creating financial crises.

It is worth reflecting upon the fact that the financial industry has been, when averaged over the long run, just 50 to 60 percent as profitable as class-leading industries such as pharmaceuticals or telecommunications or even good old fashioned railroads (Dimson et al. 2002; Fortune 500 annual rankings). This failure of finance to keep up with other class-leading industries is due to two reasons: (i) averaging, since when finance is doing well, it does as well but not much better than other industries, while the toll of repeated collapses, crises and bailouts drive down long run average profitability and (ii) splurging, as most of the potential profit is doled out to a small number of employees in the form of high salaries and exorbitant bonuses. For example, according to Bloomberg, in 2009 Morgan Stanley paid an industry record of 62 percent of all its revenues in compensation, and 2007 Goldman Sachs paid another industry record of an average US$661,490 *per employee*. It is very difficult to believe – at least to anyone outside banking – that a person competing with other people at moving patterns of numbers around computer systems (i.e. effectively a crude form of computer programmer) is many times more valuable to society than an average surgeon, an average mayor, or even an average chief software engineer at Google, Microsoft or Facebook.

The Sources of the Power of Finance

Short side power on the credit market

> Men may safely be allowed to grant or to deny loans of their own money to whomsoever they see fit. But bank resources are, in the main, not owned by the stockholders nor by the directors, but is represented by deposits. The bank has no right to use its powers specifically to build up or destroy other businesses.
>
> —*Louis Brandeis, 1913*

There would be no room for a significant role of power in finance if markets for credit and finance were fully competitive. Anybody trying to exert power would simply lose business to a competitor. However, as Stiglitz and Weiss (1981) and Akerlof (1970) have demonstrated, incomplete information means that some markets do not clear, which means not all demand is met. The market for credit is such a market. Lenders are on the short side of the market, the side of those who have what is in short supply. Lenders can normally turn down a borrower with near impunity because they will easily find another seeking a loan (i.e. they have high "seller power"). Borrowers are typically on the long side of the market (i.e. they have low "buyer power"). They ask for something that is in insufficient supply at an affordable rate of interest, if at all. If borrowers are denied credit by a certain lender, they might not find another one or might have to accept conditions that are much worse (Bowles and Gintis 2008). Indeed, just being denied a loan in itself can damage a person's centralized credit rating according to any of the "Big Three" international centralized credit bureaus (Experian, Equifax and TransUnion/Callcredit), as can applying for more than one new credit source in "too short" a time period.

The main reason that the credit market does not clear is the potential for adverse selection. Ideally, banks charge a low interest rate for loans to finance low-risk projects and a high interest rate to finance high-risk projects. If they could reliably tell them apart, they would finance every project at an interest rate commensurate with the risk. However, the bankers can only make an educated guess about the riskiness of a project and the trustworthiness of a borrower. If the bank considers a project very risky and charges an interest rate of, say, 25 percent above the rate of inflation (i.e. they calculate that at least one out of five borrowers will default), the likelihood is low that reasonable and honest investors will take it. Those who accept such terms are likely to be risk-lovers, frauds or criminals. They might ignore the high interest rate because they have decided they will either get rich with the project or fail and default on the loan. It will thus normally not be attractive for banks to offer credit at a real interest rate of 25 percent. Instead, banks will demand that the entrepreneurs come up with a significant amount of their own money or provide collateral to show that they are not gamblers. If they do not have enough money or collateral, they will not get a loan.

Even for loans of moderate risk, bankers will provide less credit and demand more collateral than they would if they were able to better estimate the risk. They will want a premium to cover not only the objective risk of projects failing, but also the risk stemming from the fact that their customers likely know said risks better than they do. They will limit the size of the credit in relation to the cost of a project. For these reasons, there are always many credit-constrained customers on the market, while banks are on the short side of the market. If banks choose not to give a loan, the borrowers suffer much more than they do.

The power to control other people's money

The fact that financial firms control vast sums of other people's money greatly enhances their short side power. They can offer or withhold from their credit-constrained customers not only their own money, but that of others as well. They control the flow of money either by virtue of being an entrusted money manager or by providing investors with judgment on the relative attractiveness of different investments. This judgment influences who gets the money of these investors.

Those who let the financial industry manage their money or who listen to investment advice from the financial industry expect that their own investment goals and nothing else determines where their money goes, an assumption that is mirrored by mainstream economic theory. Alas, they lack the knowledge to ensure this happens. A host of recent empirical research indicates that all sorts of financial firms consider individual investors easy prey. They cheat them of some of their money's revenue at every stage of the investment process. Analysts and brokers lead clients to believe they will give honest expert advice on what to buy. This belief gives them the power to twist their clients' investment decisions according to the interests of their firms. They also collude with firm managers who pay them for luring individual investors to their own firms' securities.

A notorious case of knowingly fooling investors is that of star analyst Henry Blodget, who recommended shares while calling them "crap" in internal emails to colleagues (PBS 2002). In a study titled "Do Security Analysts Speak in Two Tongues?" Malmendier and Shanthikumar (2009) have proved that this was only the tip of the iceberg, and indeed that analysts routinely lie to individual investors, who are called "retail investors" in the industry. The study compared what analysts tell their (gullible) retail customers and their (more sophisticated) institutional clients about the same stock. The comparison reveals that analysts exaggerate company prospects much less when they are addressing professional investors. If there is an investment banking relationship between the analyst's employer and the respective company, analysts will take an even more bullish stance toward retail customers than their peers.

A comparison of the recommendations of bank analysts and of independent research houses from 1996 to 2003 corroborates these findings. Independent analysts did a lot better on average, mostly because they did not issue absurd buy recommendations for bad stocks. If the bank analysts' buy recommendation concerned companies that had previously sold new stock, they underperformed independent analysts particularly badly. These results indicate that companies expect and receive supportive analyst recommendations in return for the high fees that they pay to banks for issuing their shares (Barber, Lehavy and Trueman 2007).

Analysts do not compromise their personal and professional honor for nothing. The most important factor for their remuneration and career prospects is their willingness and ability to tell retail customers a story that entices them to do business with their employer. For analysts who cover stocks that have been underwritten by their employer, their career outcome depends even more on that optimism than on the accuracy of earnings forecasts. In a hot stock market, the reward for optimism is highest. This implies that banks systematically amplify stock market bubbles by having their analysts cheer on the retail investor crowds (Kubik and Hong 2003).

The incentives of the analysts and their employers are not a secret to the companies covered by their research: if analysts treat them well, these companies return the favor. The gift exchange between analyzed companies and analysts consists mostly of privileged access to information in exchange for favorable reports. A survey of thousands of stock analysts and corporate executives, conducted between 2001 and 2003, revealed that two-thirds received favors from the companies they covered. The more favors they received, the less likely they were to downgrade a company after poor results. Analysts expect to be singled out for penalties, such as cutting off personal contact, if they downgrade the company's stock. In effect, there exists a tightly knit web of symbiotic relationships between companies and analysts, which works to hoodwink retail investors systematically into buying overpriced stock (Westphal and Clement 2008).

The scandals around Enron and Worldcom forced the Securities and Exchange Commission (SEC) to act. It punished some banks and some analysts. Now it is no longer legal to pay analysts bonuses explicitly for helping to win investment banking business. Multiple-page disclaimers have to accompany every analyst report. As soon as the latter rule came into effect, a laboratory study cast serious doubt on its efficacy. Cain, Loewenstein and Moore (2005) showed test subjects a glass jar filled with coins from a distance. Then they asked them to estimate its value. The more precisely participants estimated the value of the coins the higher their reward would be. They assigned to each participant an advisor who was allowed to inspect the jar from close up. The higher the guess of their "customers" the more money the advisors would get. The researchers informed half of the clients about their advisors' conflict of interest (in the presence of the advisors) – the other half was not explicitly informed. As could be expected, most advisors exaggerated the amount of money in the jar. Advisors with a transparent conflict of interest exaggerated the jar's contents even more than their peers did. However, clients who knew of their advisors' conflict of interest trusted them almost as much as those who were unaware. In the end, the informed group came out worse than the uninformed one, to the benefit of their advisors. It seems that people have an urge to believe that their advisors act in their best interest even if they know of conflicts of interest. On the other hand, the advisors tend to bias their advice even more toward their own interest if they have to inform clients of the potential conflict, presumably because they assume the clients will account for the bias.

To really help investors, the conflicts of interest have to be eliminated and – where this is not possible – breaches in fiduciary duties have to be prosecuted and punished seriously. General disclaimers that a conflict of interest might arise are just window dressing.

Insider power

The process of collecting and distributing large amounts of money provides financial institutions with abundant information with which they can trade profitably. Brokers obtain exclusive information about demand (e.g. when a large buy order comes in). Banks see the books of prospective borrowers and other customers.

Financial firms and their employees are certainly not the only ones privy to insider information. What sets them apart from other insiders is the privileged access to information about not just one, but many companies. While a company insider has an occasional or regular opportunity to take advantage of those who invest in a specific security, financial sector people have regular opportunities to do so in many different securities, and they can often do so on a far larger scale.

Asset managing firms and hedge funds in particular can use insider information that they obtain in the course of their daily operations to buy securities cheaply before others hear the good news, or to sell them at a high price before others hear the bad news. An SEC investigation involving wiretaps and taped conversations by informants with billionaire hedge fund founder Raj Rajaratnam provides a rare peek into the business model of many of these opaque and secretive institutions. Rajaratnam had a network of informants who would give him insider information on which he could trade. In the year 2008 alone, Rajaratnam's hedge fund firm Galleon paid US$250 million to its banks in fees, trading commissions and borrowing charges. The fund was well known for pressing the banks it was working with for hints about market developments, such as big buy and sell orders (Sender 2009).

Trading on insider information diminishes the returns of all other investors. The damage to the individual investor from the individual insider deal is minor. However, as we will see, insider dealings and similar strategies are so pervasive in the financial industry that the cumulative damage to the individual investor can be sizable.

Market power in finance

Two important conditions for the exertion of economic power are the existence of barriers to entry and the power to determine prices. High profits of big investment banks, the constant increase in government-sponsored financial institutions and many examples of extortion, which we will cover below, provide ample proof that competition does not work well to discipline participants in the financial sector. Market entry is not free. You need a license to found a bank and there is a significant regulatory burden. More important, there are what economists call economies of scale and economies of scope. This means that a large bank can provide its services at much lower cost than a small new entry. This is because administrative costs are very important in this business. The fixed overhead cost becomes less important if you have more business. Additionally, banking is a matter of trust and trust takes time to build. This puts newcomers at a big disadvantage. In addition, banking and investment banking in particular are all about contacts and information. The larger you are the more different business lines you have, and the longer you have been in business the more information and the more contacts you will have. Thus, large investment banks do many of their trades with superior information, just like a card player who can see some of the other players' cards. This puts them in a nearly unbeatable position (Augar 2005; Peukert 2010). For an illustration take Goldman Sachs: according to Bloomberg research, based on Goldman Sachs' communication to clients, the investment advice that the bank had issued at the beginning of the year 2010 was losing clients' money overall in the first quarter. In contrast, the firm itself made trading profits every single day of the same quarter – every single one of more than 70 trading days, despite the inadequate trading ideas of the firm's analysts (Xie 2010). This was not an exception. Another very powerful Wall Street firm, J.P. Morgan, reported having had only two days with trading losses in the second quarter of 2011, after a perfect first quarter (Moore 2011).

This information advantage due to size is probably the reason that there are only a few big players in investment banking, supplemented by a number of niche suppliers. Suppliers in such a market will each have some pricing power. Former investment banker Philip Augar (2005) reaches the conclusion that there is no illegal cartel, but that investment banks manage to price far above cost anyway (Augar 2005).

Your Money in the Bank – Your Bank in the Money

Wall Street bilks Main Street. Since the introduction of money thousands of years ago, financial intermediaries with more information have been taking advantage of lenders and borrowers with less.

—*Frank Partnoy, 2009*

An army of the financial industry's bank analysts, brokers and sales people are busy enticing retail investors to give them their money or, at least, to trade on the securities market. The investors, thus persuaded to ignore the time-tested advice of buy and hold, make much less money in the stock exchange than they could, while the financial institutions who are exploiting the power of their expert status increase their fees and their profits from trading against naïve investors. Retail investors tend to buy when prices are high and sell when prices are low. When the market valuation is low, investors tend to be underinvested and thus benefit only moderately from the following upswing. When market valuation is high, investors are highly invested and are thus hurt particularly badly by the following decline. Salespeople like to entice investors with the performance of a stock market index like NASDAQ, which does not take this tendency into account. Dichev (2007) has figured it in and found that the actual returns of investors in the NASDAQ since 1973 were less than half of the index gain. Simple computer-automated index tracking funds (the famous "Bogle's folly" now called the Vanguard Group) which simply return the NASDAQ or any other chosen index minus a small overhead of typically 0.15 to 0.25 percent have been available since 1975. They have not been extensively advertised, though.

Individual investors have less information and skill than institutional investors. They are therefore at a disadvantage if they trade with institutional investors. Thus the standard recommendation of economically disinterested advisors is to refrain from frequent trading, especially as it is well known that 80 percent of individual investors lose on average, which interestingly is the same ratio for gambling (Barber et al. 2004). Investors should buy and hold diversified portfolios, such as low-cost mutual or index tracking funds. Instead, they trade actively, trying to pick the winners or trying to time the market by disinvesting when they think prospects are bad and investing again when they think prospects are good. It is hard to overemphasize how costly this is – and how beneficial to the institutional counterparties of these uninformed traders. A comprehensive study for all Taiwanese individual investors found annual trading losses of almost 4 percentage points. The corresponding gains accrue to institutional investors such as corporations, dealers, foreign investors and mutual funds. The upshot is that the commissions and profits of institutional investors reward the financial industry extremely well for enticing individual investors to trade on the stock market. Individual investors lose a lot of money in the process (Barber, Liu and Odean 2009).

For Germany, the private research institute CapQM has pulled together all available information about managed funds, transaction frequency and fees for German money managers. They estimated that German retail investors paid a whopping €28 billion to banks, investment fund managers and insurers in 2007 for managing their savings, amounting to between a quarter and a third of the investment proceeds (CapQM 2009).

A Reuters news report points at another troublesome issue. In July 2009, Sergey Aleynikov, a US and Russian national, was arrested on charges of theft just after he left his job as a programmer at Goldman Sachs. He had copied the trading program of the firm, on which he had been working, and transferred it to a server in Germany. What makes this case interesting is the warning that prosecutor Joseph Faccioponte issued based on information from Goldman Sachs. He said that because of the way this software interfaces with the various markets and exchanges it could be used to "manipulate markets in unfair ways." It is up to anybody's imagination what Goldman Sachs was going to do with that program (McCool 2009).

For a large part of the typical employee's retirement savings, somebody else makes all the relevant decisions. Defined Contribution Plans and Individual Retirement Accounts (401(k)'s) hold more than 40 percent of all mutual fund assets in the US. In the US, the big prize for a money management firm running a family of mutual funds is to become trustee of a corporate 401(k) retirement plan. If such firms face a tradeoff between increasing their chances of becoming (and remaining) trustee and making the optimal investment choices for their clients, the profit-maximizing choice is simple. They do the bidding of the company that has the power to name the trustee. The retirement savers would benefit from having a diversified portfolio. In particular, they should not be overinvested in the stock of their employer since they already face the risk of low income or job loss if their employer should fare badly. However, the company has an interest in having its stock price pumped up by increasing demand. In addition, it is very convenient for the top management of the companies involved to have a large share of their stock in the hands of fund managers who want to curry favor with them. This reduces the risk that they might face shareholder opposition. Fund managers will therefore put a lot of stock of the corporate client into the funds of the employees. Worse still, they seem to buy the shares preferably at times when these seems particularly unattractive to other investors, such as when there is selling pressure on this stock. This is precisely when having a large buyer is particularly valuable to company management, but also the time when it is likely to be a bad investment. According to economists' estimates, such collusion between asset management firms and companies is robbing a large proportion of the retirees of the company of a noticeable share of their retirement benefits. Losses for investors in small fund families with large 401(k) plans can reach more than 13 percent (Cohen and Schmidt 2009).

Zingales (2009) has proposed a fairly easy and straightforward way of tilting the balance of power in favor of retirement savers. It would suffice to take the investment decisions for employees' retirement funds out of the hands of the companies and put representatives of the beneficiaries in charge. This way, asset managers would be freed from the conflict of interest between serving the beneficiaries and currying favor with company management to get business. Of course, there would also need to be strong precautions against money managers unfairly influencing the choices of these workers' representatives in charge of the retirement fund. As a minimum, they would need to be strictly prohibited from doing private business with or taking favors from investment managers. There are plenty of examples from other countries to copy: the US individual retirement account system is based on the Chilean pension reform of 1980/81 that in turn was based heavily on proposals made in the book *Capitalism and Freedom* by Milton Friedman. In response to the Chilean system facing a likely collapse in a few decades time, it was substantially overhauled in 2008 to require mandatory participation of all citizens in exchange for universal pension coverage. Another example is that of Sweden, which enacted a series of very famous pension reforms in

1998 followed by refinements in 2010 – there an individual's personal retirement account defaults to an age-determined mix of an equity index tracking fund and a fixed income fund, but that can be switched at any time into any other investment by its owner. Such a system ensures that the minority who wish to actively manage their pension may do so, while the majority who simply want a high-quality retirement can rest easy knowing that they won't be fleeced out of their savings.

Even if you can choose your fund yourself, it is not easy to avoid being taken advantage of. It has long been established that the fees for actively managed mutual funds are on average much higher than their meager performance justifies – indeed, their fees are on average some nine times more expensive than index tracking funds in the US, with some hedge funds charging ten times more again. Among other things, it has been shown that fund managers receive kickbacks for allowing brokers to charge them excessive fees, that they trade too much, inflating fees further, and that they artificially create strong track records (Phalippou 2009). Thus the standard advice is to choose a mutual fund with a reasonable long-term history, a low load (up-front charge) and low fees. However, Gaspar, Massa and Matos (2006) have shown that the fund industry manages to fleece even customers who chose low-load, low-fee funds. This is possible because asset management firms tend to run not just one fund but a whole fund family. Apparently, fund managers and firms manipulate the earnings of the individual funds in order to make funds fare better that are more rewarding for the firm, to the detriment of investors in other funds of the family. The more rewarding funds for the fund firm are those with high fees or those which can serve as showcase funds to attract new business to the fund family.

A banker on the board is stealing more than the show

> Though properly but middlemen, these bankers bestride as masters America's business world, so that practically no large enterprise can be undertaken successfully without their participation or approval. When once a banker has entered the Board…his grip proves tenacious and his influence usually supreme; for he controls the supply of new money.
>
> —*Louis Brandeis, 1913*

Financial institutions don't just use their power to take advantage of naïve small-scale investors. Their corporate clients are also targets.

The traditional economic view of bankers on the board of non-financial companies is favorable. Economists have argued that such an arrangement can address the information problem inherent in lending. The bankers can more easily and freely lend to a corporation if they are represented on its board. This lets them know that the company is managed prudently and remains creditworthy. This view thinks of the banker as strictly benevolent. The contrasting view assigns great power to representatives of financial institutions as well as a constant temptation to use it for their own institutions' gain. According to this view, if a company needs money, in particular if it is in a crisis and cannot be meticulous, the financiers have their great hour. They can attach strings to the credit they give which assure them of a lasting influence on the company for their own benefit. Many companies even find it wise to offer them board seats proactively in good times because they are too afraid of being left out in the cold during bad times.

There is certainly some truth in the first, innocuous view of bankers on the board. However, there is empirical research showing that the second view also has a lot of relevance. Several studies have shown that companies that have bankers on their boards pay for it dearly. It seems that the banker profits while the company is often hurt. Louis Brandeis, a law scholar with an interest in finance who went on to become a judge on the US Supreme Court, asserted this almost hundred years ago in the US and backed it up by case studies (Brandeis 1913). The early twentieth century was the last heyday of banking power in the US, when J.P. Morgan and the Rockefeller-controlled trusts ruled supreme. Brandeis wrote unusually frankly about how a financial oligarchy around J.P. Morgan controlled the boards of numerous railroad and mining companies and how they profited from saddling these companies with debt for financing corporate buying sprees, sometimes to the point of ruining them.

Econometric studies have shown the same general pattern in modern-day Germany and Japan. The study on Germany found that bankers on the boards of non-financial companies take advantage of their board seats by extracting information about the company and the respective industry. They increase their lending to the respective company and to other firms in the same industry. They are more likely to be awarded the lucrative role of advisor when these firms undertake an acquisition. The bankers do one good thing for "their" companies. They help them obtain funding in difficult times. Still, having a banker on the board on average lowers the respective company's performance and valuation. The fact that the deterioration of performance occurs *after* bankers have joined the board is an indication that bankers actually cause low performance rather than low-performing companies calling in bankers (Dittmann, Maug and Schneider 2010). A similar study on Japanese bank–company relations since the mid-1990s contains a clue on why companies do not profit from a banker on their board. McGuire (2009) found that firms which had strong ties with a main bank faced higher interest payments and were less profitable than other firms without strong ties.

Recent research on the global syndicated loan market further corroborates the assertion that banks routinely draw advantage from board representation, to the detriment of the companies. A syndicated loan is a large loan that a group of banks and other large institutional investors hands out. A lead arranger, who gets extra fees for this service, puts it together. When bank representatives have a say in a corporation's decisions, their bank is more likely to be chosen as lead arranger of syndicated loans and will earn higher fees at lower risk of default than other, unconnected lead arrangers (Ferreira and Matos 2007).

There is no easy way to bar bankers from exerting such influence. A limit on the number of boards a person can be a member of would certainly help. However, such abuses of power are more a symptom rather than the problem itself. One part of the solution is to greatly increase the transparency of anything involving finance. Another more important part is to reestablish society's control over banking, to make sure that the power associated with the allocation of money and credit is used for the long-term benefit of society, not to the short-sighted and particular benefit of certain banks and their managers. This would entail curbing the tendency of the financial sector to create credit-driven booms followed by busts, a topic that will be covered in some detail below. As famous American economist Irving Fisher noted in 1936, it is during these recessions that companies fall into the hands of bankers (Fisher 1936/2009).

Why banks don't like to Google

When it comes to the highly profitable business of taking companies public, financial institutions use all available methods of exerting their power. In principle, there are two techniques for initial public offerings (IPOs): one is the plain old auction, the other is called book building. The fees associated with auctions are smaller, which is bad for the investment banks and good for the companies. However, the main attraction of book building for the banks is something different. The issuing banks set the price, and they often set it rather low. They have the power to decide who gets these underpriced shares and can use this discretion to further their own interests. Whoever wants to give them valuable new business has a higher chance of having a nice share of hot new stock allocated to them. In contrast, if an auction is used and done well, the investors' maximum willingness to pay is harvested to the benefit of the issuing company. There are no underpriced shares that banks can distribute to curry favors with potential clients (Degeorge, Derrien and Womack 2007).

Despite the advantages for issuing companies, auctioning has almost died out as a method of allocating IPO shares. Why, then, do the companies go for it? If competition was working as a means of regulating the behavior of businesses and banks had no power, one would not expect severe underpricing with book building to occur. Companies would give their business to investment banks that would not leave so much of their customers' money on the table. An international team of economists has provided an answer by analyzing all French IPOs in the 1990s. The study reveals that underwriting banks issued significantly more analyst reports and recommendations on stocks they brought public via book building than on those auctioned off. In addition, stock that is taken public by book building received more "booster shots." This is traders' jargon for buy recommendations issued by analysts when a stock is tanking following its IPO. The media took their cues from the banks, reporting much more exhaustively about companies doing book building than about those taking the auction route. Overall, this is clear evidence that banks abused investors' trust in the unbiased expertise of their analysts to extract money from their corporate customers. In effect, the banks trade their power to manipulate investor demand in order to get excessive fees and underpriced stock from companies (Degeorge, Derrien and Womack 2007).

There is more to it, though. Economists and the courts have investigated an illegal method that banks have used to get company management to agree to underpricing of the company's shares. One example, but by far not the only one, was Bernie Ebbers, CEO of Worldcom. Between 1996 and 2000, he received allocations of 21 IPOs from lead underwriter Citigroup and made first day profits of about US$5 million on them. During this time, Worldcom paid US$100 million in investment banking fees, almost all of which to Citigroup.

The practice was widespread during hot stock markets, as Liu and Ritter (2010) have shown. They looked at 56 companies going public between 1996 and 2000 in which top executives of the respective companies received allocations of IPO shares from the book runner, a practice known as spinning. These companies got 22 percent less money on average for the shares than similar IPOs and 40 percent less than they could have received if the IPO had been priced very aggressively – as might be achieved through an auction. The executives collected a profit (bribe) of US$1.3 million on average, while their companies lost US$17 million on average relative to similar IPOs and about US$30 million relative to a maximally aggressive pricing. On top of that, the companies whose executives had been bribed with hot stock were much less likely to switch investment bankers in any subsequent offer: only 6 percent of them did, compared to 31 percent of other issuers.

If banks can deter companies from using an efficient way of selling their stock and coax or bribe managers into using an inferior way, something is quite wrong. No politically easy solution is at hand, though. As long as banks are allowed to use their power of credit allocation freely, they will always be able to coax companies that want to raise capital into using techniques that create new allocation powers for banks while further enriching them. Even the lawsuits against banks that bribed managers with hot stock did not weaken the dominance of book building.

Those porous Chinese walls

By their very nature, diversified banking conglomerates are awash with potential conflicts of interest and insider information that they can abuse for their own profit. If they give a loan, they get to look into the books of the company. They can then use the information to trade shares or bonds of that company. They also obtain valuable insider information if they take a company public or advise it on a merger. This includes revenue projection updates, information on unexpected losses or acquisition and divestiture plans. Trading on such inside information hurts other investors. Sometimes it also hurts the client companies. This is why it is generally illegal. Banks are required to prevent it by erecting barriers to information flows between various departments, so-called Chinese walls. "Compliance" departments have to check that employees do not abuse insider information for their own gain. One might expect that compliance departments are also charged with making sure that affiliated funds and companies do not trade on insider information, but they don't. Economists have examined a variety of roles in which bankers receive insider information, and whether trading desks and affiliated institutions are using that information. They consistently found strong indications of widespread insider trading. This institutionalized insider trading is hardly ever prosecuted.

One such study by Bodnaruk, Massa and Simonov (2009) found that many banks advising on mergers and acquisitions (M&A) break the fiduciary trust of their customers by trading on their knowledge of secret acquisition plans. They buy the stock of the target, which they know will go up in price once the acquisition plans become widely known. These insider purchases push up the price in advance of the deal and make the acquisition more expensive for their clients. The merger advisors even seem to use their influence to shape the deals in such a way as to make their insider trades safer.

With the help of one of the authors of the above study, the *Wall Street Journal* did an investigation in 2008, naming among others Goldman Sachs, JPMorgan Chase, Morgan Stanley, Citigroup and Credit Suisse as banks that had strongly increased their shareholding in companies that their M&A customers wanted to buy, before the plans became publicly known (Maremont and Craig 2008).

In a similar way, bankers who are creditors routinely exploit insider information. It is a well-established legal principle that banks' loan managers have a fiduciary duty to keep the information that they receive from clients secret. Massa and Rehman (2008) looked into how diligently banks observe this duty, and found them quite wanting. One way or another, the information that a bank has given a loan to a specific company finds its way to affiliated fund managers, who then trade on it. The strategy of using insider information from affiliated banks improved the overall performance of funds employing it by an average of 1.4 percent per year relative to similar funds without such insider information.

The same picture emerges in the market for syndicated loans (i.e. loans that are arranged by a lead arranger), with the money coming from a variety of banks and other institutional investors. If there are significant changes to the company's creditworthiness, loan renegotiations will take place. Therefore the participants in the syndicated loan know earlier than the public of any such changes. Ivashina and Sun (forthcoming) analyzed stock trades of funds which are affiliated with syndicate members. They limited the sample to trades that were executed after loan renegotiations had taken place. They found that these funds made 4.4 percent higher returns on such trades than on other stock.

It took until 2008 before the British stock market watchdog, the Financial Services Authority (FSA), started its first-ever investigation of institutional insider trading. In that year, the FSA released a study concluding that in almost 30 percent of all mergers and acquisitions, stock price movements showed patterns strongly suggesting the occurrence of insider trading. FSA chief Hector Sants emphasized that the situation in the UK was no worse than in other markets (Maisch 2010).

The implications are the same for all three kinds of insider trading. The reputational concerns of financial companies, which are the great hope of those who believe in unfettered markets, are not preventing the abuse of short side market power and informational advantage. Retail investors are put at a disadvantage and so are customers with whom financial institutions have fiduciary relationships. Chinese walls as they stand have proved to be too flimsy to provide a solution. Therefore, large banks with a multitude of business lines and with affiliated asset-managing firms have a strong and often illicit advantage over their smaller competitors.

While economists can prove beyond a doubt that information is flowing, it is notoriously hard to prove it in individual cases. Thus the prosecutor is currently not a real threat. To combat institutional insider trading there needs to be a legal rule making the financial conglomerate financially liable for a substantial portion of any stock market movements that are negative for the client after the service contract is signed. This ought to act a powerful incentive to ensure that market sensitive information remains private, that any form of insider trading whether internal or via a friendly third party is inhibited, and it additionally encourages rapid processing by the conglomerate that ought to reduce risk for the client. A useful, but much less powerful alternative would be prohibiting all trading desks and fund managers within a financial conglomerate from trading in certain securities at times when some part of the conglomerate receives market-sensitive information about these securities. The financial sector will object on the grounds that this is either too risky or too cumbersome for them. Unfortunately, the only acceptable alternative is to eradicate the underlying conflicts of interest, for example by separating the ownership of asset managers and investment banking, as Zingales (2009) has suggested, in addition to preventing investment banks from trading on their own accounts.

Carnivores at the top of the food chain

In the pecking order of power in the financial industry, the hedge fund, which invests the money of the wealthy and of institutions, stands above the ordinary mutual fund. Hedge funds derive their particular power from being almost completely opaque about what they do. This means they can borrow as much money as they can get in order to leverage the bets they make. It also means that there is nobody who checks to see if they obey the rules of fair investing as they apply to regulated financial institutions. They can use almost any dirty trick there is in the world of finance.

One might think that hedge funds are an unwelcome competition to regulated banks. This is not so. Some hedge funds are owned and run by big banks. The others live in a symbiotic relationship with them. They rely on banks for their market transactions, for credit and for sensitive information to trade on. In exchange, they let their correspondence banks take part in their extraordinary profits by paying them lavish fees. For example, the Galleon hedge fund paid the US$250 million to its correspondence banks in just one year (Sender 2009).

One way in which hedge funds (and brokerage houses) exploit other investors is front running. Front running is illegal in many contexts. It consists in taking advantage of information about trades that other parties are planning. If a broker learns, for example, that a large customer wants to buy a particular stock, the broker might decide to buy some of that stock before executing the order of the customer, which will drive up the price to the detriment of the customer. This is illegal front running, something that is very common but very hard to prove.

Just as exploitative, but not illegal, is another front running technique. It consists of trading on information about distressed mutual funds. As long as the information is obtained from public sources, this is legal. If many customers of a mutual fund withdraw their money, usually because of bad fund performance, the fund will predictably have to sell securities to get the cash needed to reimburse investors. Since mutual funds, unlike hedge funds, have to be rather transparent, other market participants can know what securities they have in their portfolio. Experts can thus guess which securities are likely to come under selling pressure soon. The front-runners short these securities. This means they borrow them from somebody and sell them, in the expectation of being able to buy them back cheaper when the borrowing arrangement expires. This trading will drive down the price of the respective security, increasing the problems of the distressed mutual fund and with it the potential gains of the front-runners. Chen et al. (2008) found that times during which many mutual funds are in distress are exactly the times when hedge funds have particularly high profits. They also found that short interest (i.e. speculation against certain stocks) rises in advance of sales of the respective stocks by distressed funds. They estimate that a substantial proportion of hedge fund revenue comes from such front running strategies.

The techniques that hedge funds and brokers use to take advantage of weaker or less informed market participants work just as well against others of their kind if they are unlucky enough to run into a tight spot. In the words of former stockbroker and hedge fund manager Jim Cramer (2002): "When you smell blood in the water, you become a shark… when you know that one of your number is in trouble…you try to figure out what he owns and you start shorting those stocks."

A famous victim was hedge fund Long-Term Capital Management (LTCM). The troubles of this huge fund during the 1997/1998 Asian Crisis brought the world financial system to the brink of a collapse. Economists have found evidence that LTCM's problems were exacerbated by brokers and business partners who had information about the short positions that the fund urgently needed to close and engaged in large-scale front running against the hedge fund. They traded in the same direction as the distressed fund did, but one or two minutes beforehand. Accordingly, many market makers made unusually large profits during the crisis. These findings support a *Business Week* report that Goldman Sachs and other counterparties to LTCM deepened the crisis by engaging in large-scale front running. This meant that LTCM, which urgently needed liquidity, could not get reasonable prices for anything it wanted to sell. The others were always on that market already and had depressed the prices (Cai 2010).

Front running might be at least jointly responsible for the depth of many financial crises, say Brunnermeier and Pedersen (2010). They have built a theoretical model that describes the role of front running in propagating and deepening financial crises. They cite as examples not only LTCM, but also the stock market crash of 1987, which appears to have been amplified by predatory front running. Their model shows how trouble for one large trader, exploited and deepened by predatory trading, can lead to a price drop for an entire asset class. This in turn brings other traders into financial difficulty, just because they hold assets in the market that is affected. These traders can become victims of predatory front running again, and so on. In this way, the problem of one large trader in one large market can develop into a crisis of many traders in many markets.

Hedge funds do not stop at trading against other hedge funds, mutual funds and individual investors. Some of them command such vast resources that they can almost single-handedly thwart the economic policies of governments, sometimes even of large industrial countries. This was proven when financier George Soros, allegedly by himself, pushed the UK out of the European Exchange Rate Mechanism, a precursor of the European Monetary Union, in 1992. He bet such large sums on a devaluation of the pound that the central bank finally could no longer resist the pressure.

Another example, one in which the hedge funds eventually lost, was their attempt to corner the Hong Kong stock market during the Asian Crisis in 1998. The Hong Kong government prevailed by throwing all restraint overboard and buying up a large chunk of the equity of Hong Kong companies. The hedge funds used foreign exchange derivatives, like forwards, options and futures to emulate large international capital flows. The plan was to drive down the value of Hong Kong stocks and to force the HK dollar out of its peg with the US dollar, leading to a significant devaluation of the currency and – in US dollar terms – also of Hong Kong stocks. Joseph Yam, at the time governor of the Hong Kong Monetary Authority, alleges that the hedge funds had allies among financial institutions. The attack on Hong Kong was accompanied by numerous pessimistic reports on Hong Kong, on its exchange rate peg and on China. There were many planted rumors that the Hong Kong government planned to give up the dollar peg and that the Chinese Renminbi would soon be devalued (Yam 2000).

George Soros apparently tried something similar to Hungary. In March 2009, his fund was fined by a Hungarian regulator for "sending out false and misleading signals" on the shares of Hungary's largest bank, OTP. Short selling of OTP shares had caused them to drop 14 percent in the last 30 minutes of trading on October 9, 2008. According to the regulator, this was part of a "significant and strong attack on Hungarian money and capital markets." The central bank had to raise its benchmark interest rate to the highest in the European Union to defend the national currency, the forint. Soros accepted the fine and apologized for the wrongdoing of his employees (Simon 2009).

A story in the *Wall Street Journal* gives another rare glimpse into the methods of the trade. According to the report, a number of all-star managers of large hedge funds, including Soros Fund Management and SAC Capital Advisors, met in February 2010 in a townhouse in Manhattan for a dinner to discuss the prospects of the euro. There can never be anything innocent about such talks, as they serve to coordinate trading. If half a dozen of the largest hedge funds coordinate their trading and make large bets, it is extremely likely that the market will go in the direction they desire, at least for a while. By letting the most influential newspaper know and write about remarks made at that meeting to the effect that the euro would fall to parity with the dollar, other market participants were informed and indirectly invited to join and push the euro down. Between the end of February and the end of May, the euro fell more than 10 percent against the dollar (Pulliam, Kelly and Mollenkamp 2010).

With all the above in mind, it might come as little surprise that managers of hedge funds and related institutions, like private equity funds, are among the highest income earners in the world. Even in the crisis year 2008, the top 25 earners in the hedge fund industry made US$11.6 billion, according to the industry magazine *Alpha*. A year earlier, they had made nearly double that amount. This is made possible because, unlike mutual funds but like investment funds, hedge funds typically charge a very substantial "performance fee" of between 10 and 50 percent of profits for any profits exceeding a "hurdle" rate (e.g. the amount one might earn if one left the investment in a bank account). Top of the list in 2008 was James Simons of Renaissance Technologies at US$2.5 billion, which he made with his 5 percent management fee and a 44 percent share of the profits. Three more hedge fund managers made more than a billion dollars in 2008.

The wealthy and moneyed institutions that invest in hedge funds do not fare quite as well. Economists have looked into what returns investors in various kinds of hedge funds get after fees are paid. The essence is that it is not such a privilege to be able to invest in a hedge fund. On average, it seems to allow you to be fooled in a privileged way. Phaliappou and Gottschalg (2009) and Phalippou (2009) have found that investors in private equity buyout on average receive a yield lower than that of the Standard & Poor's 500, the most important stock market index for the US, after the high fees for these funds are subtracted. However, most investors are not aware of this. The fee structure is so opaque and contracts vary in so many crucial details that it is exceedingly hard to get a good idea of what investors are actually paying (Phalippou 2009). For another important subset of hedge funds, commodity trading advisors (CTAs), Bhardwaj, Gorton and Rouwenhorst (2008) have also examined the industry's performance claims. They found them just as wanting as the claims of the private equity industry. According to their calculations, returns are five percentage points above those of Treasury bonds before fees, but barely higher after fees, which average 4 percent per year. This means that fund management claims almost all the profits that exceed those of standard safe investments.

Five Hundred Years of Bankers' Rule

> The real truth of the matter is, as you and I know, that a financial element in the larger centers has owned the Government ever since the days of Andrew Jackson.
>
> —*Franklin D. Roosevelt to E. Mandell House, 1933*

> The great wealth that the financial sector created and concentrated gave bankers enormous political weight – a weight not seen in the US since the era of J. P. Morgan (the man).
>
> —*Simon Johnson, 2009*

The abundance of examples of widespread abuse of power by financial institutions raises the question of why regulators and lawmakers are not stepping in. The sad answer is that it is this very power of financial institutions that prevents it. What would have sounded to many like a conspiracy theory has become commonplace since mid-2010. Wall Street in general and Goldman Sachs in particular have benefited greatly from the inordinate share of influential government positions they obtained. Printing the long list of former Goldman managers in high-ranking public offices here would be too tedious for readers. MIT economist Simon Johnson (2009), a former chief economist of the IMF, has written on that subject in the *Atlantic Monthly*, followed by Mark Taibbi's (2009) "The Great American Bubble Machine" in *Rolling Stone*. Mainstream newspapers like the *New York Times* started to quip, "If you want to talk to someone from Goldman, call the Treasury." Finally, after the SEC accused Goldman Sachs in April 2010 of fraudulently having issued subprime-related securities, politicians even started to give back campaign contributions to Goldman Sachs. This did not include Barack Obama, who received larger campaign contributions from employees of Goldman Sachs than from any other company. During the financial crisis, former Goldman Sachs employees, in their capacities in various important government offices (such as treasury secretary), did a lot of the rescuing. The rescue of insurance giant AIG is a good example. One key player was treasury secretary Hank Paulson, who came into his office directly from Goldman Sachs. Another was the president of the Federal Reserve Bank of New York, Tim Geithner, supervised by Stephen Friedman. Friedman was on the board of Goldman Sachs and had been an executive of the firm. They negotiated the terms of the rescue with the

CEO of AIG, Edward Liddy, who had been installed for that purpose by the New York Fed and who had come directly from Goldman Sachs. A key issue in the negotiations was how bankrupt AIG should honor its obligations to derivative counterparties. The result was the payment of US$14 billion to Goldman Sachs. A report by the special inspector general of the Troubled Asset Relief Program (TARP), Neil Barofsky, would later say that "there is no question that the effect of FRBNY's (the New York Fed's) decisions – indeed, the very design of the federal assistance to AIG – was that tens of billions of dollars of government money was funneled inexorably and directly to AIG's counterparties" (SIGTARP 2009). Paulson and Geithner later claimed they were not at all involved in the AIG rescue. The Fed did everything it could to conceal the details and released to the public only what Congress and the courts forced them to release.

Other financial institutions profited unevenly from TARP money, as Duchin and Sosyura (2010) have shown. Quoting the Congressional Oversight Panel, they state that the Treasury substantially overpaid for its investments under TARP, effectively subsidizing select banks who were allowed to sell securities under the program. The researchers found that the likelihood of a bank being allowed to participate in the program was significantly increased by the bank's political contributions, lobbying expenditures and whether the bank had a seat on the board of a regional Federal Reserve, even after controlling for bank size (i.e. comparing banks of similar size).

Before Paulson, two other investment bankers turned secretaries of finance, Nicholas Brady and Robert Rubin, had already saved the big American banks from severe losses due to the Mexican Crisis using public money. After that, Rubin had started the process of deregulating the financial industry, which helped him and many on Wall Street get very rich and sowed the seeds of the subprime crisis.

One could be forgiven for thinking that this takeover of government by Wall Street was an aberration. However, the tight link of finance and government has deep historical roots, which is why it is so hard to break. The history of banking and finance reveals that the few decades after the Great Depression in which the influence of the financial industry on government was limited constitute an exception rather than the norm.

In the late nineteenth and early twentieth century, the power of bankers and financiers of J. P. Morgan's type was as big as it is now. He and a few other big industrialists and financiers controlled most of the country's largest companies. A big difference, though, was that the powerful bankers of this time were also industrialists. Rather than just thinking of ways to suck money out of the real economy, they were participating in the industrialization of America. This time of great banker influence culminated in the record-setting 11-year term of investment banker Andrew Mellon at the helm of the Treasury from 1921 to 1932. The way his rule led up to the banking panic and the Great Depression shows striking similarities to the run-up to the subprime crisis. In the mid-1920s, Mellon was one of the highest income tax payers in the US. Upon his proposal, Congress enacted the Revenue Acts of 1921, 1924 and 1926, which cut the top marginal tax rate from 73 percent to 24 percent in 1929. The economy boomed, stock markets soared and the wealth of Mellon and his banker colleagues peaked in 1929. When the Great Crash put an end to the fun, Mellon had to be expedited to England as an ambassador to avoid deposition by Congress.

However, the rule of banker goes back much further. The first treasury secretary, Alexander Hamilton (c. 1757–1804), whose portrait is on the ten dollar bill, was not just a gifted practical economist who devised an industrialization strategy for the young nation. He was also a banker. He had founded the Bank of New York before taking office – one of only three banks in the US at the time. He is credited with having had a lasting influence on the structures of US banking. Before him, banker Robert Morris (1734–1806) held the office of superintendent of finance from 1781 to 1784.

Throughout history, the normal state of affairs has been that of a symbiotic relationship of government and finance. These times tended to be prosperous, when banking interests were aligned with the interest of the real economy, leading to rapid industrialization and growth. Most of the time financiers had as much power over the government as the government had over financiers. Just as with the ordinary customers of bankers, governments often found themselves on the short side of the market for credit. There would always be spikes in their expenditures, often associated with war, which they could not cover without credit. This was already true for the European rulers in the Middle Ages and the Renaissance. As one example of many, the rich German trading house of Fugger financed the "Italian Wars" of the German king Maximilian I (1459–1519). The king responded with tailor-made laws and privileges for the Fugger. The Fugger also financed the large bribes that Karl V (1500–1558) paid to be elected emperor of the German Reich. Karl, too, reciprocated with extensive privileges.

Bankers and financiers were also dependent on a good and close relationship with the rulers because most lucrative business went through them. The Rothschild family owed their wealth to the friendship Mayer Amschel Rothschild (1744–1812) had with Carl Friedrich Buderus. Buderus was the financial advisor and treasurer of Prince Wilhelm of Hessen-Kassel. Wilhelm was one of the richest princes in Germany because of a very special trade. He rented out his citizens as soldiers to warring nations. Buderus saw to it that Mayer Rothschild and his five sons got an increasing share of the prince's banking business. This became particularly lucrative when Napoleon forced Prince Wilhelm to flee into exile. Nathan Rothschild, the representative of the family in London, got to invest the Prince's fortune. Even though the details of the dealings are often not known, and it is sometimes contentious if and in what way Rothschild used Wilhelm's money for his own benefit, it is safe to assume that he could not have made his fortune without that money in the background. He earned high commissions by financing the British war effort against Napoleon and by organizing the risky transports of gold to pay the troops. Rothschild reciprocated for Buderus' patronage by making him a silent partner in the bank in 1809 (Ferguson 1998; Kaplan 2006).

An extreme form of the symbiosis of bankers and rulers was the long rule of the House of Medici over Florence and Tuscany. The prosperous Medici Bank, founded in 1397, made the Medici family the richest and most powerful in Europe. Cosimo the Elder took over in 1434 as gran maestro and the Medici became unofficial heads of state of the Florentine Republic. The Medici produced three popes of the Catholic Church, two queens of France and, in 1531, the family acquired the hereditary dukedom of Florence, which was later elevated to the grand duchy of Tuscany. Their rule ended in 1537 (though the last Medici pope, Alessandro Ottaviano de' Medici, ruled into the seventeenth century).

Be powerful or vanish

It is no accident that bankers became so powerful. It was a prerequisite of surviving in the trade. If you wanted to be successful in conducting financial business with the monarchy – and most large-scale business was with monarchs at the time – you needed to be as powerful as an absolute monarch. Otherwise you ran the risk of financial annihilation, which was the fate of the Florentine houses who dominated Italian finance in the early fourteenth century, the Bardi, Peruzzi and Accaiuoli. The defaults of two of their principal clients, King Edward III of England (1312–1377) and King Robert of Naples (1309–1343), wiped them out.

Financial strength and cooperation gave bankers the power that made them safe from physical or financial annihilation. Nobody could legally force King Phillip II of Spain (1527–1598) to pay back the millions that he borrowed to finance his wars all over Europe. The King stopped payments several times when his ships loaded with silver from Latin America did not arrive as planned. However, he always came to an agreement with his main financiers, a group of Genoese bankers, to resume payments. The secret behind the power of the Genoese bankers was a tightly knit net of social ties. They would intermarry within the banking families of the network, extend credit together in syndicates and exchange collateral, which the others could confiscate if one did not play by the rules of the group. No members of this network could step out of line and make their own special deals with the king without being seriously hurt. They effectively acted in concert, like one single lender with huge combined resources. If the king did not pay, he would not get credit from anybody in the group again and would be unable to pay his armies. Not even bankers from outside the network, like the Fugger, dared to give Phillip money while the Genoese boycotted him. The Fugger were not able to finance all the king's enterprises by themselves. Thus they had to assume that the king would eventually have to return to the Genoese. Given the chance, the Genoese would certainly insist that Phillip default on any loans from the boycott-breakers as a precondition for giving new money (Dreilichman and Voth 2009).

The Rothschild family followed the same strategy with tremendous success. The five arms of the family who headed banking houses all over Europe were knitted together over many decades by marriages within the family and by revenue and power-sharing contracts. Of 21 marriages involving descendants of Mayer Amschel between 1824 and 1877, all but 6 were between his direct descendants. True to the old adage *knowledge is power*, the family invested a lot of effort and money to develop a highly efficient network of agents, shippers and couriers to transport gold and information across Europe. They knew better than anybody what was going on in the various centers of power and how to benefit from it financially. By the 1830s, their communication network was so developed that political leaders used it as an express postal service. Often the Rothschilds were used as messengers, as they held good relations with many conflicting parties. This gave them much information and considerable influence. They had the financial power to contract with all European governments on an equal footing or even as a superior power. They did not depend on any individual ruler so much as rulers depended on them. German prince Hermann von Pückler-Muskau referred to Nathan Rothschild in 1828 as one "without whom no power in Europe today seems to be able to make war" (Ferguson 1998).

With banking such a powerful second force next to government, it is no wonder that the banking systems and regulations developed in Europe were particularly friendly to the interests of the banking community and thus not characterized by strict customer protection, general transparency or openness in their dealings, nor one that was restrained legally, morally or otherwise in their methods of making money.

Let there be money

> The study of money, above all other fields in economics, is one in which complexity is used to disguise truth or to evade truth, not to reveal it.
>
> —*John Kenneth Galbraith, 1975*

Starting in the middle of the seventeenth century, bankers slowly usurped a particularly profitable power that had until then been the prerogative of governments: the power to issue money and to determine the value of currency. They did so either in cooperation with the government or with tacit and later explicit permission of the government. This was the basis from which modern banking practices evolved. They have become so normal and ubiquitous that they seem without alternative, yet these practices brought about the latest financial crisis, and most of the other 124 systemic banking crises that economists of the IMF have counted between 1970 and 2007 (Laeven and Valencia 2008).

According to one account, money creation by banks emerged as an aberration of deposit banking starting in the 1640s. Some English merchants deposited their gold with goldsmiths or other safe keepers. In order to economize on transaction costs, it was customary to transfer documents of possession rather than the physical gold. The deposit slips started to function as paper money, entirely backed by gold. Soon, the safe keepers had an idea – one that could be called either fraud or a smart invention. They could make money by multiplying the deposit slips they issued. As most gold would stay in their vaults for a long time without being requested by its current owners, they could lend out some of their customers' gold and pocket the interest. For the banks it was essentially the same as producing gold out of nothing.

In the Netherlands, the Bank of Amsterdam did the same for many decades in cooperation with the government until the bank eventually folded. The bank secretly passed gold to the government that depositors had given to it for safekeeping. In exchange, the bank received government bonds (Rothbard 1985/2008; Fisher 1936/2009).

These practices meant that the gold in the vaults of the banks was actually owned by several people. As all these people used the inflated deposit slips to pay their bills, what they regarded as a mere substitute for physical movements of gold morphed into fiat money. This technical term for money created by the banks refers to the biblical "fiat lux" or "let there be light." It is money that has been created out of nothing and is backed by nothing but faith in its value (Rothbard 1985/2008).

The same principle underlies our modern banking system. Banks do not have to actually have the money that people deposit in accounts with them on hand. Money in deposit accounts is a large multiple of the cash that the banks actually have in their vaults to pay out to depositors who want their money in hand.

Early in the nineteenth century, judge Lord Cottenham issued a blank check to the bankers by ruling,

> The money placed in the custody of a banker is, to all intents and purposes, the money of the banker, to do with it as he pleases; he is guilty of no breach of trust in employing it; he is not answerable to the principal if he puts it into jeopardy, if he engages in a hazardous speculation; he is not bound to keep it or deal with it as the property of his principal; but he is, of course, answerable for the amount, because he has contracted. (Rothbard 1985/2008)

This is still the legal situation today. A bank can take a depositor's money, invest it in an extremely risky project, with any benefits going to him – just as Nathan Rothschild presumably did with the Prince of Hessen-Kassel's money – and get away with being an honest insolvent if it fails. No charge of fraud or embezzlement can be brought against the banker. Contrary to what most people believe, the money they deposit at the bank is no longer theirs. By law, they have given it as a loan to the bank. Because banks do not have to actually have the money that people keep in accounts with them, they can create any amount of money they want. If they give credit to a customer, they simply add to the amount in the customer's checking account. By the stroke of a pen, the sum of money available for general purchasing has increased by this amount.

Fighting over the spoils of money creation

Today, the privilege of private banks to create money is no longer seriously debated. The degree of avoidance of the subject smacks of a taboo. Economists and participants in discussions of economic policies take this state of affairs as a given. Yet a look at the early monetary histories of China and of the US clearly shows that the system has never been without alternative.

As Marco Polo reported to the astonishment of his fellow Europeans around 1300, the Chinese–Mongolian Empire under the Kublai Khan had a sophisticated and highly successful paper money system. The government issued paper money, which – according to Polo – was used for the majority of all transactions. The government controlled the amount of money circulating by buying (and selling if needed) valuable goods from (and to) tradesmen. Since the government earned the profits from creating money out of nothing, not the banks, it was spectacularly rich and powerful, as Polo reported. This paper money system worked well for decades, if not centuries, as all available research reports that the Chinese economy was flourishing during that time (Werner 2007).

The US being a fairly young nation, conflicts around money creation that had long been resolved in favor of the banks in Europe surfaced in the early decades. There were intense and sometimes violent power struggles over who should create money, the government or private banks.

In the 1780s, as the American Revolution wound down, America had a large trade deficit. This meant that a lot of the US stock of gold and silver coins, used as money all over the world, leaked to England. Coinage was in short supply in the US, in particular those regions far from the ports. At the same time, taxes were very high as the federal government and the state governments strove to repay the large debt from the war quickly. A large proportion of the population struggled to come up with money to pay these taxes, which were the same for everybody, independent of income. As prices fell for lack of money, the real value of the war debt and the associated taxes increased in value every year (Nettels 1962).

The Bank of North America and the two other US banks that existed at the time, the Bank of New York (owned by Alexander Hamilton) and the Bank of Massachusetts (a predecessor of Bank of America), were merchants' banks. They only gave loans to merchants, not to farmers or ordinary folk. To make matters worse, no uniform dependable paper currency existed. The notes of individuals, bills of exchange, various kinds of state paper and notes of the three merchant banks all circulated. Farmers and producers often had to resort to barter, exchanging goods for goods, a very cumbersome practice. Everybody agreed that more currency was needed, but there was fierce disagreement as to who should issue this money (Nettels 1962).

Merchants of port towns, who tended to be financiers and creditors, wanted privately owned and managed banks to enlarge the currency supply by issuing private bank notes. This is how the Bank of North America already provided them with paper currency. As creditors, they could live very well with falling prices and the increasing real value of debt. Given how the government had financed the revolution by effectively printing money, they feared the government would issue even more money at low interest rates. This would raise prices and devalue what their debtors owed them. If private banks, owned and controlled by these merchants, issued the money instead, they could control the amount. They would also reap the profits from creating money out of nothing, rather than the government (Nettels 1962).

The farmers, on the other hand, were not served by the existing banks in their financial needs and were deeply in debt, mostly with tax liabilities. The land banks proposed as the main alternative to the merchant banks would benefit them the most. These public entities would issue government bills of debt secured by land. Bill holders could use them to pay taxes. As producers and debtors, farmers would benefit from rising prices. Thus they wanted generous money supplied by government. As taxpayers, they would benefit from the fact that the government would earn interest on the money created and would thus need fewer taxes (Nettels 1962).

As these strong financial interests opposed each other, fights over land banks broke out in various states. Pennsylvania saw a violent collision between the proponents of state paper and partisans of merchants' banks after the state pushed through a bill in 1785 for the issuing of bills of credit by the state. Morris' Bank of North America, which was headquartered in the state, boycotted these bills by refusing to give gold or silver for them at par. In Maryland, there were armed attacks on tax collectors and creditors after the senate rejected a paper money bill. In New Hampshire, a band of armed men imprisoned the legislature and tried to force it to issue paper money. Wealthy defenders of the government raised a counterforce that drove them off. In Massachusetts, where the legislature refused to issue currency to relieve the taxpayers' burden, a serious rebellion broke out in 1786. The ultimately unsuccessful uprising became known as Shays' Rebellion, after an encounter between a force of about 800 farmers led by Captain Daniel Shays and a private militia associated with the merchants' interests (Nettels 1962).

This was the social and political environment in which the federal government had to decide how to relieve the money shortage and to create a workable national currency. They could have opted for money created by the federal government, or they could give the lucrative privilege of creating money to the bankers and merchants. As the decision was made by merchant bankers in their capacity as politicians, the outcome was clear.

Let there be crisis

Expanding credit is a good thing as long as it is sustainable, goes roughly in sync with the expansion of production capacities and is allocated to the right uses. There are essentially three different uses for credit. Firstly, it can go into investments that enlarge a country's production capacity and thus its ability to pay back the credit with interest. Secondly, it can go into consumption, raising demand for current production, but not directly raising the production potential. If this kind of credit is expanded, it tends to lead to inflation, as more purchasing power chases the same amount of goods and services. Thirdly, and most perniciously, new credit can go to those who buy claims on existing assets, be they land, housing, stocks or bonds. If this kind of speculative credit is strongly expanded, it inflates the prices of these assets, enticing even more people to speculate on price gains with even more credit. This creates a bubble, which feeds on itself, until it finally bursts (Werner 2007).

While it is in the interests of society to have most new credit allocated to the first usage, this is often the one to which banks are the most hesitant to give, as they perceive credit for the untested endeavors of companies to be the most risky. The most money and the fastest money for banks is in the third kind of credit, which is not in society's interest to expand (Werner 2007).

A credit-driven asset bubble has feedback effects on the real economy. If the new money goes into real estate, for example, construction activity will pick up, creating an economic boom. This economic boom enhances the potential for further credit expansion because the assets that people hold become more valuable. They can be pledged as collateral for still more credit. In addition, lending appears safer to banks in a booming economy. However, in the long run, in order to push the economy forward and justify the expansion, it is not enough for the financial sector to increase credit. It needs to secure an ever-increasing pace of expansion.

Increasing the pace of credit expansion is possible for quite a while due to positive feedback loops, but not forever. A boom created by credit expansion will invariably end. Once the pace of credit expansion no longer increases, the moment of truth arrives. Once speculators take on less new credit, asset prices nosedive. A bust follows the boom. After the credit contraction of the crisis has run its course, outstanding credit is depressed enough to allow for a new cycle of credit expansion.

In a careful historical examination, Schularick and Taylor (2009) revealed how a secular rise of credit in relation to the size of the economy after the Second World War sowed the seeds of increasingly frequent and severe crises that culminated in the recent Great Financial Crisis. They found that during the gold standard years from 1870 to the early 1920s bank credit evolved in a roughly stable relationship to central bank money and to the size of the economy. The credit boom of the 1920s ended this stable relationship. More money in relation to the size of the economy means that the new money (i.e. new credit) is used mostly for buying up existing assets, not for enhancing production capacity. An equally severe credit contraction followed in the 1930s. Then, after the Second World War, banks increased their loan portfolio again with steadily increasing speed. At the same time, they took on more leverage (i.e. financed themselves with borrowing rather than seeking extra capital). Banks took short-term deposits and borrowed long-term assets.

As a result, credit not only grew relative to gross domestic product but also relative to central bank money. By 2008, the relationship of bank credit to national output in the 12 countries studied had risen from about a quarter in 1950 to about one. The ratio of bank assets to national output rose in the same time from about half to twice the gross domestic product. Since the early 1970s, when banks seriously ratcheted up their debt leverage, crises have become much more frequent than in the two decades prior. According to Schularick and Taylor (2009), there was a financial crisis in the 12 countries they studied on an average of one every 20 years. Between the Second World War and

1971, there had hardly been any. In all the countries that Schularick and Taylor surveyed, bank credit expansion was a good predictor of an imminent financial crisis. For them, almost all these financial crises were credit booms gone bust.

Central banks used the freedom that the demise of the gold standard and the end of the fixed exchange rate system gave them to try to prevent the worst. Since the early 1970s, they have regularly printed extra money and lowered the interest rate aggressively whenever banks have run into trouble. This has certainly been good for the banks, but it has not prevented serious damage to the economy, or to companies and workers, because banks increased their capacity to do damage faster than central banks could follow. In the 60 years before the Great Depression, financial crises had a much smaller effect in terms of output loss than after 1971 (no serious crises occurred between 1945 and 1971) despite the efforts of the central banks to contain the damage (Schularick and Taylor 2009).

It seems clear that banks did not simply *happen* to become more leveraged and have fewer liquid assets. They collectively *chose* to do this because they knew central banks and therefore the public would have to bail them out if they ran into trouble. Those with most debt would benefit the most from the boom in the run-up to the crisis *and* from the low interest rates after the crisis erupted. That is why no bank wanted to stay behind in this game. This kind of competition also took place on an international level. A global era of progressive deregulation and increasing financial laissez-faire ensued as each country wanted to help their own financial institutions to gain a lead or at least not to fall too far behind (Schularick and Taylor 2009).

What deregulation meant, in essence, was doing away with society's control over credit allocation by banks. The US government had exerted this control in the "financial repression" era after the Second World War with tremendously positive results in terms of economic growth. The same was true in all the other success stories of this era, including Germany, Japan, Korea and Taiwan. All these countries had systems to make sure that banks allocated credit mostly for productive uses and not for speculative purposes (Werner 2007).

Give back the money

The last time such problems were discussed seriously was in the midst of the Great Depression in the 1930s. A group of Chicago economists including Henry C. Simons and his young disciple Milton Friedman advocated taking away the power of banks to create money with their proposed "100 percent banking." Irving Fisher did the same with his "100 percent money" proposal. Where Simons' group and Fisher parted was that the 100 percent banking school argued in favor of increasing the amount of money by a fixed percentage every year, while Fisher proposed a politically independent currency commission that would determine a degree of money expansion that was consistent with a preset inflation target (Huber 2007).

Milton Friedman would later become famous and highly influential with his proposal of a monetary rule, even though (or perhaps because) he had given up on the demand to control the issue of money by banks. He simply proposed to increase the amount of money created by the central bank by a fixed percentage every year. He chose to ignore the insight of the 100 percent banking school, which he had earlier belonged to, that banks can expand and shrink the amount of fiat money they create on top of this central bank money in a way that needs to be controlled by either central banks or the government.

The 100 percent proposals intended to avoid the cycle of uncontrolled money creation and destruction that is so lucrative for banks and so damaging to the economy. Under Irving Fisher's proposal, banks would have to either keep an equivalent amount to the money deposited by customers as cash in their vaults or in the form of deposits at the central bank, which are as good as cash. This would eliminate the possibility of banks enlarging the money supply (and shrinking it again in a crisis). The government would create the necessary reserves by having a currency commission buy government bonds from the banks with money that the commission printed. In this way, the money supply would remain unchanged versus the status quo, and be much less volatile. It would consist entirely of central bank money, which would be strongly expanded to make up for the decline in money created by the private banking system. The amount of money in circulation would cease to depend on the fluctuating willingness and ability of the financial sector to extend credit. The interest rate would become a reliable indicator of scarcity again (Fisher 1936/2009). It would be up to the central bank (or currency commission) to increase the money supply if rates were deemed too high, and vice versa.

If the current monetary system of the US was named in analogy with Fisher, it would be called 10 percent money. In this system, banks have to hold 10 percent of bank deposits as reserves with the central bank. The minimum reserve requirement is the lever that determines which proportion of overall money the banks can create and which proportion the government, through the central bank, can create. If banks have to obey a 10 percent reserve requirement, they can send any sum of cash customers deposit with them, say US$100, as reserves to the central bank, and extend US$1,000 credit to other customers. If banks have to obey a 100 percent reserve requirement, they can only lend out the money they get from the central bank or from savers. They cannot create extra credit by creating checking accounts out of thin air.

If the minimum reserve requirement is 10 percent, this means that the private banking system can credit their customers' checking accounts with US$10 billion for every billion of dollars in cash and central bank reserves. The banks get the profits from creating 90 percent of the money in circulation and the government gets the profits on 10 percent. If banks find ways to creating money off their balance sheets, as they did on a large scale in the run-up to the subprime crisis, they can significantly extend their share of profits from money creation. In the euro area, the minimum reserve requirement was cut from an already ridiculous rate of 2 percent to 1 percent in January 2012, and in the UK it has long been abolished altogether such that British banks can decide for themselves how much cash and central bank reserves they want to keep as a safety margin to satisfy customers' demand for cash.

The reserve requirement determines how much the banks can expose themselves – or in practice, the public purse – to the risk of a bank run. The lower the reserves in proportion to the money that customers could withdraw at any time, the higher the risk of a bank run. This does not only affect the banks with the lowest reserves. If the reserve requirement is low, the banking system as a whole has low reserves in relation to potential withdrawals of cash. This is why the problems of any significant bank routinely threaten to put the entire financial system at risk. If customers of one bank get worried that they might not get their money back, customers of all other banks have reason to run to their bank before others have the same idea. In fact, the first bank that failed at the start of the subprime crisis in 2007 was the small German bank IKB. The government rescued it, at great cost to taxpayers, based on the argument that a bank failure would damage the public's trust in the banking system.

As government-sponsored depositor insurance systems, central banks and the prospect of bailout packages in times of need insure the banks against a bank run, a low reserve requirement is a superb deal for private banks. Using their influence, they made sure that in Europe minimum reserve requirements were continuously reduced in the last decades of the twentieth century. In the US, they engineered policies so that the reserve requirement would cover less and less of the financial sector's money creation activities. The goal of the operation was usually cast as improving the international competitiveness of the banks of the respective nations or as increasing the attractiveness of the respective financial centers. These expressions cloak the goal of conferring profits to the banking sector into a respectable-seeming public purpose. The bigger the bank, the more valuable the implicit insurance subsidy by the government is. Big banks are too big to fail, and they know governments and central banks will bail them out if they run into trouble. Thus bigger banks can take on more risk and make more profit in good times than smaller banks. This is a recipe for ever-increasing bank size.

The main argument of the banking lobby against 100 percent banking or 100 percent money has always been its potential to reduce the availability of credit. Fisher never took this argument very seriously. For him, it only served to disguise the banks' financial interest in the status quo: they understandably want to preserve their profits, which stem from their ability to create money. Fisher noted that bankers like to discredit money printing by governments as inflationary but do not condemn money expansion as produced by banks. The main difference, of course, is that the proceeds of money printing by agents of the government go to the government and the proceeds of money creation by banks go to the banks (Fisher 1936/2009). Economists acted as key allies of the bankers. They let the ideas of Fisher and Simons fade into oblivion and spent all their effort devising strategies to keep central banks from printing "too much" money while almost completely ignoring the dangers of money creation by banks for price stability and financial stability. The less money central banks create, the more leeway there is for private banks to create money.

With the public finances of many industrial countries ruined by the need to bail out banks and the economy, governments are overdue in reclaiming the power to control the amount of money in circulation and to reduce net taxation using the profits from creating that money. As Fisher and Simons already made clear, this would not at all mean socializing banking. It would only mean socializing the provision of the means of exchange, a core government function, just like controlling the means of measuring weights and lengths. Banking would become more boring and less profitable, of course. Banks would basically become brokers, bringing together savers and investors.

Fisher saw his proposal also as a contribution to making government more independent from banker's influence. He wrote that in hard times, banks become creditors of the government and exert an "unhealthy influence" on politics. Reclaiming their superiority in issuing money would somewhat shield governments from this, he argued. In a similar way, banks' power over other companies would be reduced if credit-driven booms and busts were mitigated. During credit crunches and because of the threat of credit crunches, banks can demand a lot of influence over companies in exchange for helping them to survive (Fisher 1996/2009).

Chances are slim that contemporary students of economics will think about any of that. The leading textbooks in economics, for instance Mankiw and Taylor (2006), restrict the discussion of the monetary system to explaining the process of private money creation in a rather roundabout way, and as if it was a law of nature. If these textbooks mention the possibility of changing the minimum reserve requirement at all, as the one by Mankiw and Taylor does, they limit their remarks to stating that increasing reserve requirements can significantly disturb the banking business, with the implication that this would be negative for the economy. This means that banks' ability to create more claims than they can satisfy should only be increased or left constant, but never curtailed.

The strange and unusual role of central banks

It is forbidden to even pose the question "who benefits?" with respect to the Fed, lest one be smeared and marginalized as a "conspiracy theorist." Strangely, when a similar question is asked regarding the imposition of tariffs or government regulations of one sort or another, no one seems to bat an eye, and free market economists even delight in uncovering such "rent-seekers" in their publications. These economists of the Chicago and Public Choice Schools have explained the origins and policies of [many] federal agencies as powerfully shaped by the interests of the industries that they regulated. Yet these same economists squirm in discomfort and seek a quick escape when confronted with the question of why this analysis does not apply to the Fed.

—*Joseph Salerno, 2008*

Obtaining the power to print money was a good deal for the bankers but still not the best they could get. As long as money creation was unregulated and uncoordinated, the amount of money that banks could create without adverse consequences was limited. A bank that issued too many notes could easily face mistrust and see the value of its notes decrease. Notes from a more conservative bank which instilled more trust might displace them. This kind of competition is bad for banking profits. Better if there is some central coordination, some form of a legal cartel, determining the amount of money banks can produce. If every bank expands its notes at the same rate, the speed limit can be much higher. Enter the central banks.

Central banks are Janus-headed creatures. Most people think of them as part of the government, but they are also banks and often seem to have the interest of their banking constituency closer to heart than the interest of the public. There is a reason for this, of course. The history of central banking reveals that there was little of government and much of banking about them for long periods. Governments took a significant amount of control over time, but in the face of very powerful banking interests, their control over central banks remained tenuous.

The Bank of England was founded in 1694 as a private enterprise with special privileges. After a series of civil wars, the British Crown was desperate for money. A consortium led by the Scottish businessman William Paterson suggested a scheme. It would afford King William and Queen Mary a large loan and make him and his companions rich. The consortium was granted the right to found the privately owned Bank of England and to create money. They lent the money as notes of the Bank of England to the Crown against interest. Thus, the financiers did not even have to use any of their own money to lend to the Crown. The king and queen were not able to pull off the same trick by themselves. Their finances were in such bad shape that nobody would have accepted notes backed up by their word alone. The syndicate was smart enough, however, to invite in parliamentarians and the king as stockholders of the Bank of England. This secured them political support (Rothbard 1985/2008).

Robert Morris founded the Bank of North America, the first predecessor of the Federal Reserve, in similar circumstances and for a similar purpose. However, Morris did not even introduce the semblance of separation between private and public interest. Morris founded and owned the bank while at the same time holding the office of superintendent of finance. He dominated finance, politics and the economy of the early United States all at once. With the bank up and running, he borrowed money from it on behalf of the government to the benefit of himself as owner of the bank. He also conferred on his own bank a monopoly license to issue paper money and the privilege to have its notes accepted for duty and taxes on par with gold (Rothbard 1985/2008).

Morris suffered a setback, though. In the charged climate of the fights about land banks in 1785, his Bank of North America was accused of abusing political power. In September 1785, the Philadelphia legislature annulled the bank's state charter. Morris later declined the offer to be the first secretary of the treasury in 1789 and suggested instead his banker friend Alexander Hamilton. Hamilton, who would have a big role in helping to industrialize the country, pushed through Congress the chartering of the First Bank of the United States, a bank with special central bank-like money creation privileges. He staunchly opposed the idea that the government itself should issue the money needed to fund manufacturing and the settling of the West. He wanted private banks to do it, but they should have the strong backing of the government. Thus the government rewarded the predominantly privately owned First Bank of America for printing paper money by accepting these notes in duties and taxes. The government also entrusted it with investing all its funds and awarded it a monopoly as the only bank allowed to operate nationally (Nettels 1962).

The highly privileged role of bankers remained a source of political controversy for decades. After its 20-year charter ran out in 1811, a bill to re-charter the First Bank of America narrowly failed. Five years later, the banker Alexander Dallas, in his other capacity as secretary of the treasury, pushed through Congress the chartering of the Second Bank of the United States. He endowed the predominantly privately owned bank with the same privileges as the First Bank had had before (Rothbard 1985/2008).

President Andrew Jackson eventually was successful in his campaign to take away the privileges of the Second Bank in 1832. Jackson had doubts that paper money was constitutional in the first place, but if it was, he insisted that it was improper for Congress to pass the important task of creating money and regulating its value to a private corporation.

The US banking system evolved further toward its current structure when the government needed a lot of money to finance the war against the secessionist South. Jay Cooke, a banker from Ohio, helped the government find buyers for billions of greenbacks, issued to finance the war. He built on that success to push for the creation of a layered bank system with a couple of New York banks as quasi-central banks. Together with his newspaper-owning brother Henry, Jay Cooke installed Senator Salmon Chase as treasury secretary in 1861. At least, that was how their father saw it. In a letter, he congratulated his sons on this feat and added, "Now is it the time for making money, by honest contracts out of the government." The following year, Secretary Chase granted the house of Cooke a monopoly to sell the government's bonds to the public. Cooke used his public relations prowess and his power as a major newspaper advertiser to convince the public and congress that a national banking law was good idea. The new layered system had New York City–based national banks at the top, designated as central reserve city banks. They could give loans and thus create deposit money as a multiple of the amount of Treasury bonds, gold and silver they held. Other nationally chartered banks in big cities, the reserve city banks, were required to hold reserves in the form of deposits at central reserve city banks and could create a multiple of these reserves as checking accounts. National banks in smaller places had to hold reserves at reserve city banks to back up the loans they gave. Jay Cooke benefited in multiple ways from this arrangement. He earned a commission on all the government bonds that banks were practically forced to buy. He also set up a bank in New York to benefit from the privileged position of a central reserve city bank as well as several national banks, either personally or through his associates. Chase's successor Hugh McCulloch extended Cooke's monopoly. He was a close friend of Cooke's. When McCulloch left the Treasury, he became head of Cooke's London office. The result of the new system was a great expansion of the number of banks and of deposits but also, in short order, a series of financial crises. There were panics and bank runs in 1873, 1884, 1893 and 1907 (Rothbard 1985/2008).

As a reaction to these crises, the Federal Reserve System was created in 1913 upon bankers' initiative. At a secret meeting at Jekyll Island, Georgia in December 1910, they hammered out the essential features of the new Federal Reserve System. Bankers representing the interests of Rockefeller, J.P. Morgan and Kuhn, Loeb & Company, the most powerful institutions of the time, dominated the meeting. The idea was to make the process of money creation more disciplined and orderly and to have institutions with deep pockets bail out the banks if the public lost confidence in the bank notes they had issued. The bankers wanted the government involved as paymaster only, though. Other than that, it was not supposed to have any influence over the process (Rothbard 1985/2008). This is why the terms of the board members in Washington are 12 years long, such that any American president can only replace two of the six members in one term. If ever a conflict between bankers' interests and the government should develop, the Federal Reserve and the banking community can be sure to have time to use the levers of their financial power before the president has a chance to impose his will on them.

To this day, the 12 regional Federal Reserve Banks, which are in charge of regulating banks, are owned and governed by their member banks. Before the subprime crisis, this fact was never advertised and often concealed by the pretence that the Federal Reserve System was a public institution. It became a little more widely known when Stephen Friedman, board member and former head of Goldman Sachs, was forced to step down in 2009 as the chairman of the board of the Federal Reserve Bank of New York. He had overstepped by making large deals with Goldman shares while presiding over the board of a Federal Reserve, which was intimately involved in rescuing the financial sector (including Goldman) with large amounts of public money. The Friedman case exposed the fact that there are no safeguards against bankers using their control over the Federal Reserve Banks to promote the interest of banks at the expense of the public.

The Federal Reserve Bank of New York is the one in charge of regulating, overseeing and bailing out Wall Street banks with public money. Wall Street banks choose the president of the New York Fed and charge him with regulating and controlling them. A board chosen and dominated by bankers makes sure it is done in accordance with their wishes. Only during the subprime crisis did the Federal Reserve give up the pretence of being a public institution. The New York Fed, managing US$1.7 trillion of emergency lending programs for banks and brokerages, was called upon to inform the public of the whereabouts of the public funds going to Wall Street. At this point, the Federal Reserve of New York insisted that as a private institution it is not bound by the Freedom of Information Act, nor are any of the 11 other regional Federal Reserves. Why such a private institution can be in charge of disbursing trillions of taxpayers' dollars with no political oversight is another matter. That such an institution should be put in charge of consumer protection in the banking business is hard to understand unless Congress has been captured by the interests of the banking industry.

A key ingredient of any meaningful and lasting reform is to make central banks more independent from the private banking sector.

Otherwise, it is only a matter of time until the politically independent technocrats at the central banks help the banking sector to undo or circumvent the restrictions that fleeting public outrage has prevented them from blocking. Farhi and Tirole (2009) chide their fellow economists for having forgotten to push for the independence of central banks from banking interests over their successful campaign to reduce the governments' control over central banks. So far, this has remained the lonely voice in the wilderness.

The Austrian government decided in January 2010 to take control over the national central bank away from the nation's private banks, insurance companies and financial industry associations who held its shares and staffed its board until then. After some severe failures of bank oversight led to large losses for taxpayers, it dawned on the Austrian government that it might not be a good idea to have institutions oversee a central bank that is supposed to regulate and control these very institutions. It is high time for the US to make similar changes. The same goes for Italy, where the financial industry owns the central bank. According to a report in the Financial Times, Italian banks even argued that they should be allowed to declare their share in the nation's large gold reserves, held by the central bank, as their own capital (Sanderson 2011). Bank representatives later denied the report, but it is still interesting to learn that by law Italy's national gold reserve belongs to the Italian banks. It is left purposefully unclear who owns the vast gold reserves that are held in the Federal Reserve System, and thus it remains a matter of contention.

However, such formal changes are insufficient. Central bankers have to be barred from having too much influence on matters of financial regulation. They are much too aligned with bankers' interests. There has to be regulatory knowledge and regulatory powers wielded by democratically accountable people and institutions sufficiently removed from the banking industry.

A Man-Made Crisis (and a Woman Who Tried to Prevent It)

What happened between approximately 1980 and 2007 was credit creation for speculative purposes run amok. Financial deregulation – arranged in no small part by investment bankers in their capacity as treasury secretaries – allowed the financial sector to use and massively expand a series of financial innovations that ostensibly served to distribute risk and make the system safer. The real purpose was to extend the limits on money creation. By the second quarter of 2007, after two decades of exponential growth, assets held by securitization pools or at similar shadow banking institutions that buy up loans and fund themselves by issuing securities was US$16.5 trillion, or approximately the entire economic output of the United States for one year. This exceeded the assets held by banks, which were only US$12.8 trillion (Adrian and Shin 2009).

When the credit crisis hit, Alan Greenspan, Robert Rubin and Larry Summers tried to create the impression that the subprime crisis and the ensuing global financial crisis was an accident that nobody could have foreseen. However, these men knew full well what they were doing and how it endangered the global financial system. One of their most pernicious actions was to prevent other regulators from doing anything to manage derivatives. Derivatives are securities that are *derived* from other securities like stocks or bonds. "Without derivatives, leveraged bets on subprime mortgage loans could not have spread so far or so fast," claims Frank Partnoy (1997/2009), a law professor at the University of San Diego and a former derivative structurer at investment banks Morgan Stanley and CS First Boston. Without derivatives, the complex risks that destroyed Bear Stearns, Lehman Brothers and Merrill Lynch and decimated dozens of banks and insurance companies, including AIG, could not have been hidden from view. Yet regulators, most infamously Alan Greenspan and treasury secretary Robert Rubin, with bankers like Hank Paulson and their lobbyists, worked and fought hard to make sure that no rules or restrictions would be applied to derivatives.

In 1998, Brooksley Born, chairwoman of the Commodity Futures Trading Commission (CFTC), pushed for minimum regulation of derivatives. The CFTC issued a "concept release" report calling for greater transparency of derivatives that were traded over the counter (OTC), off the formal exchanges. The CFTC sought greater information disclosure, improvements in record keeping and controls on fraud. The response by Federal Reserve governor Alan Greenspan, treasury secretary Robert Rubin, his deputy Larry Summers and SEC chairman Arthur Levitt was swift: They obtained a moratorium on the CFTC's ability to implement the strategies outlined in its concept release. Then they engineered passage of the Commodity Futures Modernization Act of 2000, which explicitly exempted OTC derivatives from government oversight. At the last minute, the bill was tucked onto an 11,000 page bill sampler and passed without serious consideration by lawmakers (Partnoy 1997/2009; Levine 2010).

The derivatives that were allowed to remain in the shadows included the now infamous credit default swaps (CDS), which would later bring down the world's largest insurer, AIG. CDS are a bet that a bond (loan) will hit some adverse credit event like an arrear, downgrade or default. Those who sell the CDS get a fee and those who buy it get a payment if the adverse event should occur. CDS are therefore somewhat like insurance policies, except that there is no need to own the underlying item being insured to buy the CDS. Indeed, most buyers do not own the underlying item, as the CDS market is many times larger than the underlying bond market, so what many in the CDS market are doing is betting on the misfortune of others. However, it goes further: CDSs, as currently defined, let you do something very curious. Technically, it is entirely possible to take out a CDS on the debts of your neighbor without your neighbor knowing a thing about it. If your neighbor should for any reason, miss a payment on their debts, you receive a payout with all the very obvious incentives for misfeasance that this introduces. The fact that this is completely legal is astonishing – furthermore, the fact that it is very common throughout the financial industry as a means of leveraging extra profit from financially assaulting a firm or country, and no one does anything about it, is surely not just foolish but obscene.

CDS became extremely attractive for banks because in 1996 the Federal Reserve allowed banks to hold less capital in reserve for the bonds they held if they bought CDS as insurance on those bonds. Because the market was very opaque (and was expected to remain so due to the efforts of Greenspan and others), and because nobody really looked at the sellers of the CDS, the banking system was able to lower its overall capital requirement massively by exchanging CDS. By 2007, the largest US commercial banks had purchased US$7.9 trillion in CDS protection. Thus a huge derivatives market, which was totally obscure for regulators, increasingly compromised bank oversight. Some sellers of CDS developed massive exposures to CDS risk. For example, AIG had a notional exposure of about US$500 billion to CDSs (and related derivatives) in 2007, while having a capital base of about US$100 billion to cover all its traditional insurance activities as well as its financial derivatives business. The growing exposure of AIG and other issuers of CDSs should have – and did – raise concerns about their ability to satisfy their obligations in times of economic stress. If the seller of the CDS was unable to pay in a crisis, all the CDS would be worthless and the banks wouldn't have enough capital (Levine 2010).

Those who knew the market could guess early on where it would go. At the end of the original edition of the book *F.I.A.S.C.O.*, published in 1997, Frank Partnoy (1997/2009) predicted:

> The current path seems clear. The financial services industry will continue to pay tens of millions of dollars to lobbyists and congressional campaigns to fend off regulation. Derivatives will continue to cause billions of dollars in losses by hundreds of derivatives victims, along the way destroying reputations, twisting lives and emptying bank books. And Wall Street will continue to argue that there is no compelling reason to regulate derivatives.

Greenspan, Summers and Rubin cannot credibly claim that they remained unaware of the possible consequences. Already in the fall of 1998, the hedge fund Long-Term Capital Management (LTCM) was suddenly near bankruptcy. LTCM had piled a hundred billion dollars of debt and more than a trillion dollars of derivatives on top of a few billion dollars of equity from investors and had sold massive amounts of options (a type of derivative). LTCM's derivatives positions were so large that a relatively small decline in the world financial markets was enough to wipe out its capital (Partnoy 1997/2009). The Federal Reserve was intimately involved in saving LTCM and the financial system. Even after that, Greenspan, Summers and Rubin kept resisting derivative regulation or even the imposition of additional transparency.

There is another part to the story, one that starts a little earlier. Before Mrs. Born, Wendy Lee Gramm had headed the Commodity Futures Trading Commission (CFTC) from 1988 to 1993. Under her rule, the CFTC granted Enron an exemption from regulation in its trading of energy derivatives. Subsequently, Wendy Gramm resigned from the CFTC and took a seat on Enron's board of directors. Enron was also very generous toward her husband Senator Gramm. He was Enron's second largest recipient of campaign contributions in 1996. Phil Gramm would later be one of the key allies of Greenspan, Rubin and the bankers in their fight to keep derivatives completely unregulated (Ferguson 2009).

After Enron's giant house of derivative cards had collapsed, Congress passed the Sarbanes–Oxley Act of 2002, which imposed costly corporate governance reform on all companies. However, it had no specific regulation for the financial industry and for the dangerous financial products that had enabled Enron, Worldcom and others to cook their books and manipulate markets for so long. Cooking the books (legally) is a major side purpose of derivatives trading, as investor legend Warren Buffett (2003) emphasized when he famously warned of derivatives as "financial weapons of mass destruction." He wrote to his shareholders:

> Reported earnings on derivatives are often wildly overstated. That is because today's earnings are in a significant way based on estimates. However, the parties to derivatives also have enormous incentives to cheat in accounting for them. I can assure you that the marking errors in the derivatives business have not been symmetrical. Almost always, they have favored either the trader who was eyeing a multi-million dollar bonus or the CEO who wanted to report impressive "earnings" (or both). The bonuses were paid, and the CEO profited from his options. Only much later did shareholders learn that the reported earnings were a sham.

Timothy Geithner, then president of the New York Fed, created a taskforce in 2004 that identified the array of risks posed by CDS to the stability of the banking system. Yet the Fed did nothing to reverse its policies regarding bank capital and CDSs or regarding oversight over the market for CDS or derivatives in general. Obviously, the banks that own and control the New York Fed and the other regional Federal Reserves would not have supported any such move since the rapidly growing derivatives market enabled them to do increasingly risky but highly lucrative business. Politicians and regulators chose not to confront the big investment banks and commercial banks, who are among the most important campaign contributors for any candidate for presidency or Congress. Former regulator Brooksley Born said in a 2009 interview with *Stanford Magazine*, "Recognizing the dangers was not rocket science, but it was contrary to the conventional wisdom and certainly contrary to the economic interests of Wall Street at the moment."

It was also no accident, but the result of active deregulation, that investment banks like Lehman Brothers held very little capital in relation to their assets and that they financed these assets with very short-term debt. In 2004, Hank Paulson, while still head of Goldman Sachs, led the successful Wall Street campaign to get the SEC under William Donaldson, a former investment banker, to scrap the so called "net capital rule" which restricted leverage for large investment banks. Henceforth, financial firms were effectively allowed to decide their own leverage based on their own risk models (Gowan 2009; Levine 2010).

Lehman Brothers was by no means an exception. In September 2008, before Lehman went broke, Bank of America had capital equivalent to 1.4 percent of its assets. If the activities that the bank conducted off the balance sheet in some specially created conduits are figured in, the ratio even dropped below 1 percent (Ferguson 2009).

In a related policy change, the SEC enacted another rule in 2004 that induced the five investment banks to become "consolidated supervised entities" (CSEs): This meant that the SEC would oversee the entire financial firm including all its subsidiaries in the US and abroad. Given the size and complexity of these financial conglomerates, overseeing the CSEs was a systemically important and difficult responsibility. The SEC's stated commitment to put a lot of effort and manpower into overseeing these CSEs was instrumental in getting regulators in other countries to agree not to regulate the foreign subsidiaries of these firms. This was particularly important for those in the second global financial center, London. The London subsidiary of Lehman would later be instrumental in hiding the debt of the conglomerate. The SEC apparently never intended to, and certainly never did, seriously supervise these globally active investment banks. While the SEC had promised to hire highly skilled supervisors to assess the riskiness of investment banking activities, they had only seven people to examine the parent companies of the investment banks, which controlled more than US$4 trillion in assets. Under Christopher Cox, who became chairman in 2005, the SEC even eliminated the risk management office and failed to complete a single inspection of a major investment bank in the year and a half before the collapse or near collapse of those banks. Cox also weakened the Enforcement Division's freedom to impose fines. Still, the SEC's deputy director Robert Colby, in a bid to ward off regulation that would have imposed some oversight over investment banks, boldly – and falsely – told the Financial Services Committee of the US House of Representatives in April 2007 that the SEC "has established a successful consolidated supervision program based on its unique expertise." The 2,220 page report of a court trustee on the causes of the failure of Lehman Brothers notes that Lehman "was significantly and persistently in excess of its own risk limits" and adds that the SEC "was aware of these excesses and simply acquiesced" (Levine 2010).

Lax regulation and oversight is a terrible thing in finance since finance is already prone to what Professor William Black, a former finance inspector, calls *control fraud*. It consists of gaining control over a company in order to commit fraud, while also using the company as a shield to be safe from prosecution. Control frauds seek out companies that operate under lax oversight. They use the money they generate by their fraudulent behavior to bribe or coax regulators and politicians into keeping it lax and making it even more so (Black 2010).

Indeed, Igan, Mishra and Tressel (2009) found a close statistical connection between the amount of money lenders spent on lobbying related to mortgage lending and the aggressiveness of their lending practices. Those who spent more on massaging bureaucrats and politicians gave borrowers higher loans for a given income, repacked more loans into securities, grew faster in size and performed worse later. According to Black (2010), the business model of control frauds goes as follows: grow very fast, with no consideration for long-term profitability, with a Ponzi-like scheme. Use as much leverage as possible (i.e. operate with much debt and little capital), because this increases short-term profitability, impressing observers. To grow quickly, give loans to people with low credit standing who did not get credit before. This has the added advantage that you can charge more and increase short-term profitability further. Make sure you are being compensated with a pay-for-performance scheme giving steep rewards for good short-term performance. To get loan managers and internal auditors to give loans to people that are not creditworthy, devise an incentive scheme that rewards turnover and punishes prudence. After the first movers start to do this, other bank CEOs are compelled to do likewise, because otherwise they would not be able to meet the new industry standard for profitability and success. If such a dynamic plays out on the mortgage market, house prices will go up, making the aggressive lending strategy even seem reasonable. By the time the Ponzi scheme collapses and takes the companies down with the lending institutions, the control frauds and many of their imitators have cashed out big. If they were careful, they have not done anything for which they could go to jail (Black 2010). This may sound like an *ex post* description of what was going on in the run-up to the subprime crisis. It is noteworthy, though, that Black developed his theory of control fraud earlier, based on the evidence of the savings and loan crisis of the mid-1990s, which had followed a similar pattern.

They made a killing

Did it work for the bankers and for the regulators who helped them fend off any impediments to their dangerous business practices? It did indeed. The CEO of failed subprime lender Washington Mutual,

Kerry Killinger, reportedly extracted US$100 million before his company folded. CEOs of some other mortgage lenders reaped even more. In addition, a generous bailout by the American taxpayer made sure that even after the crisis had broken out, bankers continued to do well. According to an analysis by the *Wall Street* Journal, the top 38 financial companies set a new compensation record in the crisis year 2009, paying out US$139 billion in bonuses and salaries to their employees. In 2010 they raised this further to US$144 billion (Grocer, Lucchetti and Rappaport 2010).

Most high-ranking Wall Street bankers and regulators involved in the deregulation and credit expansion preceding the latest crisis ended up much richer even after the crisis hit. Robert Rubin became director and senior counselor of Citigroup after leaving his office at the Treasury. For his job of providing counseling and representative services, he received more than US$126 million in cash and stocks over eight years. Just as with Andrew Mellon in the 1920s, he was one of the major personal beneficiaries of the policies he had pursued as treasury secretary. His successor and protégé Lawrence Summers also shared in the wealth of the banking industry after leaving office. He became a part-time managing director of the large hedge fund D. E. Shaw & Co. and was paid US$5.2 million in his second of two years working there for one day a week (McKinnon and Farnam 2009). Alan Greenspan would become a consultant for Pimco, the world's largest bond fund, in 2007. At that point, he suddenly became much smarter about what was going on in the world of derivatives and banking. Bill Gross, the bond manager's co-chief investment officer said in 2008 that Greenspan's "brilliance in terms of forecasting the potential for exactly what happened was a big money saver for us, he's made and saved billions of dollars for Pimco already" (Bhaktavatsalam 2008).

Even the top executives of the worst-hit investment banks Bear Stearns and Lehman Brothers made a fortune in the run-up to the crisis. This made it easy for them to forget about the loss in value of their remaining shares when their companies were sold in a fire sale or went bankrupt respectively. For the top five Bear Stearns executives, the total proceeds from sales of stocks and options in the years 2000–2008, which came on top of cash salaries, was US$1.1 billion; for the top five at Lehman Brothers it was US$850 million. Figuring in cash bonuses, the amount comes to US$1.4 billion and US$1 billion, respectively. Each of the two teams sold more shares in those eight years than they held when the music stopped in 2008 (Bebchuk, Cohen and Spaman 2010).

Rating agencies were doing the dirty work

There are two superpowers in the world today in my opinion. There's the United States and there's Moody's Bond Rating Service. The United States can destroy you by dropping bombs, and Moody's can destroy you by downgrading your bonds. And believe me, it's not clear sometimes who's more powerful.

—*Thomas Friedman, 1996*

The failure of the rating agencies, the institutions charged with assessing the creditworthiness of borrowers and the credit quality of securities and derivatives, was no accident either. This failure was a critical element in making the subprime scheme profitable and possible. Without the blessing of the rating agencies, the delivery chain of junk assets from originators via investment banks to final investors would not have supported such a torrent of activity. Mortgage lenders were able to vastly expand their business and profits by selling mortgages to millions of people who clearly could not afford them. They could do so because they were sure they could sell the mortgages to investment banks. Investment banks would buy the mortgages because they were able to repackage them with the use of complex derivatives structures and sell them on to investors all over the world. They knew these investors wanted highly rated securities promising relatively high returns. Without the rating agencies giving their absurdly over-optimistic top ratings to the vast majority of these repackaged junk loans, this chain would not have worked (Levine 2010).

Rating agencies did not achieve their tremendous power on the market themselves. It was bestowed on them by a government agency. Until the mid-1970s, the rating agencies were rather modestly sized, modestly influential institutions selling their judgment to investors who subscribed to their service. Then in 1975, the SEC named the three largest ones, Moody's, Standard & Poor's and Fitch, as Nationally Recognized Statistical Rating Organizations and made the capital that banks had to hold dependent on these agencies' judgment of the quality of the securities they owned. Private endowments, foundations and mutual funds also used these ratings in setting asset allocation guidelines for their investment managers. Thus the SEC was in effect giving the agencies a quasi-monopoly to sell a license to issue securities. If they rated a security badly, demand would be very low because banks would have to hold too much capital in reserve for them. Essentially, the *opinions* of the agencies had attained the force of law. Ironically, the reports of the agencies carry a disclaimer that urges users not to rely on any credit rating in making any investment decision, advice that most investors are required to ignore by law or by statute. Around the same time, the rating agencies switched their business model to having the issuers of securities pay for their services. In 1957, the vice president of Moody's had said of such business practices, "[W]e obviously cannot ask payment for rating a bond. To do so would attach a price to the process, and we could not escape the charge, which would undoubtedly come, that our ratings are for sale." Apparently, this did not count any more after the quasi-monopoly given to the largest agencies shielded them from the kind of competition that could have prevented them from putting their ratings up for sale (Partnoy 1999; Levine 2010; White 2010).

The fact that rating agencies with a near monopoly status can make self-fulfilling prophecies further weakens market discipline. Very many large investors such as pension funds are required to act on their ratings. Thus if the agencies accord high creditworthiness to a company or government, that company or government can easily borrow fresh money to pay back bonds or loans that are expiring. If the agencies give a bad rating, the borrower will not be able to refinance and will more likely have to default. Thus, the verdict of a respected credit rating agency is self-fulfilling within reasonable limits (Carlson and Hale 2006). Even after the subprime crisis evidenced that the rating agencies had spectacularly failed, there was next to no punishment from the market. Rating agencies still keep rating all major new bond issues and market participants still have to act as if they believe these ratings.

The dangers of the extraordinary power conferred to rating agencies had become apparent a long time before the agencies helped bring about the subprime crisis. Practitioners knew about it and any regulator or legislator who wanted to know could know. After Enron collapsed in 2001, followed shortly thereafter by Worldcom, in spite of investment grade ratings by the agencies, Congress held hearings where representatives of the agencies and of the SEC had to justify themselves. This exposed the issuer-pays model and the conflict of interest that goes with it to extensive public attention. Still, nothing happened (White 2010).

Instead, unencumbered by any regulator or lawmaker, rating agencies took their conflict of interest to an even higher level. The banks associated with creating structured financial products to sell off mortgage loans would first pay the rating agencies for guidance on how to package the securities to get high ratings. Then they would pay these same agencies to rate the resulting products. The profits from these activities were huge. At the peak of the subprime frenzy, Moody's achieved 44 percent of its sales this way – with a profit margin of more than 50 percent. Documents released by the US Senate suggest that rating agencies consciously adjusted their ratings to maintain clients and attract new ones (Levine 2010).

Why did regulators and lawmakers not draw the obvious conclusions, as they had done in the case of accounting firms, who were prohibited from structuring the financial statements that they would later audit by the Sarbanes–Oxley Act of 2002? The straightforward and easy answer is that the ability to buy favorable ratings from the rating agencies was a critical element for Wall Street to allow them to expand their business and their profits so spectacularly. Therefore Wall Street, with its huge influence on regulators and Congress, was squarely on the side of the rating agencies.

There is probably another element to the explanation. One which would explain why there have been high-profile efforts to establish a European rating agency for decades and why these efforts never went anywhere. The most recent installment of these efforts was a public push by German chancellor Angel Merkel and the French government to create such an agency in May 2010. It came after the big American agencies Standard & Poor's and Moody's had stoked the fire of a severe crisis in the European Currency Union by severely downgrading the debt of Greece and other southern European countries and by issuing stern warnings of impending default. This rating action came only a week after Moody's, as the last of the three big agencies, had changed its long-standing methodology for rating the bonds of US states and municipalities. The result was that California, with its public finances near collapse, was rated three grades higher, pulling the state back from the edge of junk status and firmly into investment-grade territory. The interest rate that California had to pay for its debt decreased a great deal within weeks, significantly alleviating its fiscal troubles. The ratings of 33 other states were also raised. There was already legislation pending in Congress that would have forced the changes if the agencies had not done so on their own (Seymour 2010).

According to the age old rule *do ut des* ("I give so that you may give," colloquially "a favor for a favor"), a rating agency might have to use its power to the advantage of those to whom it owes important favors. The three largest agencies are based in New York. They depend for their near monopoly status and for a lot of their business on the benevolence of the US government. Their business depends on having their ratings hardwired into regulatory prescriptions for banks. If they were willing to reciprocate occasionally, it would be a bad idea for the US government to break the power of its rating agencies.

Conclusion

> It makes little sense for large- or medium-sized economies, like the UK, Switzerland or the US, to be deriving 20 percent or so of their gross national product from financial service activities, when finance, like law and accounting, should be about facilitating economic investment, not being the investment itself.
> —*Warwick Commission, 2009*

If governments wanted to regain control over the financial sector, rather than having the financial sector control government, they would have to make use of this crisis and cut the financial sector and financial institutions back to size. However, doing so without causing a lot of damage is not easy. One can have a financial sector that is both too large in one way and too small in another way at the same time. There can be too little of the useful kind of banking and too much of the hurtful kind of banking. In situations where access to credit expands to groups that have been credit-restricted before, a dangerous credit boom might be on the way. Conversely, a primitive and very restricted financial sector might be a safe option in terms of stability, but it can make life unnecessarily hard for a significant portion of the population.

In the years before the outbreak of the Great Financial Crisis more than 40 percent of all domestic corporate profits in the US were accrued to financial institutions, in comparison to fewer than half that many 30 years ago. The number actually understates the share of profits accruing to the financial sector since it does not include the outsized salaries and employee bonuses paid there. For calculating profits, salaries and bonuses are treated as an expense, even though treating the above-average part of them as a way to disburse excessive profits might be closer to the truth. After all, financial sector salaries have risen to twice the average in the economy, whereas three decades ago they were equal to this average (Johnson 2009).

The only time that finance has been known to have been as profitable for as long as they have been during the past 30 years was in the UK during the period leading up to 1913, as the British Empire stagnated

(Imlah 1952; Dimson et al. 2002). Are sustained abnormal banking profits a sign of hidden local economic stagnation as capital is redirected to more profitable locations in the world?

Perhaps with the long British experience of finance in mind, the British Warwick Commission noted that a bloated financial sector is a disaster waiting to happen as well as a continuous drag on the economy. The commission, named after the university that convened it, was headed by Avinash Persaud, an academic and financial market practitioner who had long warned of the dangers of the regulatory approach that would prove so disastrously wrong when the subprime crisis hit. Even if one subscribes to the theory that financial institutions were helping to put capital and company ownership into the right hands, which they obviously did not, this would not justify a 40 percent share of economy-wide profits. It is extremely unhealthy for society if all the good students in every leading university think of nothing other than joining the financial sector because pay is so much higher than in the productive sectors of the economy. If the financial sector makes such fortunes by its short-term wheeling and dealing, it draws attention away from productive long-term investments. Even good returns will look boring compared to the wealth created by shuffling financial instruments around (Warwick Commission 2009).

A financial sector that is so big and so lucrative cannot be reined in or controlled effectively by politicians and bureaucrats earning a small fraction of the salaries paid there. Billions invested in lobbying and campaign contributions will inevitably show results. If high-ranking politicians and regulators routinely get extremely well-paid consultancy jobs in finance after they leave office, they cannot be expected to be tough on banks. After all, no bank or hedge fund would make them that kind of job offer if they were unsympathetic to the causes championed by the industry. As the Warwick Commission (2009) has pointed out in unusually clear language, "To avoid financial crises we must deal with regulatory capture."

No reform will be meaningful and sustainable if it does not heed the time-tested advice of *divde et impera* ("divide and conquer"). No individual financial institutions should be allowed to get so big and powerful that national governments can no longer control them. Splitting up the huge multinational banking conglomerates into individual companies for deposit banking, investment banking and asset management would promote three goals at the same time. Government guarantees would cover deposit banking only. The individual companies would be smaller and less powerful. Competition would work much better if a few very large players were not able to use and abuse their informational advantage and the power derived from their other business activities to race ahead of their competitors. Customers would receive better service, and the public purse would be much less strained should one of them collapse.

Promoting the establishment of small banks with narrow business lines to help underserved areas and constituencies and to stimulate competition enhances growth and efficiency as well as equity. Keeping large banks from becoming even larger protects the government and regulators from being captured by the interests of the banking industry. The unfortunate policy choice of the US government to create ever bigger banking behemoths by letting the biggest banks swallow up the failed smaller ones with the help of public guarantees needs to be reversed. Traditionally when a bank fails, its shares become almost worthless, thus allowing others to inject capital by buying up large amounts of those shares (if the government does this, it is called a "bailout") or indeed perform a hostile takeover (if the government does this, it is called "nationalization"). These two options are generally presented, especially in the US, as the only two options possible when rescuing a failed bank. However, there is a third option: instead of transferring ownership to the government, it can be transferred to the bank's customers (i.e. turned into a customer-owned mutualized cooperative). One of the most striking differences in financial evolution between the US and the core euro countries (Austria, Finland, France, Germany, Italy and the Netherlands) since the 2001 recession is the rapid growth of mutualized financial services in the core euro countries that grew in every measure of market share (loan share, deposit share and branch share) by about 20 percent in the five years up to 2007, almost all of which was driven by an increase in the number of customers (Groeneveld and Sjauw-Koen-Fa 2009). As commercial banks have gotten into trouble, cooperative banks have had the spare capital to make significant acquisitions: buying out shareholders lock, stock and barrel. As a result, cooperative banking gained a still further 5–7 percent of market share in the core euro countries between 2007 and 2009 (Groeneveld 2011). One might consider this when interpreting the narrow binary debate in the US between nationalization and bailout for failing banks.

Giving more authority at the local level would help make financial regulation more accountable. The largest financial institutions have lobbied instead for moving the regulatory process up to ever more international institutions. Recently, the Financial Stability Board (FSB) has been groomed to become the main regulatory body, setting worldwide rules for banking oversight. Until September 2011, the board was headed by former Goldman Sachs banker Mario Draghi (who moved on to become president of the European Central Bank, to be followed by Mark Carney, another former Goldman Sachs banker) and made up by technocrats (i.e. ministry officials, central bankers and bureaucrats from regulatory agencies). They have a lot of contact with bank CEOs who are promoting the interests of their national banking industries and almost no accountability to any political bodies representing the general public (Warwick Commission 2009). As long as the leading globally active banks are not allowed to decide on banking regulations themselves, the FSB looks like the next best thing.

The current international regulatory system is a recipe for driving down regulatory demands on banks, because banks from countries that have light supervision and regulation will outcompete those from countries with strict supervision, while the sheer size of internationally active banks and the complex web of mutual dependencies in the financial sector make it almost impossible to let overextended banks fail in a crisis. If we ever want to regain control over the banking sector, national regulators have to be able to impose tougher rules on their banks without simply diverting local business to foreign banks operating under laxer international rule. This might make it necessary that foreign banks who want to do business in another country would be required to do so through a subsidiary incorporated in the host country and regulated by the host country. This would ensure that international rules delineate the lower bound, not the upper bound, of the strictness of regulation.

Much higher reserve requirements and capital standards would make bank runs less likely and make the payment system safer, thus reducing the amount required to bail out large banks that are failing. Financial transaction taxes (of say 0.1 percent) are an empirically proven method for reducing trading volumes (Wrobel 1996), but given the industry's mortal opposition to them they have never spread past limited application by some European and Latin American countries (and most countries eliminated them after the industry fought back). There is also the problem that empirical studies have found that transaction taxes increase volatility and decrease liquidity (Habermeier and Kirilenko 2001), which is exactly the opposite of the desired outcome. There is a simple solution for this: the first step is to levy the entire value of the investment annually rather than additions and subtractions to that investment – this also inhibits the formation of asset bubbles. The second step is to make the annual levy inversely dependant on how long the investment has been held and repayable after a sufficiently long period. For example one might be charged 5 percent of the investment in the first year, charged nothing in the second year but repaid 5 percent at the end of the third year. Such a system is extremely inexpensive to implement and very effectively taxes speculation without harming long-term investment.

The next step would be to take away banks' ability to engineer credit bubbles. This requires that the public control a much larger part of the money creation and credit allocation process, and private banks a correspondingly smaller one. There certainly was a time when autocratic governments might be less trusted than private banks to provide a stable supply of a paper currency, and therefore they had to cooperate with private bankers. Times have changed. Today, governments need not be dependent on the good will of financiers. Governments observe the rule of the law. They made their central banks independent and gave them a clear and credible mandate to limit inflation. If fulfillment of this mandate is currently in question, this is not because governments have decided to cheat, but rather because excessive credit creation by the private banking sector has caused a major crisis that ruined public finances. If they wanted, democratic governments could take over a much larger part of the highly lucrative task of creating the money that the economy needs. This way citizens and taxpayers would benefit through lower taxes, instead of extra bonuses for overpaid bankers.

To get there, central banks should not withdraw the abundant amount of central bank money they have created to combat the financial crisis, but rather they should raise the minimum reserve requirement (the cash balances that banks have to hold with the central bank) as the crisis abates. In effect, the composition of all money would be changed in favor of money created by central banks. Increasing liquidity requirements for banks is at least as important as fiddling with capital requirements, the overwhelming focus of banking regulation so far. The Basel III Accord of 2010–11 does have some liquidity requirements, but they are far from stringent and appear to assume in their design the availability of government bailouts after 30 days of trouble beginning. Nevertheless, banks are fighting them tooth and claw, as there is nothing that they detest more than any impediment to this highly lucrative prerogative of creating money. Any reasonable amount of bank capital cannot prevent bank runs if banks have a high multiple of their cash balances as short-term liabilities. The banking business would be safer, but also less glamorous and less lucrative after such a change. Banks would have less money with which to influence policymakers and outsized bank bonuses would cease to be an issue.

Another important change needed to keep the financial sector under control is regulation of financial engineering. Trading in new financial products should be prohibited until officially approved by regulatory bodies, the same way pharmaceutical companies must perform real world trials and prove both efficacy and lack of public harm in order to obtain permission before they can market a new drug. Otherwise banks will always play cat and mouse with regulators, trying to circumvent any capital or liquidity regulations with new financial products (Soros 2009).

Of course Goldman Sachs, J.P. Morgan, Citigroup, Deutsche Bank, UBS and the other outsized banking behemoths will fight any attempt to cut back their power and profits with full force. Time will tell if the fallout from the subprime crisis weakened their influence sufficiently for reform-friendly forces to overcome this resistance. In two countries with a particularly outsized banking sector, the UK and Switzerland, even the heads of the central banks broke the taboo and suggested that excessively big banks should be broken into smaller pieces. Interestingly, in both the UK and Switzerland, steps to force primary loss-absorbing capacity for "too big to fail" banks to more than twice that required by Basel III (to around 15–20 percent), and the separation of deposit operations from all other kinds of banking as the sole kind protected by government guarantee, are well under way – and up to the time of writing the dire warnings from bankers that banks would relocate in response have been ignored by policymakers. Unfortunately, the Fed has elected to implement the minimum required by Basel III for most banks, and is still deciding what capacity will apply to the eight largest "too big to fail" banks. It seems unlikely that they will be as principled and erudite as the British or Swiss.

As of now, there isn't much indication that banks are losing control. Not all hope is lost, though. It can take a while for popular opinion to force governments to emancipate themselves from the outsized influence of financial lobbyists and get tough on finance. After the Great Crash of 1929 it took many years, but when it did happen it was severe. An enlightened public might cease to accept the extraordinary influence, privileges and liberties that the financial sector enjoys and demand fundamental changes. The judiciary, which is arguably less influenced by lobbying and campaign contributions from Wall Street, might have a key role to play.

Chapter 3

THE POWER OF THE CORPORATE ELITE

Half of the directors I've met on corporate boards don't know anything about business. They are not going to do anything that not only gets them kicked off that board but that reduces their chances of getting on another one.

—*Warren Buffett, 2009*

James Cayne's most important qualification for his later job as chief executive officer (CEO) of a large investment bank was a career as a professional card player. This enabled him to befriend other bridge aficionados at the helm of Bear Stearns. Firmly installed at the top, he felt completely free to pursue his own interests. In the summer of 2007, he was incommunicado at a bridge tournament in Nashville while two Bear Stearns hedge funds suffered a severe crisis. In the following spring, he was unreachable again for days at a bridge tournament while Bear Stearns was at the brink of bankruptcy (Altaner 2007).

CEOs do not necessarily have an inner urge to do what is in the interest of shareholders, as this example shows. Mainstream economic theory recognized this at least two decades ago. It came up with principal–agent theory and proposed a solution to the problem called "pay-for-performance." Principal–agent theory revolves around the idea that the principals (i.e. the owners or stakeholders of a corporation) have to give their agents (i.e. top management) wide latitude for making decisions because they cannot specify in advance how a manager should act in every circumstance. They also lack the information to evaluate individual management decisions. This gives managers the power to further their own interests rather than the interests of their principals. One such goal can be to entrench themselves by monopolizing information and building a network of cronies. This makes it harder for principals to fire them for bad performance and further increases their power. Other selfish goals that are often ascribed to top managers are income maximization and empire building. Managers might pursue unprofitable growth or spend too much money on acquisitions just to be able to wield power over an even bigger company. Pay-for-performance was supposed to align the interest of agents to the interests of their principals by paying agents specifically for furthering the principals' interests. Something went wrong with the idea, though. James Cayne was Mr Pay-for-Performance. He was one of the largest recipients of stock options, which should have given him a very strong incentive to put the survival of his employer before a bridge tournament, according to the theory.

In this chapter, we will see how influential economists helped top managers reach unprecedented pay levels without having to give up their selfish goals of maximizing power and job security. Dissenting economists and legal scholars had exposed this well before outsized bankers' bonuses, following the pay-for-performance idea, helped cause a worldwide financial crisis. We will present two countertheses to pay-for-performance. One is that management pay is not primarily a question of efficiency or of the supply and demand of managerial talent, but rather a question of social norms and structures. The other is that legal restrictions on company stakeholders' ability to direct and depose top management should be scrapped. In the process, we will have to clarify what should be the appropriate yardstick for successful management from the viewpoint of shareholders, other stakeholders and society. The subprime crisis, the dotcom bubble and the other past crises have called into question the wisdom of financial markets in steering capital to its best long-term uses. More generally, it has become hard to believe that maximization of share prices really is the same as maximizing company value in the long run, let alone achieving the highest possible benefit for society.

Autopsy of a Failed Idea: Why Pay-for-Performance Led to Disaster

> The deck is stacked against investors when it comes to the CEO's pay.
>
> —*Warren Buffett, 2005*

For textbook economists, financial markets are the best judges of corporate performance. Therefore, they want to eliminate anything that drives a wedge between the management of corporations and shareholders' interests. They want appropriately designed payment contracts to achieve this. Michael Jensen and Kevin Murphy popularized the idea of pay-for-performance in the late 1980s and 1990s and built a great reputation on it. Jensen, professor emeritus at Harvard, is among the most frequently quoted and influential economists in the field of corporate governance. Murphy is not far behind in terms of recognition and influence.

Jensen and Murphy (1990a) urged companies to pay their CEOs more by asking, "Are current levels of CEO compensation high enough to attract the best and brightest individuals to careers in corporate management? The answer is, 'probably not.'" Apart from paying managers more, they urged company boards to use monetary incentives to align the interest of the agents (i.e. managers) as closely as possible with the interest of the principals (i.e. shareholders). This is called the "optimal contracting" approach to managerial pay. It looks quite simple: give CEOs only a relatively meager fixed salary and supplement it with a variable portion proportional to a measure of the company's success. This measure of success could be profits, or the gain in stock price, or something similar.

Management and boards were easily convinced. It soon became the norm to grant top management a large amount of stock options as a form of variable pay dependant on corporate success. As a standard procedure, the top manager receives options to buy a large number of shares at a specified future date, but at the current price. If the price were to rise in the meantime, the manager would benefit a lot. If the price of the shares were to fall, the options become worthless, at least in principle. Lawmakers fell for the economic rationale of the scheme and promoted it. When the Clinton administration limited tax deductions for managerial pay to US$1 million per person, performance-related pay was exempt from this limit. This was on top of the special low income tax rate applied to capital gains income in the US that is less than half the normal income tax rate, and of course compensation paid through capital gains does not incur payroll taxation for the company. At the time of writing, both exemptions were still in place, even though the idea that stock and option grants predominantly serve the purpose of linking pay to performance has lost appeal.

The result was an explosion of top management pay. From 1936 to 1979, the median CEO worked for a salary of about US$1 million in inflation-adjusted money at year 2000 prices. They received that pay predominantly as a fixed salary. During the 1980s, median pay rose to US$1.8 million, during the 1990s to US$4.1 million, and from 2000 to 2005 it was US$5.2 million, still in year 2000 inflation-adjusted terms (Piketty and Saez 2006). Piketty and Saez (2006) estimate that the share of pre-tax personal income claimed by the top 1 percent of tax filing units almost doubled from 6.4 percent in 1980 to 11.6 percent in 2005 (those who lived off their wealth are excluded in this figure). The richest 1 percent of tax filers claimed 80 percent of all income increases reported in federal tax returns between 1980 and 2005. Within 15 years, starting in the early 1990s, CEO compensation in the S&P 500 companies more than tripled in inflation-adjusted terms from US$2.6 million to US$8.2 million in the prices of 2006.

In Europe and in other world regions, management pay is still significantly lower than in the US. However, in Europe in particular, boards and managers like to advertise the fact that pay is much higher in the US and use it as an argument in favor of steep pay increases in order to retain talent in Europe, among other things. In the year 2006, US managers received a salary that was twice as high as that of their counterparts in 26 other developed countries who worked for corporations of similar size in the same industry. The difference stems mostly from much higher pay in stock options. The CEOs in other countries are catching up, though. In 2000, US CEOs had earned almost three times as much as the CEOs of similar corporations in other countries. If company size and industry is not taken into consideration, US CEOs have to cede the top rank to the Swiss. The Swiss made on average US$6.1 million, US managers made US$5.5 million, Italian managers were third with US$4.9 million and Germans fourth with US$3.2 million (Fernandes et al. 2009).

During the stock market euphoria of the 1990s, shareholders were happy with their profits and hardly anybody complained about escalating CEO pay. Even huge paychecks seemed negligible in comparison to the increases in stock market valuation that the average corporation recorded. It did not matter that no special management skill was required to achieve these increases during the boom years. After the stock market crash of 2001 and the corporate scandals centered around Enron, Worldcom and a number of other new-economy corporations, the premise that financial markets value corporations correctly and that there is no significant difference between short-term and long-term maximization of company valuations lost much of its credit. Spurred on by monetary incentives, top management had done everything to push the prices of already vastly overvalued shares even higher, with no regard for the damage they did to their companies in the longer term.

This experience gave pay-for-performance gurus Michael Jensen and Kevin Murphy second thoughts. Like sorcerer's apprentices whose magic spell has gone out of control, they analyzed the reasons behind the failure of their approach and tried to repair the damage. In a long paper published in 2004, they revisited their earlier judgment that CEO compensation should be higher and concluded, "As the reader of this report has undoubtedly surmised, Jensen and Murphy would not give that answer today" (Jensen and Murphy 2004). They urged boards and top managers to shed their bad habits of the past and become better people. They threatened them with the purgatory of a lost reputation and public annimosity. Their plea is worth reprinting as it could just as well have been written again six years later, after the financial elite of the US had brought the Great Financial Crisis upon the world:

> This is a time where wise and forward-looking managers and boards can achieve a competitive advantage... It is a time in which proper investments in the integrity of the organization will generate considerable benefits in both the short and long run. Wise CEOs as well as wise board members will encourage these investments because they will understand that well functioning governance and monitoring systems will help to ensure not only organizational success, but personal success. The evidence of the damage to personal reputations as well as organizations is in the daily headlines. And even for some who have succeeded in preserving wealth acquired in the face of scandal, and have succeeded in avoiding jail, the question remains, how good is life without honor and respect?

As the examples of James Cayne of Bear Stearns and innumerable others show, their plea remained unheeded. Managers of large financial corporations, enticed by huge "performance-related" pay packages, demonstrated the futility of relying entirely on their sense of duty and their interest in preserving their personal reputations.

In April 2009, the Financial Stability Forum, a committee made up by finance officials, central bankers and the financial regulators of the most powerful nations, issued a report to the Group of Twenty Finance Ministers and Central Bank Governors (G20) in which they blamed pay schemes in the finance industry for having significantly contributed to the subprime crisis. There are indeed strong indications that managers of mortgage lenders and investment banks knew well before the crisis that the loans they were indiscriminately giving to non-creditworthy customers and passing on via securitizations to investors would prove to be unsustainable as soon as the housing price boom abated. However, spurred on by their pay packages, they continued. In the now infamous words of Citigroup CEO Chuck Prince, "When the music stops, in terms of liquidity, things will get complicated. But as long as the music is playing, you've got to get up and dance. We're still dancing." This attitude afforded most of the dancers dozens or even hundreds of millions of dollars in additional profits from their stock options.

In practice, pay-for-performance ended up as nothing more than an instrument to increase managerial pay. This is particularly evident in the practice of "golden parachutes." CEOs who fall out of favor with controlling shareholders routinely get very attractive severance packages, which increase with their regular pay. This practice is the result of the fact that CEOs are well placed to do much damage if they are retired against their will, so the golden parachute is used effectively to bribe them to leave quietly. The big problem is that golden parachutes completely negate any incentive effect of high pay – indeed, a cynic might note that a CEO's personal financial interest lies in either performing well or performing extremely badly but not in between, and neither is likely to be a prudent option. Jensen and Murphy (2004) note that comprehensive employment contracts for CEOs have become common. Such contracts provide compensation if the CEO is fired because of poor performance. "We believe that these contracts have become so extreme and abusive that they call into question the integrity of important parts of the remuneration process and the fiduciary responsibilities of boards and remuneration committees," they criticize. They cite the example of Michael Ovitz, who received stock options and cash worth more than US$100 million from the Walt Disney Company when he left after only 14 months in office. One can only wonder what damage he was thought capable of wreaking to warrant such a pay-off.

The ubiquitous practice of lavish golden parachutes tells the CEO that not performing is as personally profitable as performing. This was true even before pay-for-performance spread. However, as the pay ballooned with pay-for-performance, so did the size of golden parachutes. When Pfizer forced out CEO Hank McKinnell in 2006, he left with a farewell package of US$200 million. When Home Depot fired CEO Bob Nardelli in 2007, he was comforted with US$210 million (Frankfurter Allgemeine 2007). The CEO of the investment bank Merrill Lynch, Stanley O'Neal, lost his job in October 2007 after the firm admitted that it had lost US$8 billion on mortgage-backed securities and had to be rescued by an arranged takeover soon after. His decision to push the company deeply into risky business paid off well for him. He took with him stock options, unvested shares, deferred compensation and pension payments worth more than US$160 million (Whigton and White 2007).

Incentive pay is touted to address empire building, but in truth does nothing to alleviate it. It might even make it worse. When Jürgen Schrempp, chairman of Daimler Benz AG, bought Chrysler to create the ill-fated and short-lived automobile giant Daimler Chrysler, the press speculated that the prospect of gaining access to American-style pay, including lavish stock option grants, might have been a factor in the decision. It certainly paid off for Schrempp, but not for his company. After the merger, he received stock options for the new, larger company at the very depressed price that his decisions had caused. He made a fortune from these stock options when Daimler stocks jumped after he announced his resignation. Shareholder activists estimated the windfall at US$50 million. He made another big profit when the sale of Chrysler (i.e. the undoing of his merger work) was announced.

CEOs thinking about a merger can count on the same mechanism and probably will. They can count on getting even more lucrative options of the larger company. After all, if the company gets larger, it becomes all the more important to make sure that the CEO makes the right decisions in the interest of shareholders. Therefore, remuneration consultants and boards will most likely judge it imperative to give the CEO of the bigger company more options. Any CEO with a penchant for empire building will be smart enough to anticipate this (Bebchuk and Fried 2003).

Another perverse incentive of pay schemes oriented on the short-term is the excessive risk taking they encourage. The worst that can happen to the executives if their bet fails is that their most recent rounds of options, those they had no chance to cash in yet, become worthless. This is often counterbalanced by a golden parachute. If the bet works, even it is only for a couple of years, extremely high rewards beckon. The major players behind the subprime gamble made, and were able to keep, huge amounts of money, before their gamble turned against their companies and against the economy of the whole world.

As it is usually good enough to show high earnings for a couple of years to make a killing, executives with a more unlawful bent have a strong incentive to cook the books if they have large amounts of short-term share options. This is how Worldcom CEO Bernie Ebbers made a fortune during the dotcom frenzy before going to jail to serve a 25-year sentence. An empirical investigation found that misreporting was most prevalent where the CEO's option portfolio was most highly dependent on stock prices. Despite the evidence for widespread accounting fraud, only a few managers involved in high-publicity cases went to jail (Burns and Kedia 2006).

All this indicates that the distribution of power is still tilted very much in favor of managers under current rules and corporate customs, and that managers have used their discretion to pervert monetary incentives and make them into a lever to obtain a still higher share of corporate earnings. This view is corroborated by studies examining the effects of the sudden deaths of top managers on stock prices. Such unforeseen tragic events provide an opportunity to assess how much managers contribute to corporate success in the eyes of shareholders and how much of their contribution they can claim for themselves. The results of these studies indicate that many top managers cost more, relative to available alternative candidates, than they contribute. Hayes and Schaefer (1999) found an average increase in stock price of 2.8 percent immediately after news of the unexpected death. Salas (2010) found an average positive reaction of 0.9 percent. These results are even more remarkable as one would expect the disruption caused by the sudden demise of the top manager to depress company value. Nguyen-Dang (2008) included chief financial officers and presidents in his sample and found a moderate negative reaction of stock prices to sudden deaths of 1.2 percent on average. He also found that better managers seem to be able on average to claim four-fifths of their above-average contribution to company value in the form of higher pay.

In retrospect, it is hard to understand how economists who pride themselves on their rigor could make such a colossal mistake with their pay-for-performance idea. They simply pretended that incentive-compatible remuneration schemes would fall from the sky to be picked up by grateful shareholders. In reality, these schemes had to be devised by boards on behalf of shareholders. However, these are the bodies whose lack of interest or ability to supervise managers made monetary incentives for managers necessary in the first place. When it came to arguing in favor of higher managerial pay, the propagandists of pay-for-performance ignored the principal–agent theory that was the basis of their model. It is true that shareholders would like the boards and remuneration committees to devise appropriate remuneration schemes that promote shareholder interests. However, in practice, there is nothing that forces boards to do that, and little that gives them an incentive to do it. Instead, they have strong incentive to do whatever pleases the CEO.

The small and cozy world of an unaccountable corporate elite

The CEO does most of the recruiting for the board and extends the offer to join the board. And, except in unusual circumstances, board members serve at the pleasure of the CEO. The CEO generally sets the agenda for the board. Virtually all information board members receive from the company originates from or passes through the CEO.

—Michael Jensen and Kevin Murphy, 2004

In the US, a corporation is led by the CEO, who is supervised by a board of directors. Often, the CEO also presides over the board. Board members or directors can be current or past managers of the corporation or they can come from outside. Among the external directors, there are some who qualify as independent directors, meaning that they have no close personal ties to the CEO.

The principal–agent problem of shareholders with regard to CEOs would be less severe if boards would fulfill their task of controlling the CEO. Instead, boards tend to be controlled by the very CEO they are supposed to supervise. The consequences extend far beyond executives setting their own pay level using other people's money. If there is no independent oversight, executives are free to pursue their own goals to the detriment of the company. Even if they mean well, they do not face effective checks and balances to keep them from making potentially fatal mistakes. The SEC and regulators all over the world have weighed reforms that would have made boards and management more responsive to shareholder interests, but have most often abandoned them upon the resistance of the corporate world.

The only avenue that securities exchanges and regulators in the US have pursued so far to make boards more independent from management was mandating the appointment of a majority of independent or outside directors. Outside directors are people who are not and have not been employees of the company. This has not proven overly successful. It disregards a phenomenon that sociologists (particularly Bourdieu) have long recognized but economists have eschewed, the "corporate small world" phenomenon. Each knows each other and respects each other's sphere of influence and authority of decision making.

For France, where old boys' networks based on elite academic institutions are particularly important, Nguyen-Dang (2008) found that the firm performs worse if the CEO and at least one board member are graduates from the same elite college than it does if the board has no graduates from elite colleges. Furthermore, if at least two directors have graduated from the same elite college with the CEO, the normal relationship between poor CEO performance and more firings disappears.

For the US, Hwang and Seoyoung (2009) looked at social ties between CEOs and outside directors. They found 87 percent of outside directors to be conventionally independent, but only 62 percent of them were also socially independent (i.e. they did not share alma mater, military service, regional origin and such with the CEO). As their exclusion criteria are based only on social connections that show up in publicly accessible databases, the real incidence of independence is bound to be still lower. This might explain why empirical studies looking for evidence that a higher share of independent directors would lead to improved company results have not been able to uncover much affirmative evidence. However, firms with a majority of board members who are socially *and* conventionally independent award less pay to the CEO, make pay more dependent on performance and fire the CEO more easily upon weak performance than boards that are only conventionally independent.

Cozy relations between CEOs and directors are not accidental. Being favorable, or even better loyal, to top management is a prerequisite for being invited to join the board, for internal directors as well as for independent ones. "Our results challenge the widely held view that appointments of independent directors necessarily add objectivity to the board of a firm," conclude Cohen, Frazzini and Cox (2008), who conducted a study into the employment of external directors from the analyst community. The authors examined outside directors who landed that job after having been financial analysts and found that those who were invited had shown little skill in predicting the earnings and stock price developments of the company or the respective industry. What distinguished them was that they had issued an extremely high proportion of buy and strong buy recommendations for the company whose board they would be invited to join later. On top of that, they had often issued these positive recommendations at times when these were most important for the company, for example when other analysts had just downgraded the stock. Towards other companies, these analysts had not shown any similar tendency to be over optimistic, with one exception: if these companies were related to their favored company by cross-directorships, they would receive similarly nice treatment. This indicates that there has been an implicit or explicit *quid pro quo*. Otherwise these analysts might be expected to give overly favorable judgments on all companies to increase the chance of being invited to join a board.

Direct influence of CEOs on inside and outside directors on their board is only one part of the explanation for boards' widespread ineffectiveness in controlling management. The other, potentially more important one is the culture that rules the small world of the corporate elite. There are powerful social norms that prevent directors from effectively exercising their control functions on behalf of their company's stakeholders. These norms require them to defer to the CEO's judgment on important issues and on issues that are dear to the heart of the CEO. This need not be too surprising as the majority of outside directors are or have been CEOs for other companies (Westphal and Stern 2006).

Westphal and Khanna (2003) interviewed many directors and found that those who participated in actions that reduced the CEO's control over decision making later suffered "social distancing" from the directors of other companies. They would not be invited to informal meetings anymore and their advice was solicited less often.

Social cohesion within boards is a basis for sustaining such norms. Westphal and Stern (2006) polled a large number of senior managers and CEOs. It turned out that ingratiatory behavior toward the CEO was the single most important factor in explaining who got invited onto a board and who did not. Other factors that made an invitation more likely were membership in an exclusive social club, being alumni of an elite school or university, having an entry in the Social Register, being white and being male. Ingratiatory, deferential and submissive behavior toward their CEO turned out to be significantly more important for managers who did not posess the traits white, male or member of the social elite. Male, white members of the social elite apparently have less need to ingratiate themselves and do not show this behavior to the same extent. Thus, the possibility that members from outside the social elite can obtain entry into the corporate elite by showing submissive behavior serves to discipline the social elite, which might otherwise see little need to be submissive.

The pathway to riches runs through the remuneration committee

Directors generally would like to be reappointed to the board and awarded additional directorships in other companies. A reputation of being stingy in pay negotiations with the CEO does not help – after all, it is not the directors' own money at stake. On top of that, the CEO can affect directors' compensation and perks.

Jensen and Murphy (2004) describe the process of deciding executive pay in a typical US corporation in the following way: formally, the board's remuneration committee makes all decisions before the whole board approves them. However, the recommendations for pay level and compensation plans usually come from the human resources department, which reports to the CEO. They often employ outside consultants to provide a rationale suggesting objectivity. The human resources department runs the recommendations by the CEO before they reach the remuneration committee. The committee either accepts or sends the plan back for changes. "The fact that initial recommendations are made by company management and not by the remuneration committee calls into question the integrity of the remuneration process," is the devastating judgment of the business luminaries. They add, "The fact that the committee only sees plans that have already been blessed by top managers creates an environment that invites abuse and bias."

In a written interview with one of the authors, one former CEO of a medium-sized financial corporation in the US describes his relationship with the board as follows:

> As regards our board, we mostly had to worry about entertaining them. Actually, they themselves were quite entertaining and would love to tell us their old stories. We had board meetings at least once a year in resort locations with golf courses and arranged for private jet transportation. They had a lot in common, were usually happy to see each other, and looked forward to the meetings. My preparation for our annual salary reviews was to talk about our profits. We would try to highlight some recent activity, such as a merger, purchase or sale of some subsidiary and talk about our strength and position in the industry. But the main thing was to have hired a consultant or have engaged the management consulting branch of our auditors to make recommendations on compensation. Their reports would emphasize 'comparability,' which is to say what people in similar circumstances and in companies of about the same size were making.

Often the board gets ostensibly objective outside help in establishing adequate levels of executive pay by hiring pay consultants. But how independent and objective can pay consultants be if they are hired by the human resources department, which directly or indirectly reports to the CEO? How objective can they be if the same consultancy happens to do significant other consulting work for the company, and especially for the CEO? Murphy and Sandino (2010) found that companies who use pay consultants pay their CEOs more than comparable companies who don't.

A Nice Theory and the Ugly Reality of Managerial Pay

A surprisingly large number of business school finance professors are amazingly clueless about the real world, and are of the opinion that reputation effects successfully eliminate fraud and other bad behaviour.

—Jay Ritter, 2008

Law and finance scholars Lucian Bebchuk and Jesse Fried focused on what Jensen, Murphy and their followers had neglected: the control of managers over boards and over compensation committees. They examined pay-for-performance compensation schemes as they developed starting in the 1990s and checked if their actual features conformed more to the optimal contracting approach of principal–agent theory or to what they call the managerial power approach. Their book, *Pay Without Performance*, became a watershed in the economic corporate governance discussion. It gave real world power issues in corporate governance a name and made it a stumbling block in the way of the economic mainstream (Bebchuk and Fried 2003; Bebchuk and Fried 2004).

According to the managerial power approach, managers create compensation schemes that are as favorable to them as possible under what they call the "outrage constraint." The possibility of the outrage of shareholders and the general public provides the most binding restraint on the generosity of management pay.

The best evidence for the executive power approach is provided by the details of the compensation schemes themselves. If they were to follow the optimal contracting approach closely, CEOs should only be rewarded for the part of company performance that is under their influence. In a stock market boom almost all shares go up. Only those CEOs with stock prices rising more than the average of their industry or the general market should be rewarded. This is easy to do. In reality though, it is hardly ever done. According to Bebchuk and Fried (2003), only 20 of the largest 250 public US firms used provisions to avoid rewarding managers for substandard performance. The norm is that CEOs get stock options with a strike price at the current stock price. That way, they are handsomely rewarded if the general market goes up. Therefore even if their company's stock goes up less than the market and less than inflation, they can make a lot of money (Bebchuk and Fried 2003).

If boards wanted to follow the optimal contracting approach, they would require a share price increase of say 5 percent above inflation before they started rewarding the CEO. For a two year option period and a current price of US$100, this would mean a strike price of US$110.25 for the options. That would be less favorable to the CEO, because they would only be paid a bonus when the stock market rises faster than inflation (which was just 59.3 percent of years in the S&P 500 since 1872), which is probably why it does not happen very often (Bebchuk and Fried 2003).

In a fair and symmetrical remuneration system, the other side of pay for luck would be losses to managers caused by bad luck. However, an empirical investigation by Garvey and Milbourn (2006) found that on average executive losses are 25 to 45 percent less in a bad market than they should be if pay for luck was symmetrical. This is because if the stock market goes down, the strike prices of options are often retroactively lowered to renew the incentive of the managers to perform. The logic is correct. If the current stock price and the strike price for the CEO's options is US$100 and the stock price sinks to US$70, the managers can hardly hope to get into the money before the options run out. Of course, suitable offers to exchange the near worthless options for new ones would largely eliminate the windfall, but this is hardly ever done.

Firms with more influential shareholders are more likely to use benchmarks consistently across up and down markets. "This is consistent with the view that important aspects of executive compensation are chosen as a way to transfer wealth from shareholders to executives *ex post*," reads the blunt conclusion of Garvey and Milbourn (2006).

The outrage constraint in action

According to the managerial power theory, the pay level of managers is determined by social norms, not by the mathematical solution of a profit maximization problem. What top managers get depends on what the public and the shareholders are willing to accept. After the subprime crisis hit the world economy and drew attention to the extremely large paychecks that many executives in the financial industry had collected despite having caused the disaster, the public was outraged, at least temporarily. With large losses of corporations and societies in plain view, people did not believe the pay-for-performance justification for these exorbitant salaries any more. While the worst executives who were forced out early on got away super rich, those who stayed on experienced a rapidly tightening outrage constraint. In Germany the CEO of Deutsche Bank, Josef Ackermann, "voluntarily" gave up his bonus shortly before his bank announced a record loss in the fourth quarter of 2008. Soon after, Goldman Sachs' CEO Lloyd Blankfein gave up his bonus for 2008. More and more highly paid American bank CEOs did the same.

Kuhnen and Nissen (2009) used linguistic software to quantify the negativity expressed in newspapers on executive compensation and treated this as a measure of the transient changes in public opinion. They found that if the negativity of media coverage of CEO compensation was high in a particular year, CEOs received significantly lower total compensation in the subsequent year.

Kang and Mitnik (2009) provided empirical support for the notion of an outrage constraint by examining what happens to CEO pay if a firm gets into financial distress. They matched financially distressed firms with comparable firms that were not in distress. If a firm is in financial distress, the outrage constraint tightens significantly, since shareholders, creditors, workers and the public at large pay closer attention. It turns out that not only do the incumbent CEOs of distressed firms face a steep decline in their pay, but the same is true for incoming CEOs who replace them should the incumbents be forced out or leave voluntarily. The pay-for-performance idea would not predict the latter, as the new CEOs of financially distressed firms outperformed new CEOs in the control group on average. Even more interestingly, the bulk of the decline in compensation comes from one source: the lower value of options granted. While cash compensation declines on average by US$400,000 due to lower bonus payments, the value of stock options granted declines US$2.3 million in the year of distress and another US$5 million in the following year. And this decline in value is largely explained by the fact that the CEOs of financially distressed firms do not have as much luck in picking the dates at which they have their options granted. The *option backdating game*, which will be described in more detail in the next section, does not work well under public scrutiny.

The dating game

The perk of having the strike prices of options retroactively lowered sounds like self-enrichment, but it is legal. This is not the case for a certain related benefit that has also been employed a lot. As noted, it is standard practice that CEOs get their options *at the money*. This means that they obtain the right to buy shares at the price of the day on which the option is granted. This routine makes the day on which the options are granted important. It turns out that CEOs as a group are very lucky with these dates. Their stock options routinely increase in value a great deal as soon as the options have been granted. CEOs have the luck of getting their grants on the day of the month at which the stock price happens to be very low at a disproportionate percentage (Bebchuk, Grinstein and Peyer 2010).

Some CEOs were unlucky, though, and their companies and shareholders even more so, because certain economists used their specialized knowledge of prices, quantities and timing and combined it with some forensic impetus. They proved that the boards and CEOs of dozens of large companies routinely changed the dates of option grants retroactively, conferring big benefits to the recipients to the detriment of shareholders (Ritter 2008).

A prominent beneficiary of the option backdating game was Steve Jobs of the computer manufacturer Apple, who famously was paid a salary of just US$1 annually. On January 19, 2000, the company announced that it had a week earlier granted its CEO the option to buy ten million shares at the stock price of the grant date, which was US$87. By the time of the announcement, the stock price had risen to US$106. In that week alone, the options had gained roughly US$140 million in value. Apple had to admit seven years later that the dates of many option grants had been chosen retroactively and that board documents had been falsified to conceal this fact. While several top managers of Apple had to resign over the scandal, Steve Jobs escaped legal censure (Ritter 2008).

The most notorious case was that of William McGuire, CEO of United Health Group, who lost his job because of option backdating accusations in 2006. McGuire settled to end two civil lawsuits by paying back the astronomical sum of US$620 million. Still he did not end up poor. According to the *Wall Street Journal*, he still owned options with a market value of US$800 million upon his departure (Lattman 2007).

When Yermack (1997) first unearthed the phenomenon of lucky grants, he concluded that many CEOs must be "spring loading," or waiting with the announcement of good news until they had secured options in order to benefit more from the subsequent stock price increase. Heron and Lie looked at the data more closely and found that stock prices also tended to decrease before the grants, a pattern that could not be explained by spring loading. Furthermore, it was not only the respective company stocks that behaved unusually around the dates of the stock grants, but also the general stock market. They published a working paper in 2004. Regulators took notice and the issue kept expanding. In 2005 the *Wall Street Journal* broke a story on several SEC investigations into the issue. This prompted Lie to share his information with the *Journal*, which led a few months later to a big follow-up story which named a number of companies and their CEOs as possible large-scale back daters. The backdating issue blew up into a major public scandal. Dozens of CEOs, chief financial officers (CFOs) and the legal counsels of many well-known companies had to resign and some faced criminal charges.

Still Heron and Lie's (2007) paper, and a similar paper by Narayanan and Seyhun (2008), were rejected at first by several finance journals whose referees had trouble accepting the notion that there was widespread illegal activity in corporate circles. This reluctance to admit that bad things could be happening is apparently quite common for journals and their referees. Jay Ritter confirmed to the authors that there is strong pressure from reviewers and editors to avoid legal issues and moral terminology. He experienced it when he submitted the paper titled "Executive Bribery" mentioned in the preceding chapter. He was urged to change the title. It appeared later under the bland title "The Economic Consequences of IPO Spinning." He recounted that referees were loath to accept the notion that illegal practices could be widespread in the corporate world despite the reputational concerns of managers.

In reality, the issue is not just about naïve board members helping unscrupulous CEOs enrich themselves. It seems that in many cases CEOs bribed directors into being lenient by inviting them to share the spoils. An empirical study has found that independent directors have also been recipients of opportunistically timed stock option grants. The directors' benefits from such lucky timing were associated with substantial benefits to the CEO. For any given firm and CEO, the odds of a CEO grant being lucky were significantly higher if the independent directors of the firm received grants on the same date. Director grants were more likely to be lucky when the CEO received a lucky grant in the same or prior year (Bebchuk, Grinstein and Peyer 2010).

The Sarbanes–Oxley Act, which came into effect in 2002, requires top executives to report on the receipt of stock option grants within two business days. This severely limits the opportunity to backdate option grants, at least for the CEOs who comply. CEOs became a lot less lucky with their grant dates after 2002. Only for those who failed to report on time (about 13 percent) did the old lucky pattern persist. The compliant CEOs still seem to have a non-trivial fraction of grants backdated, but the benefit of backdating is greatly reduced in such cases (Heron and Lie 2007).

Avoiding sunlight

According to the optimal contracting approach, there is no reason to conceal the overall amount that is paid to the CEO. In contrast, according to the managerial power approach with an outrage constraint, the incentive to hide the full generosity of pay deals is obvious. In reality, camouflage is rampant and companies even incur significant tax disadvantages in order to camouflage payments to CEOs. Unlike base pay and options, many of these camouflaged payments do not show up in annual reports. They are reported in much less visible SEC filings if at all. Their value is hard to calculate, they often go unnoticed and the media seldom reports on them (Bebchuk and Fried 2003).

Some common practices with executive options, such as implicit agreements to reprice options in the event of a fall in the stock price, frequently make such options packages far more valuable than what is disclosed. In many firms, such hidden pay comprises the large majority of compensation for top managers. Sometimes compensation is so camouflaged that not even the boards have a clear idea of what they are granting. In the public scandal about the US$140 million pension payments of Richard Grasso, chairman of the New York Stock Exchange, board members claimed to have been unaware and to be shocked by the amount Grasso took with him (Kuhnen and Zwiebel 2008).

A large number of CEOs who left office voluntarily have obtained continued use of corporate jets for personal travel for periods ranging from five years to life. One CEO even obtained continued control over his company's box seats at the US Open (golf). According Yermack's (2006b) econometric work, the severance packages are less transparent if larger sums are involved and if the CEO is forced out. The first result is in line with the idea of camouflaging payments to alleviate the outrage constraint. The second result also makes sense if one assumes that the outrage constraint is more binding if the CEO is forced to leave. The public will not easily understand why a failed CEO is rewarded. This makes camouflage more necessary (Yermack 2006b).

Under optimal contracting, it is hard to see why the company and the CEO should routinely contract for a lifelong company car or even a jet, or secretary and office usage, which are likely to cost the company several times as much as they are worth to the beneficiary. But if the open pay is high enough that the outrage constraint becomes binding, these perks are useful. Only when former Citigroup chairman Sanford Weill announced that he would prematurely end his consultant job with his former employer did it become widely known how expensive the perks associated with this contract were. While he received "only" US$173,000 per year for his services, this pay came with access to Citigroup facilities and services comparable to those he had when he was still chairman. In 2005, Weill's last full year in office, these perks, including the free use of company aircraft and a driver, cost US$2.65 million. The company had also agreed to pay all taxes he would incur because of his perks. While taking public rescue money, Citigroup was also paying for downtown offices and secretarial staff of former CEOs Charles Prince and John Reed as well as those of the former head of investment banking Michael Klein. The latter had quit with a US$34 million exit package in July 2008 after the billions of dollars in losses created by his department became known (Keoun 2009a; Keoun 2009b).

A study by Yermack (2006a) examining the use of company aircraft for personal travel by executives speaks volumes. Yermack finds no indication that CEOs who enjoy free personal aircraft use would have to endure compensating cuts in other forms of renumeration, compared to similar CEOs who do not enjoy this expensive perk. The stock prices of firms that permit personal use of aircraft perform a stunning four percentage points worse per year than the stock market average (Yermack 2006a).

Negotiated retirement benefits can also be very valuable without being too visible. Sanford Weill gets a retirement pension of about US$1 million per annum. Sir Fred Goodwin, who was a formidable empire builder and took the Royal Bank of Scotland from provincial bank to global player able to post the largest loss ever of a British corporation, left his job at the age of 50 with the generous pension of £700,000 per year for the rest of his life. This is not unusual by American standards, but it was enough to start a fierce debate in Britain about the conditions under which knighthood should be rescinded when it leaked to the public. Only after a sustained campaign by British tabloids (which published the specific details of where Sir Fred lived around the world with an implicit suggestion of direct action by disgruntled taxpayers) did Sir Fred agree to a reduction in his pension to just £342,500 a year, though he was able to keep his £2.8 million retirement lump sum, upon which his now taxpayer-owned employer kindly paid his taxes for him.

Some economists have used increases in CEO firings and shortening of tenure as evidence against the managerial power hypothesis. While this seems plausible at first, the argument has a flaw. In a setting where managers are choosing their own pay subject to partial entrenchment, the relationship between entrenchment and firings is ambiguous. The executives extract rents from greater entrenchment by paying themselves more, which in turn increases the likelihood that they will be fired. If executives find new ways of extracting more rents in the form of hidden payments, this may well result in more CEO firings (Heron and Lie 2007). The most important driver of CEO firings will be the earnings cycle in such a setting. If CEOs extract as much as they feel they can get away with under normal circumstances, many of them will end up not getting away with it if business conditions take an unexpected turn to the worse. They therefore have an incentive to leave early, even if they do so under a cloud, before they get snagged in a downturn.

For CEOs, who are effectively setting their own pay within the outrage constraint, the pay-for-performance movement was a godsend. It not only offered theoretical justification for very high pay, but also many opportunities to tweak the system and to conceal the true amount of pay. However, the managerial power approach and the optimal contracting view are not mutually exclusive. They describe complementary aspects of reality. Indeed, for the optimal contracting view of compensation to help managers increase their pay so dramatically, it was necessary that the theory behind it contain a core of truth.

When market discipline takes a break

A market optimist would argue that market forces can do what directors fail to. The most powerful of these forces is the market for corporate control. A company with a CEO who is taking lavish pay for mediocre performance could be taken over. The acquirer could fire the CEO and bring in a better one working for less. However in reality, the management usually has defenses against hostile takeovers in place. In the US, most companies have a staggered board, among other measures. In order to install a new board that would agree to a takeover, the acquirers have to let two annual elections pass. If they want the company faster, they need to pay a high premium, often in the order of 40 percent of the pre-offer stock price. Therefore, things have to get pretty bad for takeovers to become a binding constraint to the behavior and pay of the upper management. Indeed, the CEOs of companies with stronger anti-takeover provisions have pay packages that are larger and less sensitive to performance (Bebchuk and Fried 2003). The better-paid CEOs are also more successful in passing anti-takeover provisions. After the provisions are put in place, they increase their lead even further (Borokhovich, Brunarski and Parrino 1997). Obviously this would not occur if the optimal contracting approach to executive pay told the whole story. In particular, boards should not need to increase the relative pay of CEOs whose jobs are protected by new anti-takeover provisions. The opposite should be true under optimal contracting (Bebchuk and Fried 2003).

Liu and Yermack (2008) found a creative way to show how weak corporate governance and excessive levels of pay are related, and how their cost goes far beyond the monetary cost of executive pay. By analyzing the real estate dealings of corporate executives, they found that when CEOs acquire extremely large or costly estates, future company performance deteriorates. This makes sense if the CEOs who are buying very expensive real estate should emit the signal that they are deeply entrenched, that they do not fear removal and might not be overly incentivized to work hard in the long-term interest of the company. This gives a slight twist to the old saying, "a man's home is his castle." Executives who buy grandiose estates are likely planning to spend time enjoying the property. Only a deeply entrenched CEO should be expected to do this. Liu and Yermack actually recommend this indicator as an empirically proven warning signal for investors. If the CEO of a corporation buys a very expensive house, sell the company stock. A trading rule according to which an investor shorts the company stock if the CEO buys a very large or costly estate and buys the company stock if the CEO buys a more normally sized estates (for CEOs, at least) yielded a return of 40.8 percent after three years (shorting a stock means selling it, without owning it, in order to profit from price declines).

What Is Performance, Anyway? Shareholder Value as the Benchmark of Everything

> On the face of it, shareholder value is the dumbest idea in the world. Shareholder value is a result, not a strategy… Your main constituencies are your employees, your customers and your products.
>
> —*Jack Welch, 2009*

An economist who believes in the rationality and farsightedness of financial markets will make no distinction between short-term rises in stock prices and long-run increases in company value. According to this efficient market view, the current stock market value of a company is the best available guess of company value. This is why economists propagating pay-for-performance did not make a distinction between options that can be exercised with a short delay and others that must be held for a long time. This misguided trust in the rationality of financial markets has proved very costly to society. If the stock market does a poor job of predicting the long-term value of a company and if stock prices are easy to manipulate in the short run, the justification for linking managerial pay to stock prices falls apart.

In reality, not all shareholders are alike. There is a potential conflict of interest between short-term oriented and long-term oriented shareholders and also between current shareholders and future shareholders. Short-term investors will prefer strong but potentially unsustainable share price increases. For the same reason, current shareholders care less about the long term than future shareholders do. If managers pump up the stock price in an unsustainable way, current shareholders are compensated for future losses by the gains they make in the run-up. Anybody who buys during the run-up will miss part of this upside, while they are fully exposed to the downside, as late investors in Enron, Worldcom or telecommunications stock in general found out during the dotcom bubble. Future shareholders do not vote at annual meetings, though. Thus their interests are not represented (Zingales 2009).

Recently, the acceptance of the verdict of the stock market as the benchmark for what is good company policy has been crumbling. A particularly revealing and interesting study exposing the weaknesses of the financial market as the final arbiter of everything is an analysis of the stock prices of the companies awarded the distinction of being among the "100 Best Companies to Work for in America." It proves that analysts and investors do not understand the value of a committed workforce very well. For many years, companies awarded this title by *Fortune* magazine had higher profit growth and stock price gains than similar companies, even after receiving the awards. This means that firms employing high-commitment work practices perform better than others, and also implies that the stock market does not understand and appreciate this, even after the successful investments in human capital are made visible by a highly publicized award. Otherwise the

stock price of the company in question would jump on the granting
of the award. Instead, stock prices only gain over time as the better
company performance becomes obvious in the bottom line (Edmans
2011). This is particularly unexpected given the ample theoretical and
empirical evidence that very high-skilled and knowledgeable workers –
exactly those most sensitive to workplace conditions and those most
able and willing to relocate if they feel their employer is anything
less than committed to them – are driving ever-increasing amounts
of long-term company value as technology marches forward (Grant,
1996; Deeds and Decarolis 1999).

It is probably no coincidence that in any given year approximately
one-third of the best companies to work for are private (i.e. not listed
on the stock market). A number of business leaders, such as Richard
Branson, have spent large chunks of their own personal fortune to
re-privatize companies that they previously floated. Such business leaders
have publicly stated that they do so in order to steer the company on the
high road of workforce management on the basis that the company is
then shielded from the constant scrutiny of an excessively short-term
oriented and misguided stock market. A large-scale survey among
company executives found that, under pressure to meet the expectations
of analysts and investors, 78 percent of executives would sacrifice long-
term value to meet earnings targets (Edmans 2011).

The earnings management game

Company managers routinely make use of people's trust in investment
advice provided by the financial industry. Managers and analysts together
play a game to lure investors into buying stock expensively: the earnings
management game. They take advantage of the empirical regularity
that, when a firm produces earnings that beat the average or consensus
analyst forecast, the stock price on average rises a great deal. For
negative earnings surprises, the stock price falls. Thus beating consensus
forecasts is imperative. This creates strong incentives for managers
either to manipulate earnings or analysts' forecasts. Management gurus
Michael Jensen and Kevin Murphy complain that, "for more than
two decades it has generally been understood that part of the job of
every top level manager has been to manage earnings." They further
add, "when managing earnings means taking actions that are anything
other than those required to maximize the long-term value of the firm,
managing earnings amounts to lying. And it amounts to lying to the

very stockholders or potential stockholders to which managers have a fiduciary responsibility." (Jensen and Murphy 2004).

To have an easier time beating earnings, corporations reward financial institutions and their analysts if they make suitable forecasts and punish those who issue inconvenient forecasts. Beyond rewards for individual analysts, this can take the form of granting lucrative commissions for banking or other services to firms whose analysts cater to the management's preferences (Jensen and Murphy 2004).

Prior to the SEC's Regulation Fair Disclosure in 2000, playing the game was easier. Private communications between research analysts and the companies they were covering were commonplace. These private exchanges were dubbed "guidance." Managers guided analysts as to what earnings they should forecast. The analysts who played along started with positively biased forecasts of one year ahead earnings. They revised them down incrementally until they slightly undershot real earnings shortly before these earnings were reported. This implies that analysts systematically fooled investors into overpaying for these stocks (Jensen and Murphy 2004).

Scientific evidence regarding the degree to which management and analysts still play the earnings management game since Regulation Fair Disclosure is sparse. It seems that it has become a bit harder, but that companies still do it quite successfully. The Bloomberg Surprise Index, which tracks the percentage of companies that manage to beat the average profit forecast, averaged 60 percent from 1993 until 2000. It rose to 64 percent from 2000 to 2010 (i.e. after Regulation Fair Disclosure was enacted) and was even higher at an average of 68 percent in the five years to the end of 2010.

Managers still have their ways of rewarding analysts who issue convenient forecasts and stock recommendations and punishing those who don't. This discrimination can take many forms. Managers can invite or not invite analysts to meetings where they give useful information, and they can choose whether or not to return phone calls. They can allow analysts to ask questions during conference calls, or deny them the opportunity. Mayew (2008) found that analysts who had recently issued a strong buy recommendation for a firm were more than twice as likely to be allowed to ask a conference call question as analysts with strong sell recommendations. Analysts who had given favorable assessments of the company were allowed to ask their questions earlier than those who had given unfavorable ones.

Paying Well for Lies, Gambles and Creative Accounting

> Top executives will routinely and inevitably possess information not available to investors. In these situations, changes in short run share prices will not imply a similar change in long run shareholder value.
>
> —*Michael Jensen and Kevin Murphy, 2004*

The large amounts of stocks and stock options that top managers get, ostensibly to align their interests with those of shareholders, create a massive insider trading problem. Top management has a huge information advantage over outside shareholders. At the same time, they have a large amount of stock and stock options to unload and trade. If they use their insider knowledge for timing their trades, they are putting individual investors in particular at a disadvantage. They steal returns from the individual investors. Even though trading on material insider information is illegal in the US and many other countries, it is very hard to prove and thus very rarely prosecuted. If top managers get paid in stock and options, they will constantly have to make decisions about when would be a good time to sell. It is hard to imagine that they manage to do this without taking into account their superior knowledge of the prospects of the company.

Muller, Neamtiu and Riedl (2009) have used the observable adverse event "goodwill impairment" to investigate the prevalence of insider trading by managers. "Goodwill" is that part of the price paid by the acquirer of a company that exceeds the book value of the companies' assets. This goodwill enters the acquiring company's accounts as an asset. If it turns out that the company that it bought is not really worth as much as it cost, this asset item is written down. In this case, goodwill is said to be impaired. The authors provide evidence that insiders of goodwill-impaired firms sell a larger than normal share of their stock in the company prior to the announcement of such losses. Insider trading could help explain why other research has found little or no market reaction to the recognition of goodwill impairment, despite the magnitude of the associated accounting losses. By the time the impairment is announced to the public, the stock market reaction seems to have already happened because of insider trading (Muller, Neamtiu and Riedl 2009).

Massaging earnings, and thus the share price, at times at which it is convenient or required for senior management to sell their options, seems to be a common way for executives to raise their effective pay. Zheng and Zhou (2009) have proved that these opportunities exist and that they are used. They looked at the development of share prices of companies immediately before and after their CEOs retired. This is a time when it is convenient or even required for many CEOs to sell their stock options. It turned out that if CEOs had large amounts of options, the stock price of the company tended to be unusually high in the months around the retirement, only to fall back to normal soon afterwards. In the group of companies whose CEOs had low option holdings, this was not the case.

It would not be hard to devise rules that would take the timing decision and thus the moral hazard away from managers. Law and finance scholar Jesse Fried suggested in 1998 that executives be required to announce their insider trades in advance or that firms require that sales be carried out gradually over a specified period of time. However, it is rare that such effective measures are taken (Fried 1998). At most companies have introduced trading windows or blackout periods, which limit executives to unloading their shares at certain times of the year. This is a step in the right direction, but it is less effective because it leaves the executive with the choice of whether to sell or not to sell at these times. Worse, it does not remove the temptation for managers to manipulate the share price by withholding bad information, or by cooking the books in order to obtain a high share price at the time they want to sell their stock. Under the optimal contracting approach, this oversight is a glaring flaw. Under the managerial power hypothesis, preserving such opportunities is another form of the stealth benefits that friendly boards confer to top management (Bebchuk and Fried 2003).

The practice of handing out short-duration options to executives creates dangerous incentives to disguise the true state of the company until managers can exercise their options and sell the acquired shares, as in the Enron and Worldcom cases. Benmelech, Kandel and Veronesi (2010) have built a model that explains why it was particularly high-growth companies in new markets which suffered from this phenomenon. A company in a new market, be it a technology company during the dotcom frenzy or an investment bank during the subprime boom, initially has many very seemingly profitable business opportunities due to having first mover advantages. At some point, the company matures and the number of highly profitable business opportunities returns to normal. Executives will normally know when that will happen before investors do. If they were to act appropriately and reduce investment, investors would make their inferences and managers would have to expect a strong negative response reflected in the stock prices. This would cost them a lot in terms of options and what stock of their company that they have not exercised or sold yet. The alternative is to act as if nothing has changed and to keep investing in order to maintain the pretence. This is wasteful as many of the investments will later prove unprofitable. However, it buys time to exercise options and sell stock, and after all it is not the executive's money that is being wasted. A combination of moderate stock-based components with variable pay elements based on dividends could avoid this perverse incentive while creating the same positive incentives to elicit effort (Benmelech, Kandel and Veronesi 2010).

The incentive to pretend became even more damaging during the events that led to the subprime crisis. One can assume that executives of mortgage lenders and investment banks knew that subprime mortgages with no income documentation and teaser rates would not be viable once the housing price bonanza was over. However, playing the game as long as it lasted gave many of them dozens or even hundreds of millions of dollars in stock option rewards. Angelo Mozilo of Countrywide knowingly reaped US$121.5 million in stock options by deliberately lying to investors (later paying a net US$22.5 million civil penalty for his deceit) and Stanley O'Neal of Merrill Lynch received US$161.5 million in the year of his departure on top of US$91 million the year before (and kept all of it).

Entrenched Boards Protect Entrenched Executives

> What if the US political system meant that candidates standing up for election could only be proposed by the current executive and could be elected even if they did not obtain the majority of the votes? Unfortunately, this Soviet-like system is the current election system of US corporate boards. In the current system, boards are self-perpetuating entities that are not accountable to anyone.
>
> —*Luigi Zingales, 2009*

Effective shareholder control of boards hinges almost completely on the effectiveness of the threat that shareholders might vote in a new board if they do not like what the current one is doing. However, "shareholder franchise is a myth," writes Lucian Bebchuk (2007). According to his research, in the ten years between 1996 and 2005, only 24 boards out of 120 companies with a market capitalization of more than

US$200 million faced an electoral challenge (less than three a year on average). Only one in three was successful. This was during a time when dozens of companies had to restate earnings, leaving plenty of room for shareholder dissatisfaction. The main reasons for the low number of electoral challenges are the high cost of this measure under existing conditions, and the fact that the shareholders who would incur the costs can only benefit from the rewards according to their own share in the company (Bebchuk 2007).

In Germany, there was a sensation when British pension fund Hermes staged a proxy fight for the chairman of the supervisory board of chipmaker Infineon. It was the first time this happened in one of the 30 largest companies that make up the DAX stock market index. Shareholders were angry because the stock price had gone down to €4 from €35 in ten years. Hermes lost, and management prevailed.

The US features a large collection of legal rules and informal arrangements that help boards and managers to insulate themselves from shareholder demands. Challengers do not have the right to have their candidates placed on the corporate ballot, which will be sent to all shareholders at company expense. They have to pay hundreds of thousands of dollars to hire somebody to collect addresses and to send letters to shareholders. A majority of US public companies have a staggered board of directors, which means that usually only a third of directors come up for reelection each year. To gain control of a company whose directors are protected by a staggered board, challengers need to win two elections. This means they have to incur the cost of campaigning twice and maintain the campaign for at least a year (Bebchuk 2007). By default, votes in board elections are not secret. This keeps mutual fund managers who want to maintain a good working relationship with management from voting against incumbents. There is not even a majority of yes votes required to reelect directors. A single yes vote is good enough to elect an incumbent if there is no challenger. Shareholders in the US cannot even change the internal rules of their company; they cannot change the original charter without prior board approval, as only the board can initiate such a change (Bebchuk 2007; Zingales 2009).

In other countries, more subtle mechanisms are at work to ensure that boards are shielded from censure by shareholders and remain loyal to management. As participation at annual meetings is usually quite low, and deposit banks can often vote for individual shareholders, it often suffices for management to obtain support from a few large investors or depository institutions to make sure the board of their choice is elected.

A famous study by Gompers, Ishii and Metrick (2003) has shown that weaker shareholder rights go together with lower firm value, lower profits, lower sales growth, higher capital expenditures, a higher number of corporate acquisitions and worse share price performance. They built an index of 24 provisions providing takeover protection for management and restricting shareholder rights for about fifteen hundred firms in the 1990s. According to their research, an investment strategy that bought the shares of the 10 percent of firms with the strongest shareholder rights and sold the 10 percent of firms with the weakest shareholder rights, would have earned returns that were 8.5 percentage points higher than normal (Gompers, Ishii and Metrick 2003). According to Bebchuk, Cohen and Ferrell (2009), the 24 ingredients to this corporate governance index can be reduced to just 6 important elements, which all measure in one way or another the degree of entrenchment of top managers (i.e. how hard it is for shareholders to get rid of them).

Cuñat, Gine and Guadalupe (2010) examined shareholder-sponsored corporate government proposals in two thousand widely held US corporations from 1997 to 2007 and compared the stock market reaction to proposals that narrowly failed to those which narrowly passed. They found that narrow passage of a proposal increases the stock market value of a firm by almost 3 percent. For corporate government measures that are included in the G-index developed by Gompers et al., the reaction is even stronger.

Conclusion

Most companies in industrial countries and many in the rest of the world are rather well managed. They provide the basis for our wealth. However economic models, be they explicit or implicit, which treat the "market" for managerial talent as if it were either a perfect market or could be made to approach this ideal by suitable incentive contracts for executives miss a large part of the action. In reality, social norms and social ties are very important in shaping how companies' managers act, how much they are paid and how much power they have to further their own interests rather than the long-term interest of the firm. Japanese executives take home a fraction of the pay of US executives, but few would say that Japanese companies are badly managed.

Economic theories around incentive issues and similar efficiency concerns have turned out to be little more than an elaborate way to alleviate the outrage constraint on managerial pay, thus enabling managers to claim a steeply increasing share of the value added in their companies. At best, it has served to align the interest of managers with the interest of short-term oriented shareholders. This can hardly be claimed to be a success. The Great Financial Crisis after the subprime debacle has amply proven how the long-term interests of companies and societies can very much diverge from the interest of short-term oriented shareholders.

Simply making boards and managers more responsive to shareholders will not be a panacea for improving the lot of those long-horizon investors who hold stock in order to save for their retirement, let alone for workers interested in stable employment in a prospering company. Short-term oriented shareholders might support machinations that drive up the current share price at the expense of long-term returns and of other stakeholders in the respective companies. Therefore, managers and boards should be made more accountable to workers and to shareholders interested in the long-term prospects of the firm. Workers' interests are just as respectable, from a societal perspective, as shareholders' interests.

To increase the clout of long-term oriented investors, Zingales (2009) suggests restricting the ability to nominate directors to institutional investors who satisfy some criteria of independence from company management and who can prove that they held the company's stock for a minimum amount of time. This possibility has been in place in the UK for a long time and has been recently introduced in Italy. In addition, shareholders who nominate an alternative slate of board members could be required to commit to keeping the shares for an extended period of time if they win (Zingales 2009). This would help ensure that private equity investors do not take advantage of the short-sightedness of stock markets to oust management teams who are pursuing sensible long-term plans for their companies.

Unfortunately, mainstream economics offers very little information on the implications of the interest of workers for corporate governance rules. Workers are assumed to be easily able to move to another firm, and thus implicitly assumed not to have any serious interest in their current workplace. Another reason is that mainstream economics makes welfare judgments by considering people only as consumers and investors, not as workers. This view is very much at odds with ample evidence that people's well being is very affected, if not predominantly affected, by having a job and by the working conditions that these jobs offer.

Thus taking the stock price as a measure of social efficiency means using a yardstick that is not only too short for the timeline but is also bent. To take account of employees' strong interest in the stable development of their firm, with reasonable and reliable increases in productivity and profits, Germany is giving worker representatives seats on supervisory boards. Employee involvement is also mandatory in Austria, the Netherlands, Denmark, Sweden, Luxembourg and France, and commonplace but voluntary in Switzerland, Finland and Ireland. Empirical evidence on the effects of these policies is sparse. Econometric studies of codetermination so far have found no effect, or very little, in either direction on share prices and productivity (Becht, Bolton and Röell 2007; FitzRoy and Kraft 2005).

Worker representation on boards has its problems, too. A number of scandals in Germany have shown how easy it is, under current rules, for the management to bribe worker representatives into waving through their proposals. An executive of Siemens, the large engineering conglomerate, was found guilty of having organized and financed an "independent" union. Volkswagen's board member Peter Hartz, who has given his name to a series of supply-side oriented labor reforms in Germany, along with some other Volkswagen representatives, were heavily fined or sent to jail for having paid for prostitutes, mistresses, vacations and other expenditures for workers' council representatives, on top of paying them very high salaries. Just as with shareholder representation on boards, employee representation on boards suffers from dysfunctional rules. Workers' representatives at the top level are many levels of hierarchy removed from being accountable to their constituencies in elections. Elections are only held at the lowest level, to fill workers councils at the local production sites. Presidency of these local councils, membership at the higher corporate levels of workers' councils and finally board seats for workers' representatives are all decided by union hierarchies. Such rules can help to insulate management from answering to the demands of the workforce, just like the rules of shareholder representation can insulate them from shareholder demands. Thus to make boards and management more responsible to stakeholders with the long-term interest of the company at heart, structural flaws in employee representation *and* in shareholder representation need to be corrected. If it is relatively easy to win over board members representing workers, as it is in Germany, it will hardly be possible to make top managers more accountable to shareholders.

Workers and lower-level managers have their fortune tied to the firm for which they are working to a significant degree. If the firm does badly, they tend to do badly and vice versa. Thus a need for the top management to achieve formal or implicit agreement with lower-level management and workers can be a powerful device for aligning the interests of executives with the long-term interest of the firm (Acharya et al. 2009). This could explain why many corporations work as well as they do, even though shareholder control is often extremely remote. Junior managers want to become senior managers or CEO at some point in the future. This is only appealing if the company is still viable and in reasonably good shape in the future. Workers want to enjoy the benefits of working for the firm – and potentially being promoted – for a long time. Thus, if the CEO were to act against the long-term interest of the firm, junior management and workers would veto it if they have a say.

Internal control can work whether or not economists understand it and integrate it with their models. However, economists can do a lot to weaken or enhance it, depending on the direction in which they influence institutions and rule making. A very flexible labor market and high mobility of workers and managers might have their virtues, but they also have negative effects on the governance of companies that should be taken into account. It might also be costly in terms of internal governance to squeeze workers, customers and suppliers to the point where a long-term relationship with the firm has no particular value to them anymore.

This research can shed some light on the question of why executives have become so much more successful in extracting money from their companies starting in the 1970s, and even more so from the 1990s onwards. It supports an explanation by Piketty and Saez (2006), who argue that institutions and social norms are important for the evolution of executive compensation. They believe that the experience of the Great Depression greatly affected the public's views and social norms regarding inequality. This fits with data from the famous empirical study by Bourguignon and Morrison (2002) which found that global inequality in life expectancy peaked around 1920, thereafter falling steeply while global lifetime income inequality, having risen inexorably from 1820, fell during the period between 1950 and 1970 before resuming its upward climb. This period of inequality retrenchment led to the introduction of high marginal tax rates at the top and the adoption of large-scale redistributive programs as well as a strong role for trade unions. Corporation income taxation and payroll taxation were set to high rates, and the ability to avoid them was highly restricted. These norms and institutions restrained CEO pay, especially as fear of communism made high-income inequalities socially unacceptable lest they give support to revolutionaries.

With the Great Depression fading in memory, communism defeated and social norms changing, these restraints lost importance. This made it possible for the pay-for-performance cult could take hold in the 1990s. According to the theory of Piketty and Saez, the idea that it was okay to make many millions a year if you created commensurate value would not have been accepted so widely in the 1950s, and would not have been implicitly endorsed by the government, which carved out huge exemptions from taxation both for the companies doing the paying and the employees receiving that pay.

As much as it is said that the US has the highest rate of corporation tax in the developed world (about 35 percent), like France (joint highest with Belgium in the EU at 33 percent) it has enacted wide-ranging methods of claiming back and exempting activities and employee compensation from tax. For example, between 2008 and 2010, the 280 firms which were profitable in the Fortune 500 paid an effective rate of just 18.5 percent (Citizens for Tax Justice 2011) and in France – which is highly prone to criticizing "low tax" countries such as Ireland (which has a special rate of 12.5 percent for non-family owned trading companies and 25 percent for all other companies) – the effective rate in France was just 15.4 percent (KPMG 2012). Reducing corporation tax is not a bad thing in principal given its empirically proven beneficial economic effects. But rewarding an entrenched business elite with tax advantages for plundering companies by giving both them and their friends excessive bonuses has none of the advantages and all of the disadvantages of an ever-increasing segregation of society into a super-rich plutonomy. There is no justification that such extravagance should be subsidized by the taxpayer, which at around US$20 billion per annum (Anderson et al. 2008) is simply unacceptable in such economically strained times.

For all its mischievousness, an idea proposed by Rep. Martin O. Sabo has a certain appeal. In his 1997 Income Equity Act, he proposed capping tax deductibility per worker to a certain multiple (the act specified 25 times) the pay of the lowest-paid worker in a given geographical region, but there are many easy ways of creating loopholes to work around such a cap. A simpler measure is capping corporate tax deductions per worker to a multiple of the minimum wage or the average industrial wage for the economy in question.

Regarding personal income, a simple way of inhibiting income inequalities, without inhibiting incentives to make capital investments, is to apply the normal income tax treatment to any capital gains taken as income – as is the norm in most European countries. That way, the 13.9 percent tax paid by 2012 presidential hopeful Mitt Romney on his 2010–2011 income of US$45 million would be a far more appropriate 48 percent or so.

With the effects of the crisis still painfully felt by millions of people who lost their jobs and/or a sizeable chunk of their pensions, managerial pay in the finance industry and beyond is already back to where it was before the crisis broke out. Whether this will be allowed to persist indefinitely has yet to be seen. The solutions are broadly known, easy to implement and commonly practiced in other countries. The question is, will US policymakers finally do the right thing and close the door on the corporate elite's power and money grab?

Chapter 4

MARKET POWER

> Businessmen, who regard themselves as being subject to competitive conditions, would consider absurd the assertion that the limit to their production is to be found in the internal conditions of production in their firm, which do not permit of the production of a greater quantity without an increase in cost. The chief obstacle against lies in the difficulty of selling the larger quantity of goods without reducing the price, or without having to face increased marketing expenses.
>
> —*Piero Sraffa, 1926*

The simple version of neoclassical textbook economics has produced a set of recommendations for economic policy that most people accept as the essence of economic reason. One of these conclusions is that when companies are taxed, they produce less and employ fewer people. When they have to pay higher wages to satisfy unions, or obey minimum wage laws, it has the same consequence (again according to textbook economics). Such conclusions are based on some rather peculiar assumptions about competition. In the perfect competition case, which textbooks treat as the norm, there is no profit. Companies all ask the same price, which just covers their costs (in a broad sense). Workers are also subject to perfect competition. For a given quality of labor (where quality is defined exclusively in terms of productivity), they all get the same market-determined wage that makes them indifferent to which job they work, their own or the many others they could take at the same wage. The same is true for managers all the way up to the top, where it is implied that the most highly compensated is therefore the most productive.

At this point, economists with a good academic background will interject that this is a caricature of neoclassical economics. Many neoclassical economists use models which are more realistic at least in some respects. However, it is with this textbook-presented caricature that most students of economics, and even more of those who take only the basic economics courses, leave university. They become policymakers, journalists or managers, thinking that the idea of perfect competition, while being a little exaggerated, contains the essence of capitalist economics and delivers robust and sensible recommendations.

Perfect Competition versus Imperfect Monopolies

Profit is a dirty word for neoclassical economists. In an idealized neoclassical economy, competition between companies ensures that profits are driven down to zero. Firms are in perfect competition with each other. They price their goods at what it would cost to produce one more unit. This market price is the same for every firm. Entrepreneurs earn only the normal interest on the capital they employ, which includes a normal risk premium, plus a normal entrepreneurial wage.

What economists call supernormal profits or simply profits would entail that entrepreneurs make more profit (on average over time) than what is needed to make it worthwhile for them to run the company. Such supernormal profits are also called monopolistic profits because competition must be restricted ("imperfect") for them to occur. Likewise, workers (or managers) earn a rent if their salary is higher than what is required to make them stay with their employer.

To make sure that all producers charge the same price, textbook economics assumes rising marginal costs. This means that the cost of producing one more unit of the product, say one more car, must rise with the number of cars produced, at least from a certain (relevant) point on. If the marginal cost did not rise with more cars produced, firms would make a loss if they priced the product at the cost of the last unit produced. They would not be able to recover the fixed setup cost of their operation. Also, there would be no limit to the number of cars a single firm would want to produce if marginal costs were constant or falling. After all, perfect competition entails that producers can sell as much as they want at a tad below the prevailing price. If it were more expensive to produce the 10,001st car than the 100,001st car, and producing the latter is more expensive than producing the 1,000,001st car, then large producers would grab an ever-increasing market share and become monopolists in such a setting. Mainstream theory classifies such unruly cases as natural monopolies, and puts them aside as special cases that need attention by government. The textbook norm that is presented is perfect competition.

The problem with this theory is that due to the very high sunk fixed costs for plant and machinery before a production run begins, most

industrial goods are produced under conditions of constant or falling
marginal costs – indeed the only globally commonplace industries today
known to normally have rising marginal costs are nonmechanized labor-
intensive industries such as subsistence farming. It gets worse, because
information goods (e.g. IT, media content such as movies, music, art etc.)
typically cost a very great deal for the very first copy and almost zero
for every subsequent copy; so as Shapiro and Varian (1999) point out,
the optimal profit-maximizing strategy is to maximize sales right down
to a marginal cost of almost zero (i.e. to allow some, but not too much,
piracy) which implies a scale of mass production approaching infinity,
and therefore is exactly the textbook economics model flipped upside
down. Building 100,000 cars in a big factory tends to be cheaper per car
than building 1,000 or 20,000 in a smaller factory. Even after the cost-
minimizing plant size is reached, a company that builds another factory
and sells twice as many cars can reduce administrative and development
costs per car. Baking 1,000 loaves of bread in a large bakery tends to
be more efficient than baking 100 in a small one. One of the reasons
that Microsoft became so rich in the 1990s was due to profitability per
additional item sold going up and up and up, as the cost of that very
first item becomes ever more amortized over volume of sales. These are
not just some odd examples. It has been proven to be the norm, not the
exception, that mass production is cheaper. A team around former vice
governor of the Federal Reserve, Alan Blinder, conducted face-to-face
interviews with senior managers of 200 firms representing 7.1 percent of
US GDP (Blinder et al. 1998). Almost 90 percent of the firms reported
constant or falling marginal costs. "The overwhelmingly bad news here
(for economic theory) is that, apparently, only 11 percent of GDP is
produced under conditions of rising marginal cost," conclude Blinder
et al. Fixed costs (i.e. outlays that you have independent of the volume of
production) turn out to be very high at roughly 40 percent of total cost.
The production theory taught by neoclassical textbooks is thus largely
irrelevant, which is certainly the reason that these textbooks usually
choose not to provide any empirical evidence for what they teach.

This curious production theory featuring increasing unit costs of
mass production dates from when the early neoclassical economists
thought of it during the Industrial Revolution. This is ironic given that
the Industrial Revolution was triggered by new means of transportation
and new production methods that made cheap mass production of
many goods possible. Without the important and convenient political
conclusions of the theory, which were discussed in Chapter 1, it would

be hard to understand how such a blatantly unrealistic theory could entirely displace competing ones and achieve hegemony. Its only other real benefit is that it makes the mathematics very considerably easier, and it allows the use of Lagrangians which can be solved in a finite time. Decreasing unit costs, on the other hand, require at the very least a computer and the use of topological mathematics, and generally can only be exactly solved in special cases.

By 1926 Piero Sraffa from the London School of Economics had already pointed out that businessmen would laugh at the notion that they do not produce more than they do because otherwise their costs per product would go up. They refrain from producing more than they do because they are not able to pry more customers away from competitors without lowering prices a lot (Sraffa 1926). In other words, what restrains volume of production is the worry that one will not be able to sell one's stock for a reasonable price within a reasonable time span, i.e. there is a shortage of demand. There is usually not a shortage of supply (in the absolute sense) in industries with constant or falling marginal costs.

Neoclassical economists had to resort to the unrealistic assumption of rising marginal costs because they had defined away the problems that make real-life competition work less than perfectly. They abstracted out transportation costs, meaning that in their model it is costless to transport products from the production site to the customer and workers from their homes to the factories. They also abstracted out information costs. All customers are supposed to know all products, and all potential price points that will clear a market. They are also supposed to all have the same tastes. Goods are standardized. A burger is a burger. In this setting, all that Burger King would have to do to increase their market share is to price their burgers a tad below McDonalds, and they would have the whole market to themselves. To avoid this outcome, neoclassical theory had to assume rising marginal costs of producing burgers or any other goods. That way, a company that finds a slightly more efficient way of production cannot take over the whole market.

Businesspeople are not constrained by such silly assumptions. They know that people have tastes that favor one burger over another or one car over another, and that a few yards of difference in location makes or breaks whole classes of retail outlets such as bakeries and hairdressers. They try to use that to their advantage. They develop features of their product that distinguish it from competing products to lessen the competition. They know that customers have limited information and they advertise to inform them about their products and their special features. Or they advertise to obfuscate the fact that their more expensive products are not really different or better than others; for example, one of the techniques taught in Marketing 101 is how to sow FUD (fear, uncertainty, doubt) about a competitor's product or service. Businesspeople also know that transportation costs can give them a big advantage or disadvantage, depending on where they are located in relation to the customers and competitors. A burger place or a bakery, even if it is somewhat pricy, will not have to fear a competitor from a different town very much – it may not even need to fear a competitor just around a corner if that competitor is not easily visible from the main street. Even competitors a few blocks away might not have an easy time to steal customers that live near the pricy store – for example, seniors in the US tend to "one stop" shop irrespective of price because of familiarity with that store (Curasi 1995).

All these real-life complications give producers a degree of market power. In the case of transportation costs it can be called a local monopoly. Within a certain radius, the producer does not face effective competition and can get away with charging higher prices. The logical structure is the same for incomplete information and taste differences. Anything that constitutes a preference by some consumers for a certain producer, be it closeness, a preference for the product or lack of information about alternatives, gives the producer some pricing power.

Pricing power means that producers do not simply react to market prices with their decisions on how much to produce. Instead, they jointly decide on price and quantity. They can decide to set the price a bit higher and sell a bit less. Which price will be optimal for them depends on how much demand falls with rising prices. A car manufacturer might sell 500,000 cars for US$10,000 each, even though it could produce additional cars for US$7,000 each. If it wanted to push 1,000 more cars into the market, it might have to lower the price of all cars by US$10. This would earn it a profit of US$2.99 million on the extra cars sold, but it would lose 500,000 times US$10, or US$5 million on all the other cars it sells. Thus, an increase in production would make profit go down overall. If lowering the price by US$5 would suffice to sell 1,000 more cars, increasing production would be worthwhile.

The upshot is that producers with market power, who can influence prices, will charge higher prices than what it would cost them to produce extra units and will produce less than they could. This stands in direct contradiction to perfect competition.

Mainstream economics has recognized this phenomenon of local monopolies and calls it monopolistic competition (Chamberlin 1933) or imperfect competition (Robinson 1933). In this market structure, local monopolies compete with each other at the fringes of their respective market niches (Dixit and Stiglitz 1977). What mainstream economics, as a body of knowledge that permeates textbooks and delivers policy advice, has not embraced is the omnipresence of monopolistic competition with limited entry and the resulting monopolistic profits in the real world. This is small wonder given that the concept is incompatible with staples of the modern mainstream, like general equilibrium analysis or the concept of (downwardly sloping) industry demand curves (Bellante 2004). Textbooks and policy advice are still inspired by the unrealistic idea of perfect competition, or alternatively of monopolistic competition with near perfectly free entry, which does not allow for profits. This is despite the fact that fields just outside economics, such as management and marketing, teach business development theories in their freshman classes entirely based on deliberately creating, sustaining and exploiting local and natural monopolies, e.g. Porter's five forces strategic analysis or Boston Consulting Group's growth-share matrix. Such enormously popular and clearly empirically valid theories make economics look out of touch at best, ill conceived at worst.

Inefficiency can survive

In the world of textbook economics, only the most efficient producers survive. Since even these can only just barely cover their costs, inefficient ones will make losses and disappear from the market as soon as their invested capital needs replacement. If instead most producers were to sell their goods for significantly more than it would cost to make more of them, inefficient producers with higher costs could survive for a long time. Their profits would be smaller but they would not necessarily make losses.

As far as empirical findings go, monopolistic competition holds up better than perfect competition. Economists have shown that large and persistent differences in productivity between businesses are the norm. Syverson (2010), for example, found that even within narrowly defined industries in the US manufacturing sector, plants operate at vastly different levels of productivity. A plant that just makes it into the group of the top 10 percent most productive factories (bottom of the 90th percentile) produces on average twice as much output with the same input of labor and capital than a plant that is at the upper edge of the bottom ten percent (top of the 10th percentile). This is only the average over various industries. In some industries, the productivity gaps between plants are much larger. These discrepancies are also fairly stable over time. In less developed economies, the gaps are larger still (Syverson 2010).

At this point, economists would be tempted to say that there must be something wrong with the result. Why would the owners of the inefficient businesses refrain from using the same technology as the efficient ones and make a higher profit? The reasons are manifold and interlinked. Finding the cost-minimizing managerial and human resource practices is not something that you can do simply by choosing from a menu. Copying successful competitors can be hard, too. It is often not easy to observe what makes one plant efficient and another less efficient. Furthermore, adopting a productivity-enhancing practice often involves disruption costs: a temporary period where costs are actually higher than before instead of lower. Therefore it is anything but easy to know if a change is even going in the right direction. This makes it quite plausible that the goal of maximizing profit alone will not lead to uniformly optimal technology and procedures. Some inefficient firms also maintain a profit by paying their workers less. We will look more closely at this strategy in the next chapter.

The less pronounced the local monopoly power of firms is, the less they can afford to be inefficient. Thus competition drives out inefficiency. On the other hand, very fierce competition might stifle innovation. If nobody earns more than the minimal profit, they might find it difficult to go through an extended period of higher costs due to innovation and changeover – some would say that this was the case for the US telecommunications industry after AT&T was broken up in 1984, thus allowing the Europeans to take the lead in mobile phone development until very recently, and that this was a consideration when the decision to cease anti-trust proceedings against Microsoft was taken in 2001 (Datta 2003). Thus, the optimal level of competition under such dynamic considerations might very well be an intermediate one. In the end, it is an empirical question as to where the right level of competition is. Empirical research indicates that real-life competition seems to be less than optimal most of the time. Exogenous increases in competition tend to go together with rising productivity and innovation (Syverson 2010).

The mixed blessing of free market entry

According to textbook economics, even monopolistic competition will not lead to excess profits (beyond normal remuneration for risk, depreciation of capital etc.) if entry for newcomers into the market is reasonably free. In this case, excessive profits in an industry would lure newcomers into the market. These would add to the supply of goods and push prices down until nobody would be making excessive profits any more, and this would be a good result. There are, however, two flaws in this reasoning. Firstly, in many cases it would not be good if it happened. Secondly, it will often not happen.

Having newcomers enter the market until profits go down to zero will be problematic if average costs are falling with the size of production establishments. In reality, falling average costs are the norm as shown by Blinder et al. (1998). If small newcomers take market share from larger producers, average production volumes of individual production sites decrease and production costs overall rise. Newcomers can possibly take market share away from established producers because transportation costs segment markets. They can locate themselves at the edges of the market areas of established producers. They produce at higher costs, but they can also charge higher prices since they are located closer to their (few) customers. Therefore, they can possibly make a profit even at lower quantities and higher average production costs. The market entry of newcomers (if successful) reduces the market size for incumbents. These have to shrink and see their average costs go up, further increasing the chance of more newcomers to enter the market, and so on. If such competition would really drive profits to zero, a very large number of producers would eventually produce very few units each at very high average cost. The same mechanism would play out if newcomers' market niches are not defined by geography but by the tastes of customers. Then, newcomers would carve away demand from incumbents by offering goods that cater to special tastes. This would drive up average costs of incumbents and create scope for even more newcomers to enter.

In reality, there are strong forces that go against this atomization of markets. The most powerful of these is that newcomers are routinely at a big disadvantage. Foster, Haltiwanger and Syverson (2010) have shown what a slow and difficult process it is for newcomers in an industry to establish themselves. They analyzed information on thousands of US plants who produce a number of homogenous products like fiber boxes, white pan bread, carbon black (known as the E153 artificial coloring outside the US) and roasted coffee beans. Despite brands and quality not being a big issue with these products, the researchers found that new businesses tend to be much smaller than their established competitors for a long time. On average, this size gap takes well over a decade to close.

This is true even though new plants are at least as technically efficient as older plants. The reason for the smaller size of new plants is that they start with a considerable demand deficit, which they can only slowly erase – if they survive at all. At the same price, a new plant will sell only 57 percent of the output of a plant that is more than fifteen years old. Plants that are five to nine years old sell only 67 percent of the output of an old plant and even plants that are ten to fifteen years old only sell 73 percent as much as old plants if they charge the same price.

This will normally mean several years of losses for the newcomers. To take this risk and to find financing for it requires the expectation of significant profits afterwards. To make things worse, incumbents do not have to sit by idly and watch the newcomers establish themselves. They can and often do take strategic action, for instance predatory pricing, either in order to deter new entrants or to make it hard for others to establish themselves and make a profit. Goolsbee and Syverson (2008) have empirically proved this behavior for airlines, and in recent years the laws prohibiting predatory pricing have been systematically weakened or repealed in many Western countries (the last successful prosecution in the US, which went to the Supreme Court, was in 1993).

Lower financial strength of newcomers is also often an issue, as Boutin et al. (2009) found by analyzing the data from tax files and other sources regarding almost the whole of France's goods production industry. According to their data, only a paltry 6 percent of the leaders of an industry in terms of sales were standalone companies not affiliated to a business group. The cash that these big incumbent companies – and the groups to which they belong – had at hand was an important deterrent for new entrants. The more cash-rich the incumbent company or its group, the lower the rate of new entry into an industry. This harks back to the problem of imperfect credit markets discussed in Chapter 2. Because newcomers are credit constrained, market leaders can credibly threaten them with their higher ability to sustain losses. Typically, it is particularly hard for newcomers to convince banks or investors to entrust them with their money. The chance to make a small profit regularly will not be enough to obtain funding. It will have to be a big profit to make entry feasible.

The rule is that competition by newcomers will reduce monopolistic profits to moderate levels, but rarely to zero. Admittedly examples of newcomers quickly becoming market leaders and pushing down prices do exist, but they are rare and do not exert the kind of competition that economic textbooks describe. Highly successful newcomers do not normally gain a market share by offering the same product for slightly less. Rather they enter with a significant innovation on the product, technology or distribution side that allows them to produce or distribute at significantly lower cost, or offer something clearly better to customers.

Price competition without free entry will not push profits to zero

Apart from local monopolies and the difficulties of newcomers, there is another reason that competition does not push profits to zero. According to standard textbooks, competing producers making a profit would each try to gain market share by lowering prices. The mechanism by which this is supposed to happen is rather peculiar and will not normally apply in the real world. Keen (2001/2008) has rediscovered and further developed this insight. To see the problem with the textbook story, imagine that there are many producers and no new entrants. Let them start producing the same amount that a monopolist would choose as profit maximizing. In this case, the textbooks say, each producer would have an incentive to produce more. This is because it can produce the product for less than its price. Thus it can make an extra profit by selling more for a little less. The extra supply will depress prices a bit. However, most of the "cost" of this price decline will fall on other producers as each individual producer has only a small market share. Thus, if one company sells more and all the others keep their production the same, this one company will make a higher profit. After Company 1, Company 2 figures this out and raises its sales volume. As long as prices are still higher than the cost of producing additional units, this will continue. The price incrementally decreases and volume goes up until there is no profit any more.

This outcome hinges critically on the assumed sequential change in production volume, but, this is rather unrealistic in a market with many producers. They all have the same incentive to produce more. What happens, though, if many or all of them decide to produce more in the next period? They will collectively experience a drop in profits, just as a monopolist would, because collectively they produce so much more that the price goes down a lot. After the individual companies check their profits in the next period, they will find that raising production volume has depressed their profits. Thus, they are likely to lower production again. Keen and Standish (2006) put this in a mathematical model and did computer simulations with up to 10,000 competitors. In theory, as in the simulation, they found that prices and quantities under competition would not differ significantly from the monopoly case. In other words, if companies are assumed to maximize profits, then they will be just as happy to reduce production individually as they would be to raise it if that would maximize profits. Mainstream economics dismisses such inconvenient behavior as irrational at best, pathological at worst.

Monopolies can be good or bad

Even so, it will matter if there is competition or a monopoly, but the advantage of competition is of a different nature from what textbooks teach. According to the textbooks, it is a static advantage that comes from competition reducing prices (under given cost curves). In reality, dynamic aspects matter much more and make competition preferable in most cases. A monopolist may have little financial incentive to innovate and improve service for customers, but they do have a strategic incentive in the form of keeping all potential forms of competition out. If in a technologically advanced industry, a monopolist often has an additional incentive to innovate in order to obtain and retain talent. Either way, the customers of a monopolist have nowhere else to go, so if a monopolist invents a new method of production or a better product, it is a less profitable employment of capital than other uses. For example, Kotwal, Ramaswani and Wadhwa (2011) judge that, "It is inconceivable that, without the breakup of government monopolies and the advent of competition in the communication sector, there would have been a revolution in communication technology in India. And, without such a revolution, the fastest growing sectors (e.g. business services) would not have taken off in India. The sustained growth that we have seen since the mid-1990s would clearly not have been possible without the liberalizing reforms of 1991."

A better product that a monopolist introduces might just displace the existing one, and a new production method might make expensive machinery that the monopolist already employs redundant. Thus there might be little effort to innovate in many monopolies. A company in a competitive industry, in contrast, can gain a lot by improving customer service and by innovating. More innovation will lead to better products, better service and lower prices in many industries (Keen 2001/2008).

This is the rule for many industries, but not for all. In some industries, innovation is hardly an issue due to the nature of said industry, while falling average costs (i.e. economies of scale) are a major one (Felder 1996).

These are the industries in which a well-regulated monopoly is better than competition. One such industry where innovation isn't important is housing insurance, as Swiss economist Kirchgässner (2007) has shown. In Switzerland 19 Kantone (states) have government-controlled or government-run regional monopolies in house insurance for fire, flood and other hazards. These provide equivalent insurance for significantly lower premiums than prevail in the Kantons with competitive markets. While the Swiss who have the monopolies are very happy with them and do not want to change anything, the European Commission declared them illegal for the European Union (which Switzerland is not part of). This had the result that in Germany the federal states of Baden-Wurttemberg and Hamburg had to scrap their regional monopolies for this insurance. This resulted in 60 percent higher costs for the insured and the loss of universal cover (Epple 1996; Kirchgässner 2007). Another industry where innovation isn't important, but economies of scale are, is provision of water and sewerage. After the European Commission forced the breakup of water and sewerage monopolies in Britain, in the decade that followed prices rose by 46 percent in real terms (OFWAT Memorandum to House of Commons 1998).

There is no significant technical progress in the insurance business or in basic utilities like water and sewerage. Thus the dynamic advantage of competition is of little relevance. On the other hand, dividing the market between several or many competitors has the disadvantage that administrative and marketing costs per customer rise. As insurance is all about administration and marketing, this can be a very important drawback (Kirchgässner 2007).

Many other kinds of insurance, including health insurance, are likely to exhibit similar patterns. Thus there might be good reasons in this particular case for a government endorsed monopoly. Indeed, even though the US Patient Protection and Affordable Care Act 2010 ("Obamacare") is badly designed, if implemented correctly its fundamental economic principles are sound. Ireland, which is one of the few countries in Europe to have a fully privatized health care system, is introducing compulsory health insurance from 2014 as a means of saving public money and achieving universal coverage, exactly as the US should have. Instead of pouring public subsidies directly into the pockets of hospitals and consultants as was previously the case, the Irish are reallocating the same public expenditure directly to the population in the form of income-dependent insurance subsidies. By 2016 no hospital or medical professional will directly receive a cent of public funds. This will allow the public subsidy of healthcare, which had been growing as rapidly in Ireland as it had in the US, to be reigned in. The government will block-purchase basic health insurance for all but the richest 30 percent of the population, allowing it to drive a very hard bargain and forcing prices down to less than an estimated US$500 per person per year, through economies of scale, exactly as the empirical evidence outlined earlier proved.

The omnipresence of monopolistic profits in the real world is important, but not because these profits would discredit competition or capitalism. They don't. They are important because economic policies can have very different consequences in a realistic setting with monopolistic profits than they do in the world of textbooks. Those countries, and governments, that have realized where textbook economics are "wrong" have sustainably achieved efficiencies which are impossible when competition is misapplied.

Playing Monopoly on the Labor Market

Just as most companies have some degree of pricing power on the product market, they will not take the wage rate as given. On the labor market, pricing power by employers is called monopsony power because the firm, as a large buyer, is purchasing from many small, unorganized sellers in the form of potential employees. The word "monopsony" is derived from Greek and means a single purchase or buyer. As with monopoly power, economic textbooks teach about monopsony, but they treat it as a special case, an aberration, rather than the norm that partial monopsony really is.

The factors that make partial monopsony an ubiquitous phenomenon usually disappear due to the assumptions of neoclassical theory. Labor is held to be a uniform commodity, detached from human beings and traveling effortlessly and instantly to wherever it is needed. The commodity labor does not have preferences. Whoever pays the most gets it.

In real life, labor is inseparably attached to human beings. These human beings have to live from renting out their time and selling their work, a fact that is important for determining negotiating power. The human beings to whom the labor units are attached have preferences with regard to what work they do. Such preferences can severely limit their choices. If they would rather be journalists than work in public relations, if they would rather work in childcare than in selling cars, their choices of work within an acceptable distance of their family's living place are often rather limited. Closeness to work is an important factor because, unlike the ethereal unit of labor that neoclassical theory assumes, actual workers have families living in a certain place and have to expend time, effort and money to get to work (Kaufman 2009).

A pure monopsony is rare. However, most employers will at least have some monopsonistic wage-setting power over a significant portion of their employees. A retailer can get people from the same neighborhood for a smaller wage than an employer further away. This makes the wage it has to pay dependent on its demand for labor, which is the economists' definition of market power. A large employer will have to attract workers from farther away, and thus will have to offer higher wages than a small employer located near potential workers.

Employees can be physically close to a particular employer, or figuratively close (e.g. by liking to do the kind of work for which the employer asks). Closeness by preference has the same impact as physical closeness. Employers can offer less money to those who are close in either way. Just as workers will demand a higher wage for travelling to an otherwise identical employer who is further away, they will demand more money if they are expected to do work which they do not like as much (Bhaskar, Manning and To 2002).

Empirical research has provided ample direct and indirect proof of the importance of market power on the labor market. An indirect proof lies in the fact that the law of one price routinely does not hold. If competition worked as neoclassical theory assumes, there would be one price for labor of a given type and quality. However, there is a large body of literature dating back many decades that shows that wage rates can be very different for a given type of work in a given city. One such study from 2002 cites, as informal but impressive evidence, a survey of six fast food restaurants located within a one mile radius. The six restaurants made offers of starting wages to new employees that ranged from US$5.15 to US$6 per hour, a range of 16 percent. Getting a pay rise of 16 percent is a big deal for most employees, especially those close to minimum wage (Bhaskar, Manning and To 2002). Even for highly compensated, highly skilled and highly mobile knowledge workers such as top end IT workers earning well over US$100,000 a year, there is significant monopsonistic power employed to hold down compensation and work against the interests of employees: In 2010 the US Department of Justice ruled against Adobe, Apple, Google, Intel, Intuit and Pixar for entering into secret agreements not to solicit one another's high-skilled employees, and a class action civil suit is due to be heard in the courts during 2012 (Forbes 23 January 2012).

Like monopolistic supply-restraint on the product market, monopsonistic demand-restriction on the labor market leads to supernormal profits. Distributing them is up to management, capital owners, workers or the government, depending on relative bargaining powers and on politics, or they can be wasted through inefficiencies.

To each according to their contribution

The presence of monopolistic profits is particularly important with regard to the issue of how much of the proceeds from production should (or will) go to capital and how much will go to labor. For lack of an objective measure of individual output, Adam Smith explained the division of the proceeds from production between capital and workers by relative bargaining power (see Chapter 1). Today's neoclassical textbook theory of wages and capital income is very different. This theory says that labor and capital are paid exactly what they contribute to the value of the product at the margin.

However, there are huge practical and theoretical problems with this account. It is often not possible to determine how much each worker in a team contributes to revenue. Most workers work in a team in a wider sense. The value that an extra hour of their work produces depends a lot on what other workers do. Even if individual workers are assembling a product more or less by themselves, what this product is worth will depend on how well their colleagues in the sales and marketing departments do their work. In many contexts, there is simply no practical way of figuring out an individual worker's contribution to the overall result (Adler 2009).

Neoclassical theory deals with that problem by defining it away. The different team members are not really different in this theory since it defines labor as a standardized commodity, measured by the representative labor unit. Therefore the theory cannot contribute to solving the problem of how to measure the contributions of different team members. John Bates Clark, the pioneer of this theory in the US, and his neoclassical counterparts in Europe were interested in something different. They were only interested in the distribution of the proceeds between labor and capital.

Clark's (1899/2001) theory focuses on the question of how the ideal combination of labor and capital is found (i.e. how many workers should work with a given set of machinery, or how many bus drivers should be working with a certain number of buses). He suggested the thought experiment of holding capital and labor constant in turn and seeing whether it pays to use more or less of the other factor. If you hold labor constant, for instance if you have ten workers and start with one workbench, you can calculate how much more you can produce if you add another workbench. The value of the extra goods that the ten workers can produce with this second workbench (i.e. the marginal product of an extra workbench), is the maximum the owners of the factory will be willing to pay for a second workbench. If the price of the workbench is lower, they will use two of them. The same calculation can be done for the third, fourth and fifth workbench. Adding a sixth workbench adds less in extra value of production than a workbench costs because two workers are needed to make efficient use of a workbench, and there are only ten workers. Then the factory owners will only use five workbenches and the price of a workbench will correspond to the value of the marginal product of a workbench.

The same thought exercise can be done while holding the number of workbenches constant and seeing how much more can be produced by an extra worker. Only if the extra output is worth at least as much as the worker costs in wages will the factory owner employ the extra worker. Thus the value of the marginal product of the last worker employed will equal the wage rate. There is no exploitation.

One crucial assumption is necessary to arrive at this outcome. The marginal product of adding more workers to a given number of workbenches must fall if more workers are added. This is entirely plausible. The same must hold for the marginal product of additional workbenches (capital) if the number of workers is fixed. This is also plausible, as more workbenches will not do much good if there are no workers to work on them.

So what percentage of the fares that a bus company takes in is due to the effort of the bus driver and how much is due to the bus? A bus without a driver will contribute nothing. Thus all proceeds can be attributed to the driver. However, a bus driver without a bus is not much use either.

Moving from the level of the individual workbench–worker combinations to the level of the firm, the theory looks even odder. It does not explain how many combinations of workbenches and workers the factory will employ because there is nothing justifying the assumption that the second workbench–worker combination will be less productive than the first one. If anything, it is likely to be more productive, because overhead costs can be distributed more widely in a larger factory.

If pressed, neoclassical economists will say that only on the level of the economy as a whole does the theory work. The economy has a stock of capital, they would say, which can be assumed constant in the short run. Labor will be added until the value of its marginal product has fallen to the level of the wage. The result is that the wage equals the value of the marginal product. The same thought experiment is performed when holding the amount of labor in the economy as fixed and adding capital. The result is that profit equals the value of the marginal product of capital. Everybody gets what they deserve.

However, the assumptions behind this result, which are reasonable at the level of the individual production unit, cease to be reasonable at the level of the economy as a whole. Why should the productivity of additional capital decline with each additional unit that is used in the economy as a whole? After all, a street is more productive if it links into a network of other streets. The fact that a large city or an industrial country has a large amount of private and public infrastructure makes new investments in these often more productive than investments in the countryside or in under-capitalized developing countries. Like reinforces like. Additionally, if more labor is demanded and used at the level of the economy, why should this leave the wage rate unaltered, as the thought experiment requires? More demand for labor should lead to higher wages, which in turn provides additional income for workers. These workers will want to buy more goods, which in turn means higher prices for goods and a higher value of using additional labor. Thus using more labor might raise instead of lower the value of the marginal product of labor, in which case the determinacy of the theory breaks down (Keen 2001/2008).

One of the pioneers of neoclassical economics, Vilfredo Pareto, already pointed out that the mainstay of the neoclassical theory of income distribution among labor and capital was rather fragile. He noted that it would break down if competition was less than perfect and if the amount of labor to be employed with each unit of capital could not be varied freely (e.g. as in the case of the bus and bus drivers where you cannot use a bus efficiently at any given time without a driver, or with more than one driver) (Fonseca 2009). Both of these complications are omnipresent in reality. Textbook economics consistently ignores this fundamental problem, however. In effect, neoclassical theory cannot say anything about how much of the jointly produced revenue is contributed by the bus drivers (labor) and how much by the buses (capital).

If these theoretical considerations do not adequately demonstrate that marginal product does not determine wages and profits, consider the enormous differences in wages between workers doing identical work in different countries. As Ashenfelter and Jurajda (2010) have shown, entry-level workers at McDonalds in underdeveloped countries have to work up to twelve times as long to buy one of the Big Macs they produce than workers in some industrialized countries. This is true even though they do the exact same job with virtually the same equipment (Ashenfelter and Jurajda 2010). According to *The Economist* newspaper's famous Big Mac index, the most expensive Big Mac in the world at the end of 2011 was in Switzerland at US$6.81. The cheapest was in the Ukraine at just US$2.11. Yet a Swiss worker earns nearly three of their Big Macs per hour, while a Columbian worker earns just 23 percent of one of their Big Macs (Ashenfelter and Jurajda 2010; The Economist Big Mac Index January 2012). In fact, as Ashenfelter and Jurajda show, there is a low correlation between wages and Big Mac prices in all but Western countries, where high minimum wage rates force the price of a Big Mac.

Capital is what capital does

Thus far, "capital" has been accepted as a given in the neoclassical theory of income distribution. But what exactly is capital? In what unit is it measured? Is there a difference between financial capital and capital invested in buildings, machinery, equipment or inventory? How can a truck, a building and a computer be added together to get to the capital stock of the nation? These are fundamental questions that a theory of capitalist economics is expected to answer. Unfortunately, neoclassical economics cannot answer them, calling into question its ability to deliver a convincing explanation of how the proceeds of labor cooperating with such an ill-defined thing as *capital* would be distributed between labor and capital.

According to neoclassical theory, factories combine labor and capital to produce goods, which they deliver to households. The households in turn deliver labor and capital. Since households only consume, they can only deliver capital in the form of money (i.e. the income they have not spent on consumption). However, labor combined with money will not produce anything. The money must be transformed into capital goods, and the method for doing so is not part of neoclassical theory. Any attempt to model this transformation inevitably points to fundamental problems of the neoclassical theory of capital and income distribution (Keen 2001/2008).

The 1960s and '70s saw a protracted fight over neoclassical capital theory, the so-called Cambridge Capital Controversy. Neoclassical economists, including Paul Samuelson and Robert Solow from MIT (the Massachusetts Institute of Technology), defended neoclassical capital theory against an attack from economists working in Cambridge, England, chiefly Joan Robinson and Piero Sraffa. The English economists attacked the neoclassical notion that the (relative) price of the two factors of production, labor and capital, determines how much of each is used.

Since capital has very different forms, the neoclassicals resort to adding up the market values of capital goods to measure the aggregate capital. Everything is assumed to be in the same category: a sum of money, a crane, a barrel to store wine in. However, as the English economists pointed out, this practice introduces circularity into the argument. The net present value of physical capital, like a building, consists of the future profits it can generate. If the real rate of interest is lower, that physical capital will be worth more relative to an equivalent sum of money. For instance, if the real interest rate is 100 percent and a capital good yields a return of US$100 in the next period and only in this next period, then the capital good is worth US$50 today, as US$50 could be placed in a bank at 100 percent, resulting in US$100 for significantly less work. If the interest rate is instead 10 percent, the capital good is worth about US$91 today. This means that the net present value of existing capital depends (inversely) on the real interest rate. Worse still, this effect is different for different forms of capital, depending on their lifespan, because the longer the lifespan, the more the present value will go down with the level of the interest rate (and the greater the uncertainty regarding future real interest rates will be). This effectively makes it impossible to add up different forms of capital with different life spans and come out with a meaningful value. The Cambridge economists were able to show that a higher real interest rate could lead to both more and less capital being used (Cohen and Harcourt 2003).

This implies that the labor market and the capital markets cannot be treated as if they work in the same way as a perishable commodity market like the market for potatoes. There would be a menu of different possible equilibriums, both better and worse. They would have to be chosen, by chance, the government or somebody else. As the different equilibriums are likely to be associated with rather different distributions of income between capitalists and workers, whoever had the power to see that their side's preferred distribution was selected would be of key importance.

Paul Samuelson admitted defeat at the first World Congress of the Econometric Society in Rome in 1965, which is documented in the November 1966 edition of the *Quarterly Journal of Economics*. Samuelson concluded the Congress by stating that the neoclassical rule that falling interest rates lead to increasing capital intensity cannot be universally true, admitting in effect that the neoclassical theory of capital is faulty. However, for lack of an alternative acceptable to the rest of neoclassical theory, the economic mainstream kept ignoring or downplaying this fundamental problem and acted as if nothing had happened. After Robinson and Sraffa had died, no other influential economists ventured to keep the unpleasant controversy alive (Cohen and Harcourt 2003; Keen 2001/2008). After all, it does not aid career success to be unpleasant or controversial except when it aids wealthy benefactors.

If capital is ill-defined and usage of more capital is consistent with either a higher or a lower remuneration of capital, the whole neoclassical theory of income distribution (between capital and labor) cannot work. Throwing out the neoclassical innovation to theory as faulty leaves classical economics and the notion that the negotiating power of the various social classes determines wages and profits. This is exactly what first year classes in practical business skills teach: an overview of the main points of Pierre Bourdieu's economic sociology (e.g. *The Social Structures of the Economy*, 2005) and Porter's five forces strategic analysis (barriers to entry, threat of substitutes, buyer power, seller power, competitive rivalry). Both are absolutely centered on how negotiating power between economic actors works in the real world.

Conclusion

Companies make profits beyond the assumed remuneration for taking risks and for the entrepreneur's work. Mainstream economic theory has no theoretical basis on which to determine how these rents should be distributed among capital owners, management and workers. Neoclassical attempts to provide such a basis suffer from inappropriate assumptions and from a failure to define what capital is and how it should be remunerated.

In effect, rents will be distributed according to the relative negotiating power of the parties involved. There is plenty of theoretical and empirical evidence supporting this conclusion in literature. This means that many things economists like to treat as issues of allocative efficiency involve a strong element of distribution and fairness. This is true for the assessment of the effects of taxes, for example, or for the effects of wage rises. If there are no profits, such changes will directly translate into changes in production. If there are rents, a large part of the consequences might consist of redistribution. General equilibrium models which assume the absence of profits become suspect as tools to assess the impact of policies or economic developments.

The empirical fact that most producers operate under conditions of increasing returns to scale and have local monopoly power has important consequences for theory and policy. Perfect competition is not only unrealistic, it ceases to be desirable under such conditions. Too much competition would lead to inefficiently small producers if economies of scale are important – and mass production only makes sense if there are economies of scale. The main issue regarding market power is not so much its effect on prices, but rather its effect on the development and use of new technologies. Where technological progress is not a big issue, a government-endorsed monopoly might be the best choice.

A large part of producer rents typically goes to the workers. This requires economics to augment the typical consumer-centered analysis with one that includes the interest of workers in their current job and in the success of their firm. This will be further elaborated on in the next chapter.

Chapter 5

POWER AT WORK

Workmen are disposed to combine in order to raise, masters in order to lower the wages of labour. The masters upon these occasions never cease to call aloud for the assistance of the civil magistrate, and the rigorous execution of those laws which have been enacted with so much severity against the combination of servants, labourers, and journeymen.

—Adam Smith, 1776

Tire manufacturer Bridgestone had to learn the hard way how dangerous it can be to follow the teachings of neoclassical labor market theory. Dozens of people died as a consequence of faulty Bridgestone tires on Ford Explorer SUVs (sports utility vehicles). The value of the company dropped by billions of dollars due to victim compensation, a ruined reputation and the recall of millions of tires. Management had unilaterally imposed large pay cuts and an unpopular new 12-hour plan of shifts rotating from day to night. In response, the United Rubber Workers of America had called a strike in the Illinois plant of the company. For a period of about three years, the union was either on strike or working without a contract. During that time, the company employed about 1,000 replacement workers. After a year, the union unconditionally offered to return to work without a contract, but management announced that it would permanently retain the replacement workers and offered to recall the striking workers only as needed. Only in December 1996 was a contract settled that included provisions to recall all strikers (Krueger and Mas 2004).

Following a rash of highway fatalities, the company recalled 15 million tires. Krueger and Mas (2004) established the causal relationship between the strike and the subsequent deaths from defective Firestone tires. Based on claims for compensation for property damage or personal injuries, they discovered that tires from the Illinois plant, produced during the labor controversy, were 15 times more likely to have a defect than tires from the company's other two plants at which the same type of tire was produced. Everybody came out as a loser in this battle. The stock market valuation of the company fell by more than US$8 billion to almost half its former valuation. The top management of Bridgestone/ Firestone lost their jobs, as did the workers. The Illinois plant eventually was closed (Krueger and Mas 2004).

There are many such cases that show that it can be expensive to treat workers in a way that they consider unfair. Another case that economists have examined was a hotly disputed pay cut at Alaska Airlines. The dispute led to a massive increase in flight delays lasting several months. In contrast, pay cuts in a number of other cases, when airlines were on the brink of bankruptcy, did not cause excessive delays (Rupp 2007).

In both cases, employers did what mainstream economics recommends. If market conditions are such that it is possible to get workers who will do the same work for less, it is appropriate to cut wages. What the workers did, however, does not fit this theory. They worked together to fight wage cuts. According to the theory this is wrong on two counts. The theory says they should not bother, but rather just go to a different employer. If they did care, despite the assumptions of neoclassical theory, they should not risk their jobs, but rather free ride on the efforts of their colleagues. "Rational" people let others strike and protest and reap the rewards without taking the risk. The workers' perception of how fairly they are treated should not matter much for the production process. According to neoclassical theory, work is a homogeneous good with well-specified properties. Contracts are also well specified and easily enforced.

In short, mainstream economics assumes *homo economicus* on both sides, the strictly egocentric, self-absorbed person who is "rational" in the peculiar sense of mainstream economics. Although few consider this a reasonable representation of human nature, most economists working with it think that, in a competitive context, people act this way. This chapter will first give an account of what modern behavioral research has determined about the actual nature and behavior of human beings in economic contexts. These patterns will help explain why it is not the cold rules of competition but rather social norms of fairness which regulate relationships within a firm. As established in the preceding chapter, such behavior is made possible by the market power that firms have, not as the exception, but as the norm. This market power produces excess profits or rents, which have to be distributed among owners, managers and workers. This is where fairness considerations and bargaining power come in. Conflict between employers and workers over the distribution of profits does not even exist in the textbook narrative, despite the long history of placing that conflict at the center of economic discourse (e.g. in pre-twentieth-century and Marxian economics). We cannot hope to understand much of what happens in real-life labor markets, for instance during outsourcing and union activities, without considering this omnipresent distributional conflict.

Homo Economicus at Work

> Mainstream economics are the economics of primitive economies with minimal market integration and economic cooperation. They are thus not suited to analyze modern capitalist societies.
> —*Samuel Bowles and Herbert Gintis, 2006*

An almost uncountable number of field studies and laboratory experiments that have tested the notion of *homo economicus* have unfailingly found it wanting. Strong feelings of solidarity, fairness, cooperation and revenge seem to be hardwired into human nature.

Behavioral economists have used a laboratory experiment called the ultimatum game to show these feelings. The experimenters pair participants and designate one in each pair as the proposer. They give each pair a sum of money, say US$10, and the proposer can suggest how this money shall be divided between the two. The responder can either accept or reject the proposal. If the responder rejects the proposal, both get nothing. *Homo economicus* would offer $0.01 to the responder and the responder, if also a *homo economicus*, would accept, as $0.01 is better than nothing. However, only children come close to this outcome. Adult proposers rarely give less than 30 percent to the responder and many responders reject offers of less than 30 percent. Even in the dictator game, where the responders have to take what they get, dictators routinely give a significant amount, though less than in the ultimatum game (Bolton and Ockenfels 2000).

On the other hand, a simple auction game shows that competition can indeed induce behavior conforming to the *homo economicus* assumption. In such an experiment one player gets the right to auction off money, say $10, provided by the experimenter. Several other participants, perhaps ten, compete with their offers for the money. The same people who reject an offer of $1 in the ultimatum game and so take nothing voluntarily offer more than $9 for a ten dollar bill, netting less than $1 for themselves and leaving more than $9 to the lucky auctioneer (Bolton and Ockenfels 2000).

Bolton and Ockenfels (2000) have developed a theory called ERC, which can consistently explain these seemingly contradictory results. ERC stands for equity, reciprocity and competition. It assumes that people have two main motivations. They want to make more money so they will be able to consume more and they want to get their fair share. The two motivations are in conflict in the ultimatum game. As the share offered to the responder gets smaller, the distribution becomes very uneven. In this case, many responders prefer an equal distribution of zero and zero rather than getting a little more money in a very unfair distribution.

The theory can also explain the modesty of bidders in the auction game. The bidders would like to get a higher share. However, if they bid low and others bid high, they will get a very low percentage (0 percent) *and* a zero absolute amount. They have no chance to trade off less money for more equity and thus act as if fairness were not important to them (Bolton and Ockenfels 2000). If competition of this kind ruled within firms, the management of Bridgestone would not have struck out so badly. However, workers did think that fairness mattered and they felt they could impose a fairer deal by cooperating to further the group interest. This is the other part that many economists need explained. Why did they cooperate rather than free riding on the efforts of others? Why did workers at Bridgestone risk their jobs, rather than counting on others to go on strike?

The first part of the answer is in the conclusion of Chapter 4: there are profits to fight over. Workers will increase their share of the profits if they build up negotiation power. Thus it is rational for the group to cooperate. However, according to the modern individualistic rational-choice mainstream, group interests are not relevant to "rational" individuals. As only individuals act, only the interests of individuals should matter. Individually, free riders fare better. Thus, the only rational thing for individuals is free riding. To accept or pretend to accept this dogma has long been an essential part of initiation rites for economists.

Rather than being a sign of irrationality, as economists like to assume, the prevalence of group solidarity is a sign that a society is advanced. *Homo economicus* is a concept for primitive societies, as Heinrich et al. (2001) have proven. They conducted a series of ultimatum games in 15 small cultures all over the world. The experiments with participants from cultures at different levels of economic development showed a strong pattern in the results. Players from societies with more market integration and more cooperation in production are more inclined to reject unfair offers. Proposers in such economically advanced cultures have a stronger tendency to share. Thus the conclusion by the researchers seems justified that the notion of *homo economicus* is only adequate for children and primitive societies (Heinrich et al. 2001).

The idea of *homo economicus* conforms to the interpretation of Darwinism popularized by the book *The Selfish Gene* by Richard Dawkins (1973). "If you look at the way natural selection works, it seems to follow that anything that has evolved by natural selection should be selfish," writes Dawkins, thus providing a rationalization for taking *homo economicus* as the norm. However, this view ignores that cooperation helps individuals to survive and reproduce in a hostile environment. If human beings were indeed the autistic creatures that Dawkins and the economic mainstream assume, wild animals and the adversities of nature would have long done away with us. Charles Darwin himself did not think of evolutionary selection as simply individual selection. For him, group selection was at least as important. According to Darwin, tribes with a greater number of courageous, sympathetic and faithful members, who are ready to warn each other of danger, to aid and defend each other, would spread and be victorious over other groups (Bowles 2009).

Humans had hundreds of thousands of years to develop the norms and preferences that would enable us to live together in prosperous societies. These norms encourage us to put aside narrow self-interest, to act pro-socially and to punish those who don't. Humans would not be here, with highly elaborated civilizations, without having developed these norms (Bergstrom 2003).

It is clear that there are economic rents to fight over and that it makes sense for workers to cooperate to grab a larger share. What is left to explain is why competition between workers within the firm and with workers outside does not prevent workers from exercising power. If we take into account that in many US states workers have very little protection against being fired relative to most other countries (including most developing countries), it is not obvious what keeps managers from copying the Bridgestone example and simply firing everybody who wants a larger share than the one dictated by supply and demand on the labor market.

To understand why this is not the norm, it is worth looking at the assumptions that would make it the norm. As mentioned in the previous chapter, according to textbook economics, labor markets function no differently than the market for potatoes. The employer and the worker trade units of labor at a price that is determined by the law of demand and supply. A unit of labor of a given quality is well defined, according to this view, just like a potato of given size and quality is well defined. Also the standard requirements for perfect competition need to hold: there can be no transaction costs, information must be complete and contracts can be perfectly enforced without cost. If these conditions are all met, the law of demand and supply will work beautifully (Kaufman 2009).

There is no power in the neoclassical labor market. Everybody has plenty of alternatives and everybody is thus indifferent as to whether they are hired by a specific employer or not, and whether they are fired or retained. Armen Alchian and Harold Demsetz (1972), two influential members of the market-emphasizing Chicago school of economics, made that explicit:

> The firm has no power, no authority, no disciplinary action any different in the slightest degree from ordinary market contracting between any two people. Wherein then is the relationship between a grocer and his employee different from that between a grocer and his customer?

This is obviously a caricature of the labor market, albeit a very influential one. Kaufman (2007) calls the perfectly competitive labor market not just unrealistic but logically impossible. He is certainly correct. If the labor market were perfectly competitive, it would not exist. With no transactions costs, full information and perfectly specified contracts, firms would not employ workers. In fact, there would be no firm and no labor market, and this is why:

A firm is an organization with a certain amount of capital in the form of buildings and equipment, and a number of workers who are hired for an extended period to do work together using that equipment according to the orders of the employer. If the assumptions necessary for perfect competition were met, the entrepreneur would rather buy intermediate products from other self-employed entrepreneurs, so an economy would consist entirely of single-person companies. There would be no point in drawing up ill-defined work contracts with all the associated problems they entail. The whole economy would work in the same way in which some services are auctioned on internet sites like 99designs, oDesk or guru.com. Users can specify on such sites that they have an apartment to be remodelled and choose an interior designer who asks the lowest price for their services. In the same way, industrialists would buy all the specific tasks to be performed in the factory on an auction website. Thanks to the assumption of zero transport costs, the sellers would instantly materialize, perform the task just as contracted and disappear again (Kaufmann 2007).

This makes it easy to answer the rhetorical question of Alchian and Demsetz concerning what distinguishes the relationship of employer and worker from the relationship between the grocer and the customer. The assumptions of complete information, negligible transaction costs, complete contracts and costless enforcement of contracts are even more unrealistic on the labor market than they are on many product markets.

Those ugly market forces have to stay outside

> Only social exchange tends to engender feelings of personal obligations, gratitude, and trust; purely economic exchange as such does not.
>
> —*Peter M. Blau, 1964*

Employment relationships involve complex tasks that can rarely be specified in a complete contract. While the baker can easily make a new contract to sell bread with every customer, this is rarely feasible on the labor market due to high transaction costs. This is why employment relationships tend to be ongoing. Such long-term relationships help to solve the problem of incomplete information. Employers have difficulty verifying in advance the quality of the work offered. The candidate, on the other hand, cannot be sure that the employer is giving a correct representation of the tasks and working conditions of the job. Retaining workers who work to the satisfaction of the employer helps both sides to build a reputation to overcome this problem. For this to work, there must be a surplus that allows employers to give good workers an incentive to stay with them. An employer who has a reputation of paying workers only the minimum dictated by current market forces cannot credibly offer a share of the surplus that would give workers a reason to stay (Fehr, Goette and Zehnder 2009).

Laboratory experiments that reproduce the give and take of an employment relationship can help explain the reasons that perceptions of fairness are more important for most labor relationships than market forces. The Swiss economist Ernst Fehr has pioneered the use of the gift exchange game for this purpose. The name of the game refers to an influential theoretical paper by Nobel Memorial Prize winner George Akerlof, called "Labor Contracts as a Partial Gift Exchange." In the gift exchange model, the effort of workers depends on whether they consider their pay as fair. Therefore many firms pay more than the market clearing wage in order to elicit more effort. One consequence of this policy is that the market does not clear and there is involuntary unemployment (Akerlof 1982).

The typical results of such experiments confirm that higher wage offers by firms, on average, induce workers to provide more effort. This contradicts a fundamental neoclassical assumption that the quality of the labor unit is independent of what is paid for it. Actual effort is significantly higher than the minimal effort predicted by self-interest. However, if the game is only a one-shot interaction, it is still far below the level that would maximize the combined payout of workers and employers. There are many fair-minded workers, but there are also substantial numbers of selfish workers who do not reciprocate kind treatment. The presence of selfish workers often restrains employers from offering wages that would be high enough to induce efficient effort levels from the fair-minded workers (Fehr, Goette and Zehnder 2009).

Experiments that come closer to an ongoing employment relationship by introducing repeated interaction have shown that a chance for reputation building can make even the selfish types act as if they were kind. They do so in order to get a reputation as fair-minded and thus induce employers to offer them a good share of the gains from cooperation. If the selfish types were to provide only minimal effort in the early rounds, they would reveal their egoistic nature and could not expect high wage offers in the later rounds. Employers in the experiments (as in real life) only pay wage rents to workers who they hope will reciprocate generous treatment with high effort. Thus even the presence of a limited share of fair-minded workers can have a large positive impact on performance (Fehr, Goette and Zehnder 2009).

The fairness concerns of workers have important implications. Piore and Doeringer asserted as early as 1971 that a sharp distinction exists between internal and external labor market arrangements. In writing this, they already correctly predicted that mainstream economics would not be able and willing to take such internal labor markets into account in a meaningful way. The essence of such internal labor markets is that most workers are largely insulated from outside labor market conditions once they are employed in firms (Fehr, Goette and Zehnder 2009).

The evidence is pervasive. Any study in any country that has looked into the distribution of wage changes has found that insiders are largely insulated from market forces as long as the company is not in jeopardy. This has two facets. One is that employers rarely cut wages. A related one is that the salary you negotiate upon entry tends to stick for a long time. This means that being at the right place at the right time can be more important than how productive you are. A number of empirical studies on the influence of luck alone have provided additional proof for what common sense has always known: the neoclassical presumption that workers are paid strictly according to their productivity is wrong. College graduates who happen to enter the labor market during a recession have much lower lifetime earnings than those beginning their work life in good economic times. The weaker graduates suffer particularly from the bad luck of graduating during a recession. They never make up the earnings disadvantage compared to the equally weak but luckier graduates (Oreopoulus, Heisz and von Wachter 2006; Von Wachter and Bender 2006).

Similar firms pay different wages to similar workers starting their jobs at different times. Workers with high starting wages have higher and more persistent wage losses if they are made redundant. This implies that a large part of wage differences is due to being at the right place at the right time rather than any difference in ability (Von Wachter and Bender 2008). Ironically, this has been shown to be true even for the academic economists who clung to the notion of competitive labor markets for so long (Oyer 2006).

Employers can only shield workers from market conditions if salaries and wages do not closely reflect demand and supply of labor. They need some market power to be able to absorb some or all of the ups and downs they face. There needs to be a monopolistic profit, a surplus that can be shared between employers and employees. If employers had no market power, competitive pressure for labor inputs would drive up wages in good times and force companies to cut them in bad times.

Surveys have shown that workers regard it as highly unfair if their wages are cut due to changes in demand or supply of labor. This can explain why small wage cuts are exceedingly rare, while small wage rises are very common (Fehr, Goette and Zehnder 2009). Obviously, companies do not find it worthwhile to offend their workers by making small wage cuts. They seem to only cut wages if they really need to or – more recently – if they can cut them in a big way.

The prevailing attitude of workers is different when they are looking for a job. Before employees have entered into an ongoing relationship with the employer, they accept the verdict of demand and supply. Therefore, entry-level salaries do vary significantly with the labor market conditions at the time of entry. If market conditions change, employers cut or raise the salaries of new entrants, but the salaries of those already in the firm are largely insulated from these changes in market conditions. Only the rate of increase tends to be modulated according to labor market conditions, because once workers have an ongoing relationship with the employer, they compare any changes in pay to what they perceive as the status quo, rather than to the best outside opportunity. They consider it as a breach of trust if a firm wants to cut pay simply because a larger pool of job seekers allows them to (Fehr, Goette and Zehnder 2009).

Campbell and Kamlani (1997) conducted a survey of 184 firms to investigate the reasons for downward wage rigidity. The strongest explanation, according to the answers of the managers, lies in the negative effect of wage cuts on effort and in adverse selection in talent retention. Adverse selection here means that the companies are concerned that the best employees will leave if they cut wages. Bewley (1995) summarizes the answers he received in many interviews with high-ranking personnel managers: "Workers have many opportunities to take advantage of employers so that it is not wise to depend on coercion and financial incentives alone as motivators… Employers believe that other motivators are necessary, which are best thought of as having to do with generosity." Generosity is incompatible with wages that are determined predominantly by market forces.

A field study by Kube, Maréchal and Puppe (2008) corroborates the importance of generosity. The authors employed students for a one-time task of cataloguing library books. They announced a wage of €36 for the three-hour work episode. The reference group received the advertised wage. A second group was informed upon arrival that the wage had been raised by €7 to €43. A third group did not get this pay rise but received an outdoor thermos bottle worth €7 as a present for showing up. The wage increase of 19 percent induced the subjects in the second group to enter 6 percent more data than in the baseline treatment, making the extra pay a bad deal for the employer. However, the subjects who received the present of the same value entered 30 percent more data than the reference group, making the wage cost per data entered actually decline. In a follow-up survey, respondents explained that they would consider the higher wage a payment for their effort and not much more, while they would interpret the gift as signaling kind intentions on the part of the employer. They felt that kind intentions should be reciprocated. Workers seem to appreciate having an employer who cares for their welfare and this appreciation leads to higher effort levels (Kube, Maréchal and Puppe 2008).

The high road to profit is not easy to find

The workers of Safelite Glass Corporation are the darlings of neoclassical labor market economists. These workers have done a lot to make the self-interest–centered theory look relevant to the labor market. They have reacted to monetary incentives as if they were of the species *homo economicus*, helping the company to increase profits in the process. Lazear and Shaw (2007) examined how Safelite changed its pay model from an hourly rate to piece rates, with great success. The number of windshields that the average worker replaced per day increased by almost 50 percent, whilepay increased by only 7 percent, causing a strong rise in Safelite's profits. Lazear and Shaw traced half the productivity increase to individual workers putting in more effort than before. The other half resulted from a favorable selection of workers enticed by the change. Less productive workers were the first to leave and highly productive workers took their places.

In contrast, workers of a certain large, anonymous US bank are the darlings of human resource consultants who advocate employee involvement and providing employees with fulfilling tasks if possible. The vice president of this bank, who was in charge of exceptions processing, reorganized the department. He believed that a broader reorganization could improve productivity, achieve better customer service and better jobs utilizing more skills. Managers held focus groups with clerks, asking them what aspects of their jobs were irritating and what changes would make their jobs better. The consensus was that work should no longer be divided by exception type but rather by customer account. The same representative should be able to deal with all exceptions – stop payment requests, overdrafts and so on – connected to the given account. Despite the training cost involved, the management accepted the plan. The result was a major improvement in productivity. Before the reorganization, 650 workers processed 65,000 exceptions each day. Soon after, only 530 workers were needed to complete the same workload (Autor, Murmane and Levy 2002).

Both approaches have been successful: the Safelite approach, treating workers as if they were only interested in material rewards, and the holistic approach, aiming to preserve and strengthen workers' intrinsic motivation to do a good job. A look at the conditions present in the two workplaces shows that Safelite is something of a special case. Safelite did not face the problem that many other companies have, namely that individual workers have different tasks, some of which are more easily measured than others. Replacing windshields is the dominant task and worker productivity is easy to measure. Individual workers fulfill the task by themselves. Thus the common problem of how to measure individual contributions in a team is not an issue. If there are no teams, individual incentives cannot damage team spirit. Quality control is straightforward, and a decline in the quality of work was not a serious issue. If a windshield should prove defective, the responsible worker could be identified (Lazear and Shaw 2007).

If the production process is more involved, as in the bank example above, reliance on performance-oriented pay can hurt more than it helps. Monetary incentives send a very powerful signal of what employers want and reward – and what they do not. If this signal does not correspond to the employer's real intention, the damage can be substantial. Workers might not care about making customers happy in a meaningful way, keeping stock volumes down, or keeping quality at a high level if these actions are not explicitly rewarded while other tasks are (Fehr, Goette and Zehnder 2009). In New Orleans, where police districts were explicitly rewarded for declines in incidents of serious crime, the winning district succeeded because it reclassified a larger number of serious crimes as minor offenses than competing districts did. Drivers of garbage trucks who were rewarded for finishing quickly were found overfilling their trucks, driving dangerously, neglecting the servicing of their vehicles and frequently leaving full garbage cans behind (Pfeffer and Sutton 2006).

If individual contributions are difficult to measure objectively, the losers of performance pay will rightly or wrongly consider the result unfair. They might reduce their work effort and even sabotage others as a consequence. Research has shown that the impression of unfairness is often justified. Those with the power to assess other people's contributions are rarely objective. They have self-serving biases or they might assess people strategically according to how important or friendly these people are to their own interests. One study found that performance ratings by supervisors depended more on whether or not the supervisors themselves had hired the respective worker, rather than on objective performance (Pfeffer 2007).

For all these reasons, modern personnel management theories depart from the traditional economic mainstream. They stress the high cost of control if a large proportion of workers are intrinsically predisposed to work well. This valuable intrinsic motivation can be damaged by the mistrust signaled by tight control. Furthermore, workers who identify with the goals of the firm cannot use their hands-on experience and ingenuity to solve problems "on the floor" if they have to follow strict rules. This is why modern high-performance work systems decentralize information gathering and the processing of information. They grant authority to employees to act on this information as they see fit in the interests of the firm. This strategy reduces the cost of control, but it makes the company vulnerable. It remains at the employees' discretion whether to use their leeway to benefit the company or to shirk their duties. Thus building commitment to the company goals is essential if the management wants to use such work systems (Bartling, Fehr and Schmidt 2010).

Management research and consulting firms have identified a set of high-performance management practices which have been proven to help establish a committed workforce. According to Towers Perrin (2008), a leading personnel management consultancy, the most important factors are a sincere concern on the part of the management for their employees' wellbeing, a reputation for social responsibility, sincere communication and decentralized, team-based decisions when possible.

There is a well-established relationship between the quality of personnel management and company success (Pfeffer 2007). According to Towers Perrin (2008), workforce engagement is one of the most important factors in shaping relative competitiveness. The firm refers to this relationship to explain why they focus on employee engagement in their regular Global Workforce Study, in which they poll no less than 90,000 employees worldwide.

In many cases, instituting practices that foster employee engagement does not seem to be expensive, but the reality is quite different. The majority of workplaces in the West show pervasive job dissatisfaction, distrust and disengagement. A Conference Board survey conducted in 2004 found that two-thirds of employees in the US did not feel motivated to help their employers to achieve their business goals. One-quarter said they were just showing up to collect their paycheck and nearly half said they felt disconnected from their employer. Surveys show that employee commitment has sharply declined over the past decades. In the UK, a Gallup poll found that 80 percent of workers had limited commitment to their employer's goals and a quarter were described as actively disengaged, meaning that they sabotaged at least some aspects of their employer's goals. This was also an attitude found in a fifth of US employees (Pfeffer 2007). For the companies, employing such disaffected workers means that they have given up on the profits to be gained from a more committed workforce.

The Global Workforce Study by Towers Perrin (2008) shows that in the US, despite having less than stellar results, workforce management is actually comparatively good. At 29 percent, the share of highly engaged workers is 12 percentage points higher than in Germany, for example. While in the US a quarter of the workforce is disengaged, in Germany it is a third.

Efficient markets would imply that only good labor management practices survive. Firms that employ bad practices would have to imitate the more successful ones or be weeded out over time. Why would so many people be so dissatisfied on their jobs if labor management practices were generally efficient and people could easily find an employer that suited their preferences?

One famous study published in 1994 by Jeffrey Arthur compared performance outcomes among a specific type of steel mills, so-called minimills, using different labor management practices. He found that those using high-commitment systems had higher productivity, lower scrap rates and lower employee turnover. Still, both types of management practices were performed in parallel in this one narrow industry. One reason may be that part of the benefits from higher productivity go to workers, while the capital side alone makes the decisions about management systems. After all, productivity and profits are not the same (Arthur 1994). Another reason might be that some employers simply don't understand or care about the effects of their labor management practices. Workers generally react negatively to employers who maintain tight control when there is no obvious rationale for it. If they are treated as untrustworthy, they act as if they were untrustworthy, apparently vindicating the prejudice (Bartling, Fehr and Schmidt 2010).

A related reason for the persistence of inefficient practices is the interdependence of management practices. If a disenfranchised and disaffected workforce is suddenly expected to work in teams and make their own decisions, productivity might very well suffer for a while. Therefore a management wanting to turn to the high road of employee management needs to be convinced of the value of what they are doing and aware of where they want to go. They need to be willing to work through setbacks. Figuratively speaking, they need to be willing to go down the hill and through a valley in order to climb to the top of a higher mountain (Lazear and Shaw 2007; Pfeffer 2007; Sutton 2006).

Having such a long-term view is not easy for a top management that is constantly evaluated by a very short-term oriented capital market. Financial institutions that control the capital markets have become the most powerful institutions in recent decades. This has also shifted power within companies. While CFOs have become the power brokers, the influence of unions and personnel departments has declined steeply in private industry. The latter have even been prime candidates for outsourcing, next to menial tasks like janitorial services. With these two traditional advocates of employee concerns being marginalized, there is simply nobody left to speak out against measures that cut short-term costs but hurt employee morale and long-term returns (Pfeffer 2007; Sutton 2006).

What managers and analysts regard as the right policies in managing the workforce has a lot to do with their assumptions about people and organizations. Surveys have shown that the attitudes of most managers conform to the language and assumptions of economics. They regard people as self-interested and effort-averse such that close monitoring and incentives are necessary and sufficient to bring their actions in line with company goals. This view of what drives people is not very conducive to high-commitment employment practices focusing on mutual trust, respect and fairness. As mentioned above, such assumptions have a tendency to self-justify (Pfeffer 2007; Sutton 2006).

A large-scale German study using the questionnaire of the Great Place to Work Institute found the same link. Managers who regarded employee satisfaction as most important for company success tended to implement employee-friendly policies and had a very committed workforce with very few disaffected workers. Managers who did not give much importance to employee satisfaction had a much less committed workforce and a much higher ratio of disgruntled employees. The managers of the first type were the more successful ones, as judged by company performance (Hauser, Schubert and Aicher 2005).

Rent Sharing and its Consequences

To preserve worker commitment and morale, employers are forced to pass on part of their monopolistic profits to workers. How much they pass on voluntarily depends on the size of production sites, on the personnel management strategy they pursue and on how much the production process lends itself to supervision or depends on worker initiative. A firm that has to man large production sites needs to pay more to attract workers. If worker initiative is important, workers will get a larger share of the surplus. If tasks are simple and clearly structured, tight supervision with little rent sharing might work well instead.

Workers are not necessarily satisfied with the share of profits that the company passes on to them voluntarily. They may have recourse to collective action and demand a larger share. The negotiation power of labor varies according to how much there is to distribute and how much the other side has to lose. Plant size, profits and production methods are different according to company and industry. In addition, workers are not equally well organized and equally ready to fight, which makes for varying negotiating positions.

The negotiating power of industrial workers tends to increase with the capital intensity of production. If only a few workers need to go on strike to let a great deal of expensive machinery fall idle, capital owners will be loath to risk a serious labor dispute. Satisfying the wage demands of only a few workers is not so expensive in any case. If, in contrast, production is labor-intensive, the situation is reversed. It is much more expensive to satisfy all workers' wage demands, while a strike is relatively less expensive. This difference in the negotiation position is amplified further because it influences the chances of unions organizing the workers in a company. If production is labor-intensive, unions have trouble showing tangible results and thus have difficulty convincing workers that it pays to organize. The opposite is true in capital-intensive firms. This is a prime reason that large, capital-intensive firms like automobile producers have always been the ones with the strongest unions (Bhaskar, Manning and To 2002).

The factors that influence relative negotiation power are interdependent. As long as the company can keep wages low, Taylorism (a management approach most associated with nineteenth-century factories, but still very common in any mass production setting today) is attractive. It keeps workers exchangeable, such that they do not have to be motivated by higher wages and premiums and can be easily replaced if they demand more. If unions manage to push through high wages, this can make other production systems, which make better use of worker initiative and commitment, more attractive.

Large industrial production sites tend to be the ones working with the most capital. This is an important reason that unions are strongest (if the role of the government is left out of the equation) and wages there highest. The wage cost disadvantage of large production sites helps smaller, less capital-intensive companies to keep up. They compensate what they lack in efficiency by paying lower wages. The owners of large companies, which have to pay higher wages, consider these extra wages a cost. From the viewpoint of society, however, they are not socially a cost, as one party gets what the other party pays. This difference in perspective between decision makers and society means that one can expect that there will be fewer (good) jobs in highly productive companies than there could be from a technological efficiency viewpoint (Acemoglu 2001).

Empirically, profit levels per employee explain about half of the wage differences between sectors. According to one recent study, a doubling of profits per worker on average increases workers earnings, all else equal, by between 2.2 and 3.2 percent. Outside the knowledge and creative industries, it is usually a more capital-intensive mode of production that brings about the higher profits per employee. The best-paying sectors are such capital-intensive industries as the electricity, gas, steam and hot water supply sectors, followed by the manufacture of coke, refined petroleum and nuclear fuel industries and the manufacture of chemicals and chemical products. In these sectors, workers receive wages, which are on average between two and two and a half times as high as those of comparable workers in the labor-intensive hotel and restaurant sector (Du Caju, Rycx and Tojerow 2009).

The bargaining power of workers does not only differ according to occupations or sectors. For the individual worker, personal characteristics like gender, family status and place of residence will often be more important. Rupert, Stancanelli and Wasmer (2009) have estimated the negotiation power of different groups using a large survey of French workers. They found that negotiating power is much larger for men than for women, and that the bargaining power of women with young children is close to zero. According to their calculations, workers get 42 percent of the value of a job–worker match on average. Men get 72 percent, while women get only 16 percent. Among women, married women have a still lower negotiating power at 9 percent and women with young children obtain less than 2 percent of the value of the pairing (Rupert, Stancanelli and Wasmer 2009).

While these specific numbers certainly should be taken with a grain of salt, the study does show clearly that there is some surplus over the cost of all factors that is divided up between the cooperating factors of production, with negotiating power a major factor in determining the result.

Good job, bad job or no job

Textbook theory only includes the unemployed and those who are employed at market wages. In reality, there is a continuum ranging from good jobs on the primary labor market over those employed in less attractive or (involuntary) part-time work to those in precarious employment conditions. There are jobs with attractive working conditions and high wages, and others that combine unpleasant working conditions and low wages. These combinations are the opposite of how textbook economics describe the situation. Textbooks pretend, against all experience, that normally you are compensated for less attractive working conditions with higher wages and vice versa. This is rarely the case as most of the reasons for companies to pay more than others are also reasons for offering better working conditions, or these reasons go together with better working conditions. We have also seen above that insiders in good jobs are shielded from market forces and good jobs are rationed. There is thus no mechanism that would allow workers in bad jobs to obtain a good job by asking for less money than the person who currently holds that job is paid.

The dichotomy of good jobs and bad jobs has important consequences for labor market policy. Under the pure neoclassical theory of labor, all unemployment is either voluntary, transitory or the fault of governments and unions who push wages above productivity. A critical assumption for this view is that the unemployed just have to lower their wage demands in order to get a job. This is an assumption that has been shown to be very far from the truth. You simply cannot "buy" yourself into an attractive job at a large employer by offering to do the work at two-thirds of the going wages, even if you would be just as productive as the current workers are. The main reason is not unions or government. The fundamental reason is that employers who offer the good jobs do not let you bid down wages to replace existing workers. The norm is that good jobs are scarce and rationed. If you are not lucky enough to get in, you will have to work in the secondary labor market where the bad jobs are offered, where employers do not necessarily assume high worker morale, and where tight supervision, easy firing or piece rates are the norm (Kaufman 2009).

To see how such a dual labor market works differently from the textbook norm, assume there is a decline in exports due to an excessive appreciation of the currency. Jobs in the primary labor market will be lost. Workers cannot bid their way back into the primary market by accepting lower pay because employers largely shield their existing employees from downward pressure on wages. Thus the redundant workers have to find work in the secondary market where the bad jobs are offered. But the secondary market is also suffering from the recession. This means that low-wage workers in the secondary market are supposed to cut their wages even more in order to create enough demand for their own labor and for the labor of those descending from the primary labor market. Most modern neoclassical theorists will admit that the wage cuts needed to achieve this can be steep. There is no guarantee at all that you can live on the market-clearing wage (Kaufman 2009).

In an open economy with exports, external demand might eventually solve the problem at low enough wages, but there is certainly no guarantee. With flexible exchange rates, the exchange rate often appreciates if wages and prices go down. This can cancel out the improvement in competitiveness brought about by lower wages. However, the most important problem is that low-wage workers in the non-export sector have to take the brunt of wage cuts to put the labor market back into equilibrium. For them, wages do not have to fall much before going below the minimum needed to support a family. If there is no welfare or unemployment benefits, which neoclassical economists frown upon as alleged destroyers of employment, workers cannot exit the labor market. Instead, they have to put in more of their own work or send other family members to work to make up for the shortfall of income. The increased supply of labor depresses wages even more. Thus market forces can make the disequilibrium even more pronounced. Child labor laws, which were introduced in the US during the Great Depression, were specifically intended to break this vicious downward spiral which neoclassical economics neglects (Kaufman 2009).

One might be tempted to think that this argument applies only to very poor people in underdeveloped countries. In fact research has shown that even in industrial countries people often work less, or at least not more, if their wages rise. This can explain why massive increases in real wages since the start of the Industrial Revolution have been accompanied by significant declines in annual hours per worker in industrialized countries (Keen 2001/2008).

For those not convinced by these bird's eye observations, Ashenfelter, Doran and Schaller (2010) have taken a close look at the working time decisions of a group of workers who can actually make them without being constrained by standard working hours and such. The researchers obtained data on the mileage and revenue of all New York taxi drivers from inspection records. After regulatory authority raised fare prices, drivers worked fewer hours as their hourly income increased. They could reach their desired level of income with fewer hours. This income effect turned out to be stronger than the incentive effect arising from the fact that stopping work costs them more, in terms of forgone income, at higher hourly wages (Ashenfelter, Doran and Schaller 2010).

Neoclassical economics avoids the problem of an unruly labor supply curve by assuming that workers do not have to live off their work because they either have savings or can borrow without a problem. Both assumptions are absurdly unrealistic for most low-wage workers (Kaufman 2009).

As we have seen, a laissez-faire economy does not create enough good jobs because decision makers' calculation of benefits and costs differs from society's. If there are relatively few good jobs and many bad jobs around, the unemployed have limited incentives to hold out for a good job, as the chances to find one are slim. They will therefore settle for a bad job. A dearth of good jobs also damages incentives to spend time and effort to build up the qualifications for a good job. This in turn makes it harder for those offering the good jobs to find qualified staff. This vicious circle can be turned into a virtuous circle by measures to increase the proportion of good jobs (Acemoglu 2001).

This is an example of how the neoclassical approach of thinking in unique equilibrium terms can be misleading. If a bad job equilibrium is accepted as the unalterable outcome of market forces, the system will never reach the good job equilibrium, even though the transition would have huge benefits for large parts of the population. However, neoclassical economics does not even acknowledge the distinction between a good job and a bad job. This is the reason why neoclassical economists condemn any public support for companies that offer good jobs as a subsidy that distorts the market. Such support tends to be popular even with those who do not directly benefit, a fact that economists disparagingly brush aside as proof of ignorance. The truth of the matter might well be that the public understands better than most economists that large, well-paying employers offer something that is worth preserving through adversity.

An extreme form of bad job is sweatshop work. This is an exploitative form of employment that is mostly confined to illegal immigrants in developed countries but can be rather prevalent in underdeveloped countries. Work in sweatshops means excessive overtime, wholesale disregard of safety and health conditions, low wages and lack of rights and representation. The fact that people work in them at all makes it clear that decent jobs are rationed; otherwise, nobody would choose the very bad working conditions at lower pay which prevail in sweatshops (Chau 2009).

Once in a sweatshop contract, excessive overtime, exhaustion and declining health due to bad conditions often make it hard or impossible to search for a better job. To allow for sweatshops and decent jobs to coexist on a large scale in the same economy, the efficiency advantage of companies offering decent jobs must be moderate. Otherwise sweatshops cannot compete. This is the main reason that sweatshops are essentially a feature of underdeveloped countries where inadequate infrastructure and other deficiencies limit the profitability of the more advanced form of production (Chau 2009).

Sweatshops have a tendency to beget more sweatshops, because a high share of sweatshops means the share of decent jobs in the economy is low. The lower this share gets, the more sweatshop work will seem the norm and the less promising it will seem to an unemployed worker to hold out for decent work. Luckily, it is possible for economies to get out of this vicious circle. One way out is by enhancing the profitability of decent jobs, for example by improving physical and legal infrastructure. Another is the enforcement of minimum standards for labor conditions for all workers irrespective of migrant status. A third way is to improve the social safety net and access to credit, making it possible for workers to spend a longer time searching for a decent job. This in turn helps decent employers by making it easier for them to fill their vacancies (Chau 2009).

On the other hand, costly improvements of labor standards for employers offering decent work can be counterproductive. If they lower the surplus of decent employment, they put decent employers at a disadvantage relative to sweatshop employers. Therefore it is very important for regulators or for concerned consumers to make the right comparison when deciding on whether to impose higher labor standards. Higher standards should only be forced upon the worst employers (Chau 2009). This was the case when, during the 1990s, anti-sweatshop activists in the US and other industrialized countries campaigned to improve conditions for workers in developing countries. A particular target was Nike, whose subcontractors in Indonesia gained notoriety for not respecting the national minimum wage. It took a long time for economists to evaluate the effects of this extensive and ultimately successful campaign. Harrison and Scorse (2010) did so and found that the campaigns led to large real wage increases for the workers of contractors in the targeted enterprises. Firm profits fell, investment declined somewhat and some smaller plants closed, but the researchers found no significant negative effects on employment in the affected regions (Harrison and Scorse 2010).

When a series of suicides at the Chinese factories of Foxconn, a subcontractor of Apple, created unwanted publicity for the extremely bad working conditions there, Foxconn was suddenly able to double wages within a few months (Associated Press 2012). Apple's concerns for the image of its high-priced gadgets did what workers' initiatives in the region had not achieved in years.

Divide and rule – Outsource and cut

Henry Ford built a factory in the 1920s in which the raw materials for steel went in and finished automobiles came out. This integrated method of production has become unfashionable. As Holmes and Snider (2011) point out, any automobile producer or other industrial firm in a developed country would be ridiculed today if it were to think about producing its own steel. Instead, the modern Ford Motor Company has been busy spinning off a significant portion of its parts-making operations as a separate company. General Motors has done the same.

The reason for the powerful trend toward outsourcing has its roots in the power of employers on the labor market and the countervailing power of labor, exerted mostly through unions. It is mostly a means of pushing down the share of the surplus that labor can claim. We have seen that the wages a company has to pay tend to increase with the size of the company and the capital intensity of production, because large, capital-intensive companies have a lot to lose from labor disputes. Therefore outsourcing is not mainly about increasing flexibility and making the production process more market driven. Gains reaped that way are likely to be overcompensated for by increasing administrative cost. Rather, outsourcers achieve their purpose of pushing down the wage bill by dividing up their workforces into smaller independent units and by separating capital-intensive and labor-intensive lines of production. Labor-intensive tasks like janitorial services or labor-intensive parts production are outsourced, while the final assembly line, which involves lots of expensive machinery and few workers, is operated in-house (Holmes and Snider 2011).

This separation worsens the negotiating position of the outsourced workers. In effect, outsourcing is following the ancient "divide and rule" principle. Strikes are not so costly, since not so much capital is involved. This is true at least as long as the outsourcing company manages not to become too dependent on any individual outsourced provider. On the other hand, any pay increase will drive up the cost of the outsourced company a lot, because the wage bill is a very large proportion of the cost. For this reason, management of these companies will be able, and have an increased incentive, to resist demands for higher wages. In the main company, outsourcing labor-intensive tasks improves the negotiating power of the remaining labor within that main company. As a result, the wages in the parent company rise and the wages in the outsourced company fall. The net effect will always be a fall in the wage bill, because the pay increase affects the less labor-intensive lines of production (Holmes and Snider 2011).

In the transition period, during which management can threaten workers with more outsourcing, they might even be able to push down also the wages of the remaining workers in the core company. This transition period can be quite long.

There is plenty of empirical evidence supporting this theoretical reasoning. Airlines spin off short routes to regional airlines whose pilots have less negotiating power and receive lower pay. Short routes with small planes are less capital-intensive than long-haul routes with large planes. General Motors spun off Delphi, its labor-intensive parts operations, and subsequently Delphi has tried to cut wages by two-thirds. Another spinoff, American Axle, succeeded in cutting wages by about a third (Holmes and Snider 2011).

For Germany, a study of the automobile and telecommunications industries has shown that outsourcing parts has cut the wage bill. The vertical disintegration of major German employers contributed to the disorganization of Germany's dual system of in-plant and sectoral negotiations. Subcontractors, subsidiaries and temporary agencies often have no collective bargaining institutions or are covered by different firm-level and sectoral agreements. Moving employers to these firms introduced new organizational boundaries and disrupted traditional bargaining structures to the detriment of unions (Doellgast and Greer 2007).

For the US, a different study shows that contract cleaning firms and security guards employed by a service contractor receive substantially lower wages and benefits than employees doing the same jobs employed by manufacturing firms. Higher wage firms are more likely to contract out cleaning and security services. Union density is much lower in the outsourced companies than in the companies that use the services of these contractors. All these findings fit well in a model featuring incomplete competition and a struggle for rents between capital/management and labor (Dube and Kaplan 2010).

The trend toward outsourcing is reinforcing the separation of jobs into good jobs and bad jobs. The trend implies that companies use additional resources to overcome the frictions that are inherent in outsourcing. Separate organizations have to build up. Service or supplier contracts have to be negotiated and enforced, bills have to be written and extra transport costs are incurred. These are social costs. Companies do this mostly in order to redistribute income from labor to firm owner or managers, which is not a net social gain. This means that resources are wasted for redistribution, that the pie gets smaller as a consequence of one group trying to get a larger share. (Holmes and Snider 2011). Whether this is socially bad depends on whose interests in the distribution struggle or what take of the negotiation process is favored. If unions are considered too powerful and abusive of their negotiation power in ways detrimental to society, this cost may be considered worth bearing. If you think unions are in general behaving reasonably or are weak enough not to overdo it, the large-scale outsourcing trend would be considered quite detrimental to society.

How to profit from discrimination

In perfectly competitive labor markets, discrimination by gender or race should be a very rare phenomenon. A woman or a black person with a higher productivity than a white man should beat him to a job. Otherwise the company doing the discriminating would be hurting itself. Discriminators would eventually be driven from the market by competitors who employ and pay strictly according to productivity. Based on such reasoning, Chicago economist and Nobel Memorial Prize winner Gary S. Becker instilled confidence in the profession that free markets, if left to do their work, would largely eliminate discrimination (Becker 1957/1971).

Members of minorities have many stories of how they are discriminated against in the labor market. Pager, Western and Bonikowski (2009) conducted a field experiment to check if these subjective experiences can be verified in a controlled setting. They recruited white, black and Latino job applicants as testers. They put teams together of one white, one black and one Latino applicant with very similar age, verbal skills, interactional styles and levels of physical attractiveness, gave them equivalent fake resumes and sent them to apply in tandem for hundreds of entry-level jobs. Black applicants were only half as likely to receive a callback or job offer as whites. A white applicant received 31 percent positive responses, a Latino 25 percent and a black applicant 15 percent. The experimenters had to assign a white applicant a fictitious 18-month prison term for a drug felony to get his success rate down to the same level as a black applicant with a clean record. In a number of cases, the black and Latino applicants were sent away without even being interviewed, while the white applicant was interviewed or employed on the spot (Pager, Western and Bonikowski 2009).

The Organisation for Economic Co-operation and Development (OECD) Employment Outlook found in 2008 that 20 percent fewer women than men have a job, on average. They are paid 17 percent less than their male counterparts. Similar gaps are found when comparing ethnic minorities with their majority counterparts. The OECD has estimated that if all OECD countries liberalized their product market to the level of the country with the most pro-competitive regulatory stance, the average gender employment and wage gaps would fall by a modest one to three percentage points respectively (OECD 2008). Apparently even in a liberalized economy competition among employers on the labor market is not very intense.

This result does not come as a big surprise if you have a real-world labor market in mind, instead of the idealized perfect competition world of standard economic models. In a real-world labor market where there is a surplus of workers to decent jobs, each worker has few employers to choose from, due to commuting cost, job preferences and other reasons. If Firm A is an active discriminator and Firm B is the single second-best choice of a woman or black person, the discrimination in Firm A will have an effect on wages in Firm B. Those who are discriminated against by Firm A will be in a weaker position when negotiating with Firm B, for lack of a good alternative, and will tend to accept lower wage offers. This situation is attractive for employers as a group, since they can pay lower wages to a large proportion of their workforce. Therefore no financially powerful lobby is likely to form and work in favor of change (Bhaskar, Manning and To 2002).

Policies and Institutions Revisited

In a perfectly competitive world, institutions and rules restricting the freedom of individual contracts, such as union bargaining, minimum wages, employment protection, maternity protection and minimum paid leave, must be inefficient and will often cause unemployment. The standard economic advice is based on this foundation. It recommends dismantling any such institutions and rules. The euphemistic shorthand for this type of advice is "structural reforms." As we have seen, perfect competition is only a theoretical construct. In reality, employers have market power. The question, then, is whether the essence of the standard economic prescription will stand in such a world. Often, it does not.

A little over a century ago, the neoclassical ideal of a well functioning labor market was in place. Employees had few rights other than leaving their employer if they felt they were treated unfairly. Terms and conditions of employment were only very lightly regulated in Europe and basically unregulated in the US and elsewhere. There was no child labor law in the US until 1938. For classical economists from Smith to Mill to Marx this was a problematic state, because it often led to wages too low to feed a family. Circumstances were very rough for most industrial laborers. Employers could fire any worker who suffered an injury. Famous neoclassical economists like Pigou and Marshall criticized this state of affairs, even though their theoretical work should have steered them to conclude that the workings of the free market would achieve a good result. To see millions of laborers and their families living in abject poverty while a few capitalists got very rich was an indication for them that something was wrong. Distributional concerns had not yet been banned from economic reasoning at that time (Schmitz 2004).

This is not the case anymore. The more tightly regulated European labor markets are not judged kindly by the current economic mainstream, since they are characterized by government imposed *rigidities*, like just dismissal policies, minimum wage and mandated social security contributions by employers. All these are considered distortions, which inhibit the labor market from performing as well as it would without interventions. A legally imposed minimum wage or union-negotiated wages are clearly bad in this view, because uninhibited markets work perfectly according to neoclassical assumptions. Workers are paid what their labor is worth to the employer. Employers pay for an extra hour what they net from selling the products that can be produced with that extra hour of labor. If the wage is artificially raised, the cost of an extra hour of work is pushed above its marginal product. Some workers, whose wage is pushed up in this way, will be made redundant and become unemployed.

The argument is also used the other way around. If there is involuntary unemployment, it is proof that wages are too high. If they were lowered, people would offer less work and employers would demand more. The main victims of wages that are artificially set too high are considered to be workers with relatively low productivity, like inexperienced young people, the unskilled and certain disadvantaged groups. Thus mainstream economists like to denounce the minimum wage or union-negotiated wages as antisocial.

Similarly, employment mandates like minimum notice of termination, mandatory health insurance and minimum vacation are generally suspicious to mainstream economists and also denounced as rigidities. It is argued that if these benefits were worth as much or more to the employee than what they cost the employer, competition for workers would make sure that these side benefits are provided. The dominance that this view of economics has achieved in the second half of the twentieth century resulted in worldwide moves to deregulate the labor market.

This consensus is summarized in the OECD's 1994 jobs study, which recommended that countries deregulate labor markets to increase flexibility in working time, make wages and labor costs more responsive to market pressures and weaken employment security provisions and unemployment benefit systems (OECD 1994).

This consensus among economists has been crumbling in the last two decades, but the mainstream advice lingers on. To this day, policy makers in Europe, from the European Central Bank to many government officials and most EU bodies, recommend "structural reforms."

Unions are doing more than destroying jobs

It is increasingly recognized that economic information is far from being as perfect as the competitive model assumes. As we have already seen, information on what the exact tasks of an employee are going to be is too limited to set up contracts that specify everything important. The two parties agree to enter into a relationship in which the employer gives orders and the employee acts on these orders. Job seekers would be deterred by the prospect of an unlimited right on the part of their future superiors to give them commands. Thus both parties have an interest in keeping the extent of this right in the range of what is reasonably needed to achieve an efficient production process. Specifying all facets of possible commands that are allowed or not allowed would be too cumbersome. Legally imposed general rules and minimum standards can significantly reduce the cost of contracting. Up to a point, such rules are in the interest of all honest employers and employees alike (Kaufman 2009).

Beyond that, there are very important asymmetries of information at work. This is why "Legal Restrictions on Private Contracts Can Enhance Efficiency," as Aghion and Hermalin (1990) have shown in their aptly and provocatively named paper. The gut feeling of most economists is that if the restrictions are not binding they are useless, and if they are binding they prevent parties from entering into mutually beneficial contracts. However, such negative judgment presumes that both parties can honestly express their preferences in individual negotiations. This is not necessarily true if information is asymmetric. If one party has important information that the other does not have, the ignorant party will try to infer the information from the terms that the informed party prefers in the negotiations. The informed party knows this and might not reveal their preferences. This distorts the outcome of the negotiation (Aghion and Hermalin 1990).

The job seekers know much better than the employer what type of worker they are and thus what quality of labor they offer. Are they diligent or careless, hard workers or shirkers? The employer will try to figure this out during the contract negotiations. Smart job seekers will consider this. They will refrain from asking for extensive restrictions on what their supervisor can tell them to do lest the employer take such a demand as a sign that they are insubordinate or lacking in trust. They would also not be well advised to state their true preferences as to weekly or annual working hours, if this amount is not above average. Doing so would expose them to unflattering judgments about their eagerness to work hard. In contrast, stating an (untrue) preference for working long hours with little leave time to make more money will create a favorable impression and increase the chances of landing the job. If applicants ask for a more generous health plan, employers might become suspicious that their health is less than perfect or that they have an unhealthy lifestyle. Asking for generous maternity leave likewise gives the employer a bad impression of the worker. If, on the other hand, applicants try to negotiate more pay, they will not suffer any of these negative judgments and may even be seen as even more desirable by the prospective employer. All this implies that smart job seekers with limited job opportunities will routinely refrain from revealing their true preferences in individual contract negotiations. If this is the case, free contracting cannot make sure that the preferences of both sides are reflected in the outcome of the negotiation.

From the perspective of the employer, the same mechanism manifests itself as a problem of adverse selection. Employers who offer a more generous health plan face the possibility that people with poor health will be particularly attracted to the positions they offer. Employers who offer less generous plans but better pay will attract only the healthy. Employers who insist on a long work week in exchange for high pay can count on predominantly attracting people with a very high work ethic. Even if the work week is longer than most of the employees or even the employer would ideally like it to be, this can be profitable for the employer (Kaufman 2009).

There are two major ways of solving the problem. One is for governments to level differences. If they mandate minimum standards for issues sensitive to adverse selection or signaling problems, they can prevent a race towards the bottom (Kaufman 2009). Alternatively, unions can negotiate such issues for large groups of workers. A union, which negotiates minimum leave times, can truthfully represent their constituencies' average preferences. If the union negotiates with individual employers, this can take care of the signaling problem. If they negotiate with an employer organization over standards for the whole industry, this will also take care of the adverse selection problem for companies who are willing to satisfy union demands. The downside of collective negotiations is, of course, that individual preference differences around the average cannot be taken into account.

Failure to deal adequately with the issue of asymmetric information might well explain why Americans have so much less vacation time and longer workweeks than Europeans. The US labor market is much closer to the neoclassical ideal of free contract. In most of Europe there are long minimum vacation times and extensive restrictions on the length of the workweek imposed by governments or unions. There are no indications that voters or union members are dissatisfied with this state of affairs. The relatively unrestrained freedom of contract that Americans enjoy might not be a blessing after all. It might work against their best interests.

As an aside, there is another type of signaling issue with vacation time and working hours. Many people's concern over income is driven in large part by their desire to consume for the sake of the status that conspicuous consumption confers, as much as for the sake of the consumption itself. In a famous laboratory experiment, people were asked if they would rather earn $100,000 when everyone else made $200,000 or $50,000 when everyone else made $25,000, with prices assumed to be the same in both situations. A majority chose the second situation, in which they would have only half the consumption level, but would be at the top of the consumption hierarchy (Solnik and Hemenway 1998). Visible income and consumption are strong positional goods. For vacation time it is different. Vacation time is mostly valued in itself, without too much regard for how much of it others have. Therefore there is an inefficient rat race under free contracting in which workers trade off more income for less vacation time in order to keep up with the Joneses. It works for the individual, but if all workers do it, everyone ends up with too little vacation time and no status gained in exchange. A mandatory minimum vacation ends this rat race and makes most workers better off (Layard 2006).

Minimum facts about minimum wages

In places and occupations where wages are low because low-grade workpeople are being "exploited" by employers, paid less than they are worth, there is no reason to expect that the forcing of the wage rate up to a fair level will cause a [loss of jobs] for it will not pay employers to dispense with their services.

—*A. C. Pigou, 1920*

The verdict of textbook economics on minimum wages has traditionally been quite clear: they destroy jobs. Workers on a low wage are of correspondingly low ability and productivity runs the argument. If the government comes in and mandates that they cannot be employed for as low a wage as they ought to get, they will not be employed at all, and that is that. Of course, this verdict is built on the assumption of a perfectly competitive labor market with full information, in which workers get paid according to the marginal product of their labor. There is no surplus that employers could share with workers. If they have to pay more, it is not worth it for them anymore.

In the early decades of the neoclassical era, the attitude of economists was quite different. A survey of the professional journals from 1912 to 1923 by Prasch (1999) yielded a consensus in support of minimum wages among American economists. This consensus included famous early neoclassicals like John Bates Clark. Neoclassical pioneer Alfred Marshall wrote that, "if a minimum wage could be made effective, its benefits would be so great that it might be gladly accepted" and his equally famous colleague A. C. Pigou showed a significant amount of skepticism toward the power of competition when he wrote the lines quoted above. Several British economists were fiercely opposed, but the only prominent American economist to categorically rejecting minimum wage legislation was Laurence Laughlin from the University of Chicago (Prasch 1999).

Until early in the twentieth century, economists took it as a given that there was unequal bargaining power between employers and individual workers. The axiom of perfect competition had not completely done away with reality yet. Employers who paid wages below the threshold of what could be considered living wages were regarded as placing a burden on society, since those earning nonliving wages would need to make up the shortfall somehow, be it from theft, charity or other family members. There was also less trust in the notion that all employers would be working at the point of maximum efficiency. Economists considered it desirable to make managers compete on an equal footing with a floor under wages, rather than using the loophole of squeezing workers wages to compensate for inefficient practices. A legislated minimum wage was also believed to promote social peace and preserve the free market in the face of socialist temptations. The early twentieth century was marked by frequent and often violent labor disputes (Prasch 1999).

The axiomatic change starting in the mid-1930s eliminated the support for minimum wages among economists. It would take six decades until the 1990s for a significant number of recognized economists to switch sides on this issue again. Behind the switchback is the relaxation of the assumption of a perfectly competitive labor market under the weight of accumulating counterevidence. Employers who are not taking the wage rate as given but have some market power restrict employment. They do this because they don't want to bid up the wages of their existing employees. If a minimum wage is imposed that is moderately higher than the going wage in these firms, one of the reasons for restricting hiring disappears. As employers have to pay more to their existing workforce anyway, they might as well employ the extra people they can attract at these higher wages (Card and Krueger 1995).

To illustrate this point, imagine there is a town with one bakery, employing ten people. If the operators were to raise capacity and hire two more employees they might not find enough personnel at the current wage of $5. They might have to pay $5.20 to the new employees as well as to the existing employees. Even if each new hire would bring in net revenue before wage costs of $6 per hour, this would not be worth it for the employer. The wage bill for the ten existing employees increases by $2 (ten times $0.20) as a consequence of the expansion, plus the two new employees cost a further $10.40. All in all, wage costs therefore increase by $12.40, which is more than the $12 gained in extra revenue. A minimum wage of $5.50 would make this consideration irrelevant. The owners would employ more people as long as they can get them for a wage of $5.50.

There is another positive effect to top this off. A firm that pays better is likely to have a more satisfied, more committed, more productive workforce and better worker retention. Thus the increase in labor costs per unit is likely to be smaller than the increase in wages (Kaufman 2009).

Obviously, the countervailing effect is also there. It can be less profitable to start a business that is affected by a binding minimum wage. Therefore it is possible that fewer new businesses are founded or that some existing ones go out of business. Thus minimum wages have two influences on employment which lead in opposite directions. Which one prevails is an empirical question. Plenty of empirical evidence has accumulated in the UK, where a minimum wage of £3.60 an hour was introduced in 1999. It was raised in several steps to £5.93 an hour (US$9) by April 2011. Roughly a tenth of the British workforce works for the minimum wage (Metcalf 2008).

There is probably no labor regulation that has been more thoroughly examined for its effect than the British minimum wage. David Metcalf (2008), a long-term member of the politically independent British Low Pay Commission, which was set up to help determine the appropriate level of the minimum wage, has surveyed the empirical evidence on its employment impact. All available empirical techniques have been thrown at the problem in the UK, with largely consistent results.

Between March 1999, just prior to the introduction of the minimum wage, and March 2006, total employment in eight low-wage sectors rose from 6.3 million to 6.7 million and their share of total employment remained virtually unchanged (Metcalf 2008). At the time when the minimum wage was introduced there was none for 16–17-year-olds, but 18–21-year-olds were covered. Still, the employment share of 16–17-year-olds fell, while that of 18–21-year-olds increased. A thorough study of individual employment probabilities found that the introduction of the minimum wage had no statistically significant impact on the probability of remaining in employment for all four demographic groups (male, female, adults and youths) (Metcalf 2008).

Several empirical studies used the fact that wages in poor, low-wage areas were more affected by the minimum wage than wages in higher-wage areas. A comparison of regional change in employment and the fraction of workers initially below the minimum wage revealed no negative effect of minimum wages on employment. Neither did a comparison of employment changes between poor and rich areas. A comparison of individuals who work in high-impact areas compared with low impact areas also revealed no significant impact on employment probability, even if the sample was restricted to those most at risk – women, unskilled workers, those in their job for fewer than 12 months or in low-paying industries. Net creation of establishments and aggregate employment increased in all low-wage sectors except textiles. In poorer areas, where the minimum wage bit harder, the net growth in establishments or in employment was only modestly below that in areas where it was softer (Metcalf 2008).

A representative sample of some 2,000 British workplaces determined in 1998 the percentage of employees in the workplace who were paid less than £3.50 an hour a year before a minimum wage of £3.60 was imposed. There was a follow-up survey in 2004. Workplaces with a quarter or more of the workforce earning below £3.50 an hour in 1998 had a closure rate (21 percent) that was virtually identical to that of the complete sample of firms, even though profit margins fell by 8 percentage points to 11 percent in firms affected by the minimum wage (Metcalf 2008).

Thus all the empirical studies on the British national minimum wage consistently suggest that the positive and negative employment effects have roughly canceled each other out, with no net negative effect on employment (or a very slight one). The significant improvement of the living conditions of the lowest paid came at little or no cost in terms of employment (Metcalf 2008).

The absence of the feared negative employment effects led to a marked shift in political attitudes in the UK. In 1991, Conservative employment secretary Michael Howard had declared that a minimum wage would cost up to two million jobs. By 2005, even the Conservative shadow chancellor Oliver Letwin announced that a Conservative government would implement the latest recommended increase in the minimum wage by the independent Low Pay Commission. There was by then an almost complete political consensus in favor of ambitious minimum wages, which was part of a larger program called welfare to work. This program included income subsidies to low-wage workers as part of performance-related targeted welfare (having any paying job, attending skill training, or relocating from the worker's birth city counts as performing). Part of the role of minimum wages was to make sure that employers do not take advantage of these subsidies by cutting wages (Metcalf 2008).

For the US, the famous fast-food industry studies by Card and Krueger (1995) even found slightly positive effects of minimum wages on employment. They investigated employment trends in the fast-food industry in New Jersey and neighboring Pennsylvania, after New Jersey raised the minimum wage by almost 20 percent to US$5.05. Despite the higher wages, employment in fast-food restaurants grew more strongly in the following years in New Jersey than in Pennsylvania, where the minimum wage remained at US$4.25. The consumer paid at least part of the bill. In comparison to Pennsylvania, fast-food prices rose in New Jersey. Five years into publication, a comprehensive critique by Neumark and Waescher (2000) was published, which challenged these results. However, Card and Krueger had the last word. In an extensive reply, they reproduced their earlier findings with an improved set of data (Card and Krueger 2000).

Dube, Lester and Reich (2010) took the methodology of Card and Krueger to the national level. They compared the employment performance and wage developments in the low-paying industries of all neighboring counties located in two different states, only one of which saw changes in the state minimum wage. They found no evidence for employment loss, but strong evidence of an improved income situation for low-skilled workers in these industries.

Neumark and Wascher (2007) did a number of studies in which they found a negative impact for young workers in France in particular. Young workers tend to be less productive. This makes it likely that for relatively large numbers of them a minimum wage which might be moderate for experienced workers is far above what is justified by their own productivity level. Many countries with minimum wage rules, including the UK, take this into account by exemptions or separate rules for young workers. As the French minimum wage is among the most ambitious in the world and has only small discounts for teenage workers, it is quite plausible that it might lead to a significant deterioration of the employment opportunities for this group.

The upshot, though disputed by Neumark and Wascher (2007), of the existing empirical research is that minimum wages moderately above the lowest market wages raises the income of low earners without significant employment loss (Metcalf 2008). The evidence suggests that improvements of efficiency absorb part of the higher wage cost. Of the remaining cost, a part is borne by consumers in the form of higher prices. Another part is borne by employers in the form of lower profits. However profits apparently were still high enough, as evidenced by exit rates that are little affected by the minimum wage (Draca, Machin and Van Reenen 2011).

These conclusions are not easy to accept for employer-friendly economists. They try to ignore the new evidence as best they can. One example is the Council of Economic Advisors to the German government Sachverständigenrat zur Begutachtung der gesamtwirtschaftlichen Entwicklung. In their 2004 report, they concluded, "The fear that a legally-promulgated minimum wage will have a detrimental impact on employment is amply supported by economic theory as well as empirical studies. Minimum wages should therefore be rejected as an ineffective, even counterproductive instrument" (Sachverständigenrat 2004). Following a newspaper report by the Häring and Storbeck (2006) which alleged that the Advisory Council had seriously misrepresented the state of research, the council addressed the issue again in 2006 (Sachverständigenrat 2006). Now the conclusion was that "for the United States, no unequivocal effects on employment can be found." The extensive evidence from the UK again was not mentioned. Instead, the council insisted that the US evidence did not apply to Germany because the US labor market is more flexible and income tax there is lower. They failed to explain why a more flexible labor market and lower taxes implied that a minimum wage would do less damage.

So far, we have only looked at the direct effects of minimum wages on the affected industries and companies. The indirect, longer-term effects on the economy could be even more important. A floor under wages can change the relationship of good jobs and bad jobs. As we have seen, too few highly paid good jobs are created in a laissez-faire economy. A reasonably ambitious minimum wage can help take an economy out of a bad jobs equilibrium. Thus even if minimum wages were to reduce the creation of firms offering low-wage jobs, this would not necessarily be a bad thing. It helps shift employment away from bad jobs and into good jobs. In such a dynamic framework, even an increase in unemployment is no proof that minimum wages are hurting more than they help (Acemoglu 2001).

One thing is clear, though: since a minimum wage makes sure that more of the surplus from the cooperation of labor and capital goes to the workers, most employers and their allies will oppose a (high) minimum wage.

Money for nothing – Unemployment insurance

When Karl Marx, Adam Smith or Arthur Pigou complained that employers exploited workers who were desperate for every penny, there were no unemployment benefits and only the most rudimentary social security. In many underdeveloped countries, this is still a sad reality. In modern industrial countries, however, most of the unemployed get unemployment benefits or reasonably generous welfare payments. These do not only have a charitable function. Rather, they are critical for determining the negotiating power of workers in general. Better social security improves workers' negotiating position and increases the share of the corporate surplus that they can get. Employers have to offer minimally qualified workers more than what they would make without working. This sets a lower limit for wages. Those who want better qualified workers have to offer more. Thus for the low-wage sector it is not the market, but the generosity of social assistance, which determines the level of wages.

Unemployment benefits allow the unemployed to hold out longer for better jobs rather than taking the first available (bad) job that is offered. They can afford to look longer for a job that makes full use of their qualifications. This is a very different perspective on unemployment benefits from the one which produces the traditional negative economic verdict. Labor market researchers have known for years that more generous unemployment benefits increase the length of unemployment spells. The more generous transfer payments are, the longer people will be out of a job. Studies in the US have found that when unemployment compensation rises by 10 percent, the duration of unemployment goes up by 4–8 percent (Chetty 2008). Mainstream economists usually call this a costly distortion. They assume that the unemployed enjoy getting money for not working and prefer it to an honest wage. This is why they stay unemployed for longer. Of course, this is true in some cases. Everybody knows or has heard of people collecting unemployment benefits while not really looking for work.

However, the fact that unemployment spells are longer if unemployment benefits are higher does not necessarily prove that.

Helping people to take the time to find a job that makes good use of their capabilities is beneficial to society. It is inefficient for society to force unemployed skilled workers without financial reserves to take a job flipping hamburgers or driving a taxicab rather than looking for a more suitable job. Their know-how is easily lost, along with the tax and social security contributions that a better paying job would entail (Chetty 2008).

To find out if unemployment benefits are used for their intended purpose or abused, Chetty (2008) compared the search times of those with money in the bank to the search times of those without financial reserves. He found that only those with limited assets take more time to find a new job when unemployment benefits are raised. Financially more secure households, those who could afford to search long enough even without benefits, do not extend their search times if benefits become more generous.

Pink slip economics revisited

In most continental European countries, permanent employment relationships are the norm and job security legislation protects these jobs. It restricts the firing of workers to cases of wrongdoing, firm reorganization or downsizing. Individual workers usually cannot be fired at will without good cause (Schmitz 2004). In the Anglo-Saxon countries and especially the US, workers can be fired much more easily and cheaply. The US has a long-standing legal presumption that workers and employers may freely terminate their employment relationships at will, without notification, financial penalty or requirement to demonstrate just cause (Autor, Donohue and Schwab 2006), with the only major exception at the federal level being the prohibition against firing reservists for having been called up for service.

Most US state courts have adopted exceptions to the employment at will doctrine that limit an employers' ability to fire. The most important is the implied contract exception. This protection comes into force when an employer implicitly promises not to terminate workers without good cause. Another one, the public policy exception, prohibits firing employees because they are performing jury duty, or because they have been filing a worker's compensation claim, reported an employer's wrongdoing, or refused to commit perjury. Three states – Florida, Georgia and Rhode Island – have never altered the employment at will doctrine. Surveys have shown that workers in the US vastly overestimate their degree of legal protection against arbitrary dismissal (Autor, Donohue and Schwab 2006).

Several studies have analyzed the effects of employment at will exceptions on labor market outcomes. Most found either modest negative effects or no effects on employment levels (Autor, Donohue and Schwab 2006). Studies for other countries came to similar conclusions (Schmitz 2004; Autor, Donohue and Schwab 2006).

Theoretically, it is not too surprising that employment protection has only modest effects on employment, as there are countervailing effects at work. It might make employers more reluctant to employ workers, thus raising unemployment and/or depressing wages. On the other hand, unemployment protection prevents firings, thus reducing unemployment and/or raising wages. As firings are decided only by the employer, while they also affect the surplus of the worker, many of the firings that are prevented would be inefficient from a social perspective. For instance, if the employer hires the worker and shares the surplus, something unforeseen may happen which cuts the surplus from the employment relationship in half. If renegotiation does not work for practical or legal reasons, then the employer does not benefit from the relationship anymore, while the employee does. If the employer fires the worker, an employment relationship with positive value is ended. Thus the decision of the employer does not maximize total surplus. A restriction curtailing such inefficient firings raises the total surplus. Only if and to the extent that it prohibits firings where the employer gains more in surplus than the workers lose would employment protection be inefficient (Schmitz 2004). Even in the US with its flexible labor market, the losses to workers from losing their jobs are very large on average. According to an examination of "Displaced Workers Supplements" from 1984–2004 by Farber (2005), more than one-third of displaced workers are not employed two years later. A further 13 percent of those who lost a full-time job were subsequently holding part-time jobs. Even if they found a new full-time job, they suffered an income loss of 17 percent.

An economist's knee-jerk reaction against accepting this as an argument for employment protection would be that workers could ask to have job security written into their labor contracts without government interference. This should happen, according to mainstream theory, if employees valued additional job security more than employers desired to avoid additional costs (Schmitz 2004). However, employers who offer a high degree of employment protection will find that this offer is particularly attractive to workers who – unbeknownst to them – are lazy, insubordinate or not very productive. Such workers might know they have the highest chance of being fired and thus would most easily make sacrifices in terms of pay to get job security. Workers who would try to negotiate better protection would run the risk of being suspected of being less productive and therefore not being employed. The effect is that all employers offer too little protection – as judged by the preferences of workers – in order to try to skim the milk (Levine 1991).

The downside of job protection laws is that employers take into account how easy or hard it is to terminate employment when they decide how many workers they want to employ. If it is very hard, they are afraid of getting stuck in a relationship with negative value for them. Thus employers might not commence some employment relationships that would create value.

One of the best known examples of this phenomenon is in Spain, which since the early 1980s has operated a two-tier employment system. The first tier gives indefinite employment rights, but costs the employer six and a half weeks of salary per year employed if an employee is fired. The second tier can only be employed for a certain maximum period (no more than two years) before they *have* to be fired, but the employee can be fired at any time for no cost since the reforms of 1994. This system incentivizes the worst of both worlds: the first tier is full of "baby boomer" workers nearing retirement who can refuse to be retrained or transferred into new roles, some of whom are so unproductive that they are assigned worthless tasks just to keep them busy. Meanwhile, the second tier is almost entirely the purview of the steadily aging, highly educated and highly skilled children of those workers, few of whom can legally retain a job for more than two years no matter how hard they work or how good they are at their jobs. Between 1987 and 1998, the average age at which workers made it into the first tier rose by 0.42 years per year (Rica and Iza 2006). As a result, the 2007–2008 recession had a particularly devastating impact on the young: in 2011, some 46.2 percent of those under the age of 25 were unemployed, as were a full 19 percent of graduates under the age of 30 with nearly half of employed graduates working menial jobs. Rica and Iza (2006) note that men without first tier jobs are at a significant disadvantage in retaining women long term, and by 2011 the average age of becoming a father in a second tier job was trending towards 40 years old.

Such are the consequences and social devastation of badly designed employment protection. Spain stands in sharp contrast in this regard to Germany, despite a similar employment protection design and a similar level of firing costs. The differences in protection seem minor, but their effect is considerable: though costly, first tier workers are more easily fired in Germany, and employers can therefore more easily give incentives to workers to retrain in new skills in Germany. If they are not up to the task, they can be dismissed. Second tier workers can't be fired without cost as in Spain, and after six months of employment they gain a set of employment rights even though they usually must still be fired or made permanent after a maximum of two years.

The relative success of Germany indicates that there may also be some value to high firing costs for employers. If employees do not have to be on the lookout for new jobs all the time, they will be more committed to and concentrated on their current work. If they expect to have their job for a long time, they will be more willing and able to identify with the employer's goals and more inclined to acquire skills that are valuable for the current employer, even if they are not easily transferred to a new employer. This is why many employers in the US have implicitly promised their employees to restrict firings to cases where there is a good cause, even when they were not legally required to do so (Schmitz 2004). The implied contract doctrine derived by US courts requires companies to make good on such promises, which they have given in order to secure their workers' loyalty.

In short, well-designed employment protection prevents inefficient firings, but also prevents efficient firings and might reduce job creation. Which effects prevail overall depends on the circumstances and the details of the rules. It is not necessarily the case that high firing costs automatically means lower job creation as is so often assumed in the US discourse. Rather, it has more to do with the specifics of how the rules are written as we saw in the Spanish and German cases.

So far, this has been an exposition of the narrowly economic arguments for and against job protection laws. However, these arguments are not necessarily the most important ones. The value of job security to workers is obvious to most non-economists, but most of the components of this value do not fit into the economic textbook model. People and their families who have to frequently move to find new jobs cannot build stable relationships like those who are in a long-term employment relationships in one place. As has been amply shown by psychological and sociological research, and by the recently popular happiness research in economics, a network of close interpersonal relations is among the most important determinants of a good and satisfying life (Layard 2006).

Economists often disregard these large and obvious values because they do not fit into the consumption-maximizing framework and because they can be hard to quantify (Schmitz 2004).

A recent study by Alesina et al. (2010) attempts to include such considerations. It explains voters' support for growth-reducing employment protection legislation with their unwillingness to be exposed to excessive demands on their mobility, which would hurt their social ties. The researchers examined the relationship between the strength of people's family ties and their attitudes toward labor market regulation. If workers are not mobile, firms with regional labor market power can take advantage of their immobility and push down their wages. Thus, the authors argue, individuals with strong family ties should prefer regulated labor markets to avoid the need to move and to limit the market power of firms. Answers from the "World Values Survey" indeed show that countries with strong family ties implement more stringent labor market regulations. They also show that, within countries, individuals with strong family ties are more likely to believe that job security is a critical feature of a job and would like government regulation to ensure it (Alesina et al. 2010).

In summary, employment protection is not only and not predominantly a question of efficiency but a question of whose interests are to be served, labor's or employers', and who can obtain government and public support to push their interests.

Conclusion

Empirical studies on the impact of labor market institutions on economic outcomes have found only one robust truth: The income situation of most workers is improved by the presence of labor market institutions and protective rules. The more deregulated the labor market, the more concentrated income is. In contrast, efforts to prove empirically the detrimental effect of labor market institutions on outcomes like growth and unemployment have not yielded strong conclusions. This led the OECD, in its 2004 employment outlook, to downgrade their own assessment of negative effects of high minimum wages to a "plausibility" and to admit that the evidence is fragile. By 2007 the attitude of the organization had changed even further. According to the OECD's new assessment, empirical evidence does not support the claim that only countries that emphasize market-oriented policies, characterized by limited welfare benefits and light regulation, can have low unemployment with strong labor productivity growth. The OECD stressed that the labor market institutions of various low-unemployment countries in Europe differed a great deal. This implies that there is no unambiguous right or wrong with regard to achieving a low rate of unemployment. Stringent employment protection for regular contracts is now considered to have only a small negative impact on long-run productivity, while higher minimum wages and a more generous level and duration of unemployment policies have a positive impact (OECD 2007).

Why then did such a strong consensus among economists develop in the first place? The answer is likely found in the distributional consequences of the policies advanced. Unlike the consequences for growth and employment, these are pretty clear. They are without fail in favor of the wealthy and high-income earners and to the detriment of labor (Freeman 2007).

The alternative view of the labor market sketched out here should not be read as an apology of ever greater regulation of the labor market. It just explains the rationale for some degree of regulation of the labor market and for many of the institutions that have developed in real life. If there is no social safety net and no unemployment insurance at all, even companies who normally benefit from low wages can be badly damaged. The economy might go into a tailspin of declining wages and declining demand, as it did in the Great Depression. On the other hand, if you make labor regulation too stringent and minimum wages excessively high, the counterarguments of textbook economics will increasingly become relevant and come to hurt even those groups who are the main beneficiaries of such measures applied in moderation (Kaufman 2009).

The same is true with job security. If it is exceedingly difficult to fire nonperforming workers, this can be an obvious drag on productivity. It improves the negotiating position of labor tremendously, but much of labor's gains may be eaten up by inefficiencies. A moderate amount of job insecurity spurs even people who are not intrinsically motivated to put in reasonable effort and to be reasonably flexible. If job insecurity is very high, on the other hand, workers might put in a lot of effort and be very flexible to retain their jobs, but they will have little incentive to invest in skills that are predominantly useful for the current employer and they will show little commitment to their employers' goals. Firms' bargaining power is much higher under this arrangement, but again, their gain might be eaten up by inefficiencies.

In between the extremes, it is not a fight of economic reason against irrational activism that determines where the balance is set. It is a competition between the interests of workers, management and capital owners over who gets how big a slice of the pie. This competition plays out in the political arena where the rules are set as much as at the workplace. The results, however, can be seen in the market. Crushing the negotiating power of workers by weakening unions and employment protection or lowering unemployment benefits will lead to lower wages and higher profits. This in turn will allow management to pay themselves higher salaries and bonuses and get away with worse management practices without dissatisfying shareholder demands. This will lead to higher differences in pay, which have been shown to damage workers' morale and thus their productivity. The outsized bonuses of top management that created such outrage after the subprime crisis are clearly not unrelated to decades of pushback against the negotiating power of non-managerial employees.

However, in the political arena and in economists' discourse, the arguments in favor of and against certain labor market institutions are rarely ever framed around group interests. All sides pretend that they are talking about what is best for the country on economic grounds, as if economic theory could be an objective arbiter in such a fight. Instead, as Kaufman (2009) has pointed out, whose interests are to be served and what kind of world we want to live in will determine the choice of rules and institutions. No appeal to efficiency can reveal a value-free and determinate outcome. Efficiency cannot be calculated until whose preferences or interests are being maximized is decided.

Chapter 6

THE POWER TO SET
THE RULES OF THE GAME

A democracy is nothing more than mob rule, where fifty-one percent
of the people may take away the rights of the other forty-nine.
—*Thomas Jefferson*

If liberty and equality, as is thought by some are chiefly to be found
in democracy, they will be best attained when all persons alike share
in the government to the utmost.

—*Aristotle*

When the victorious French revolutionaries unseated the monarchy and
introduced democracy, they were careful not to go overboard. Only
men aged more than 25 who owned a certain minimum wealth were
allowed to vote. The founding fathers imposed similar restrictions in the
US. They restricted voting rights to property owners. In the UK, only
one in seven adult males was allowed to vote in the years after 1832.
In 1884, 40 percent of male adults were still disenfranchised. In Prussia,
a three-class franchise system (*Dreiklassenwahlrecht*) was introduced after
the revolution of 1848 for the election of the Lower House of the
Prussian state parliament. It was completely abolished only after the
revolution of 1918. Those paying a third of all taxes were allowed to
select a third of electors, those paying the next third selected another
third of electors with their vote and those paying the last third chose
the final third of electors. According to Anderson (1981), in 1849 the
first class constituted 4.7 percent of the population, the second class
12.7 percent and the third class 82.6 percent. Thus the vote of the
wealthy citizen had 17 times the weight of the vote of the average
citizen. A three-class franchise system was also used for local elections in
parts of Prussia. One result was that industrialist Alfred Krupp was the
only person to vote for the electors in the first class in the city of Essen.

These examples show that economic and political elites can be (and usually are) tightly connected and overlapping. Sometimes they are even the same. Thus one cannot talk about the regulation and limitation of economic power without taking into account what motivates the political elite and how the two spheres influence each other.

History Never Ends

The interplay of economic and political power is complex and cannot possibly be understood within the ahistorical equilibrium analysis of mainstream economics. History teaches that the same event or innovation can have very different consequences, depending on the specific social, economic and political system of a specific time and place. Daron Acemoglu and Simon Johnson from MIT and James Robinson from Harvard are foremost among a new breed of economists who have rediscovered history, power and elites. In a series of influential articles, they have demonstrated that a lot depends on who had the power to set the rules of the economic game at important crossroads in history. Their approach can explain why economies developed along very different paths, even when they started with comparable economic conditions and opportunities.

Take the rise of Europe from the sixteenth to the nineteenth century. This was the time when some countries in Europe, all of them Atlantic traders, left the rest of the world far behind in terms of economic development because they made great riches from colonialism and the slave trade. However, not all Atlantic traders achieved lasting development. Portugal and Spain were governed by absolutist monarchies, while in the UK and the Netherlands there were already significant checks on royal powers. These countries took very different paths. In the UK and the Netherlands, Atlantic trade produced a large class of rich and influential traders. These traders put their money and influence behind efforts to restrict the power of the Crown even further. In the UK, they financed the Parliamentary coalition's victorious civil war against King Charles I and helped to push through the Bill of Rights in the Glorious Revolution of 1688/89. This bill, and the further weakening of the Crown, protected their wealth against expropriation through taxes or coercion. In the Netherlands, the money of those who had obtained riches in the Atlantic trade financed the military revolt against the Habsburg monarchy, an unwelcome government that used to tax the country quite heavily and at times unpredictably (Acemoglu, Johnson and Robinson 2005).

Conversely, in Spain and Portugal the absolute power of the Crown put them in control of the exploitation of the Latin American colonies, making them richer and even more powerful in the process. The Crown used this money and power to make sure that nothing changed and everybody depended on its favor. Thus while in the UK and the Netherlands Atlantic trade helped the emergence of the institutions of free market economies, in Spain and Portugal it hindered the emergence of such institutions as property rights and free trade. In Spain and Portugal, the riches from the colonies financed only a short-lived boom and expensive wars of overarching monarchs, but did not set the basis for sustainable development (Acemoglu, Johnson and Robinson 2005).

These historical experiences influenced the classical economists. Quite rightly, they emphasized the importance of an open economic system for economic development. A rigid system preserving the privileges of a closed (noble) elite is an extremely unfavorable starting point for economic development. A market economy in which people can rise up if they offer something that other people want is much more promising for development. This is why the classical economists focused on the establishment of ownership rights and on pushing back the influence of a defensive political and clerical elite on the economic system (Acemoglu et al. 2009).

During pre-democratic times, those who were economically successful had to be afraid mostly of the government, as the government could take away their wealth through heavy taxes or in some other way, such as confiscation or arbitrary imprisonment. As the economic elites became richer and more powerful, government became less of a threat and even became an ally in many countries. Instead, the economic elite as well as the government increasingly had to fear revolution by impoverished and disenfranchised workers. Acemoglu and Robinson (2000) suggest that it was this threat that lead to the extension of voting rights in the nineteenth and early twentieth century, until it covered the whole male (and later female) adult population. According to their theory, elites would grant extended voting rights as a credible commitment to give a larger share of the wealth created in the country to the working masses indefinitely, in order to keep them from grabbing power by force. Aidt and Jensen (2011) have empirically tested that hypothesis. They take revolutionary events in neighboring countries as a strong indication that the elites of a country faced a heightened threat of revolution themselves. For the period between 1820 and 1938, they find that an increased threat of revolution preceded extensions of voting rights and made reform of voting rules more likely in the following years. As anecdotal evidence they cite the British parliamentarian Lord Grey, who introduced the reform bill of the year 1831 with the words, "the principal of my reform is to prevent the necessity of revolution... I am reforming to preserve, not to overthrow."

The early neoclassical economists' penchant for redistribution, which was described in Chapter 1, can also be seen in the light of this threat of revolution. On the basis of their theory, they judged that the poor had more urgent needs than the rich. The political structure was such at the time that the poor and destitute did not have any political power and could not effectively demand redistribution. Thus in effect what the early neoclassicals proposed were systematic rules and rationales for providing generous alms to the poor. Some members of the elite considered this water on the mills of the revolutionaries, but certainly not all. Even an authoritarian, antisocialist ruler like Otto von Bismarck (1815–98) found it wise to put Germany on the road to becoming a welfare state in order to fend off the socialists. To that purpose, he introduced compulsory employer-funded health, accident, old age and disability insurance. The leading German economists both inspired and supported these policies.

By the 1930s, when Lionel Robbins and his followers started the push to redefine economics as a science exclusively concerned with the allocation of scarce resources, voting rights were universal almost everywhere. The perceived risk for the economic elites had shifted from revolution to the threat that democratic governments seeking to maximize votes could levy high taxes on the rich. In such a political context, a redistribution-friendly economic theory was dangerous for the elites. It would provide a left-leaning government with a scientific justification for taking away from the rich and giving to the poor. Prohibiting economists from comparing the needs of the poor and the rich did away with that economic justification. Also, discrediting government as a coercive Leviathan encroaching on individual liberties, as the rational choice and public choice schools did, was fully consistent with the interest of the wealthy and powerful in a democratic setting.

Politics for the Apolitical

Economists feel on election day a little like Jews feel on Christmas. Participating makes them feel like a traitor to their kind but boycotting the extravaganza makes them feel estranged from the rest of society.

—*Aaron Edlin, Andrew Gelman and Noah Kaplan, 2007*

The dogmatic prohibition of interpersonal comparisons of needs and preferences introduced by Robbins prevented mainstream economics from developing a reasonable theory of how and why people vote. For decades, economists preserved the rather primitive, democracy-skeptical notion that a majority of (relatively) poor people would always try to grab the wealth of the rich by voting in favor of very high taxes. For delivering arguments in favor of restraining government, this primitive notion did well enough. However, reality is a lot more complex and does not conform to the assumption underlying this notion.

Since Downs (1957) published *An Economic Theory of Democracy*, mainstream, rational choice-inspired economics has struggled and largely failed to explain why people vote. The effort of voting is not negligible, but the gain is. No strictly selfish individual can hope to influence the outcome in a nationwide election, making it "irrational" to vote. The fact that so many people vote anyway seems proof that there is something wrong with the notion that collective action is not possible without coercion. Economists found a peculiar way out. They termed the act of voting as an act of consumption, creating pleasure akin to sounding off over a beer with friends or colleagues. Their votes are not seriously intended to achieve anything, as this would be folly. According to the rational choice school, collective decisions are irrational in any case and the only function of democratic elections is to remove bad leaders.

There are other less cynical and more realistic ways to think about voting, though. If human beings are recognized as the social animals they are, then it becomes very easy to rationalize voting, even if each individual is only one in a million voters. Edlin, Gelman and Kaplan (2007) show economists a more reasonable way out of their dilemma. Just admit that people have altruistic preferences and like to improve the wellbeing of others. In this case, the stakes of the election increase with the size of the electorate. If one candidate or party makes global depression, nuclear war, or global climate change less likely, a significant monetary equivalent per person can be placed on the better candidate winning. Multiply that number by the 300 million people in the US, or the 7 billion in the world, and even tiny chances of being pivotal will justify the time and expense of going to the poll booth.

Based on opinion polls, Edlin, Gelman and Kaplan (2008) calculated the chances of being the pivotal voter for the 2008 presidential elections in the US that were as high as one in a few million in embattled states. If they were rightly or wrongly convinced that in the event of casting the pivotal vote they would improve the lot of 300 million or more people, even economists could go to the poll with a clear conscience. They would not have to fret that they were committing the mortal sin of acting irrationally, as the authors point out.

An Improbable Love Affair with the Median Voter

The predominant theory for economists to think about democratic voting is median voter theory, popularized by Anthony Downs. It assumes that all voters vote for the politician who commits to a policy position closest to their own interest. In a majority election between two candidates and with only one issue at stake, both candidates will maximize their votes if they position themselves exactly in middle, where the interest of the median voter is maximized. The logic of the theory and its limitations can easily be understood with an example. If the single issue to be decided is the speed limit on a country road, a particular voter might prefer 70 mph. This voter will be the median voter if there are equal numbers of voters preferring a higher limit as there are voters preferring a lower limit. Median voter theory says that if Party 1 goes for 75 mph, then Party 2 should go for 74 mph and win, as all voters preferring 74 mph or less would vote for Party 2. Assuming reliable opinion polls, Party 1 would anticipate this and switch to 73 mph and so on, until both parties would end up proposing 70 mph. This is a theory which respects economists' self-imposed prohibition against comparing intensities of preferences between people. It does not matter for the result if those preferring a lower limit feel very strongly about it and those wanting a higher limit do not care very much.

In a representative democracy, it is hardly ever appropriate to assume a single-issued policy space. Elections are about large bundles of policies, not about a one-dimensional policy issue. It is almost universally recognized that the median voter theory breaks down in such cases. For lack of an accepted alternative, many economists use it anyway. It fuels their belief that there is a tendency towards the exploitation of the few by the poor in any democratic setting.

Adherents of the public choice and rational choice schools would instead let Arrow's impossibility theorem kick in, saying that almost anything could happen in multi-issue elections. Cycling majorities could form, which would make the outcome unpredictable and political choices erratic. Any economist with the median voter theorem or rational choice in mind must fundamentally mistrust the political process, as many indeed do.

Both these points of view hinge, however, on the dogma that intensities of preferences cannot and must not be measured and thus cannot be included in any economic theory of democracy. This dogma is hard to justify. In multiple issue elections, voting itself is the way to compare the wants and needs of different voters. A government in a representative democracy regularly decides about many different issues before voters go to the poll. Voters give their verdict on how candidates have met (or are likely to meet) their preferences overall. That helps them to express the intensity of their preferences. Their vote will depend a lot on policies that are important to them and fairly little on policies unimportant to them. They will largely ignore small deviations from their preferences, while large deviations might sway their vote. If the political process works well, a government that wants to be reelected will try to enact policies that meet the preferences of as many voters as possible to the largest possible degree. They would give the most weight to preferences that they perceive as intense and less weight to others. Over time, parties learn which policies get candidates elected and which don't. Choosing policies accordingly is often labeled populism, even though it simply means giving voters what they want most urgently.

The theory behind the mechanism sketched out here has slowly been gaining a foothold since it was formulated in the 1980s under the name probabilistic voting theory. It is called *probabilistic* because the metric used to compare intensities of preferences is the probability that a certain policy choice makes voters switch their vote in a representative election. To give an example, if one party offers higher unemployment benefits (financed by higher taxes), the likelihood that unemployed people switch their vote in favor of that party will be rather high. On the other hand, the likelihood that safely employed (selfish) taxpayers will vote for that party will decrease. These likelihoods can be empirically compared, even between different people. This is what pollsters and election analysts do. If the theory of the early neoclassicals was correct, a certain amount of redistribution can be expected to be vote maximizing, as unemployed people with important unfulfilled needs value an extra dollar more than the well-to-do value the first few tax dollars they have to give up. The result of an unbiased attempt by all parties to maximize the sum of probabilities of receiving the votes of individual voters is akin to trying to maximize the sum of all voters' utilities. More informally, it results in a fair compromise among all voters' preferences, taking the intensity of these preferences into account (Coughlin 1992).

Redistribution will be limited by several factors. The two most important ones are the decreasing marginal utility of income and the cost of redistribution. As income discrepancies get smaller with increasing redistribution, any further redistribution will gain fewer votes. On the other hand, increasing redistribution will raise the cost associated with it, potentially even exponentially. Levying taxes from earned income and handing out money based on need damages work incentives. Thus redistribution reduces the pie that can be distributed, which is bad for vote-maximizing politicians. The fear that a majority of poor people will always vote to fleece the rich, with no regard to the interests of the rich, is thus not supported by probabilistic voting theory, nor is it supported by empirical evidence. The likelihood that rich voters will switch their votes if money is taken from them counts as much as the likelihood that the poor will switch their votes as a reaction to receiving this money (Coughlin 1992).

A recent example of a paper using probabilistic voting theory is Farhi and Werning (2008). They use this approach to explain why progressive (but limited) taxation is observed as a vote-maximizing outcome, which median voter theory has trouble accounting for. The similarity to Irving Fisher's 1927 paper "A Statistical Method for Measuring 'Marginal Utility' and Testing the Justice of a Progressive Income Tax" is striking. After many decades in which such papers were not publishable in quality journals, mainstream economics seems about to rediscover the insights of the late nineteenth century.

The idea of probabilistic voting suggests an attitude toward government very different from the fundamental skepticism instilled by median voter theory and the rational choice movement. While the latter two see government as a necessary evil that should be kept as small as possible, the former can point to an ideal democratic process that serves to find a good compromise between competing interests. While the process is distorted in reality, it can suggest changes that reduce such distortions of the public will.

Buying Protection with Votes and Money

Distortions of the political process abound. People and institutions with money and well-organized interest groups can exert disproportional political influence. Businessmen sometimes go into politics, like Silvio Berlusconi, who used his money and his influence as a media mogul to become prime minister of Italy. This enabled him to change laws so that he would be safe from prosecution for breaches in business laws. Another celebrity example is Dick Cheney, who changed from the office of US secretary of defense to the CEO of the large energy and military procurement corporation Halliburton and back to US vice president under George W. Bush. The volume of government purchases from Halliburton rose very strongly during this time.

Alternatively, people and institutions with money can use it to buy privileges by conferring material benefits to politicians. It has become very common that high-ranking politicians take on well-paid posts in private business upon leaving office. It seems rather obvious that during their careers as politicians they are aware that they will reduce their chances of getting such an offer if they alienate important constituencies in private business. This route of influence is the most open to industries with high profits and high pay. Public opinion can hardly deter such implicit bribery, since the respective politicians (or bureaucrats) no longer need to care about votes at the end of their political careers.

There is no lack of prominent examples. The chief economist of the European Central Bank, Otmar Issing, went to Goldman Sachs immediately after his departure, joining dozens of former high-ranking politicians and bureaucrats who earn their very generous pittance there. Former president of the Federal Reserve Alan Greenspan was hired by Pimco, the world's largest bond fund. German chancellor Gerhard Schröder took on a job at Russian gas company Gazprom. After he had already been voted out of office, but before leaving, his government had given Gazprom a high debt guarantee (supposedly without Schröder's knowledge).

It would be very easy to defuse this conflict of interest. Politicians and bureaucrats, and their relatives and immediate family, could be barred from working for organizations within their sphere of influence for five years during and after their departure. In exchange, they would need to be paid well enough to reach an income level which is commensurate with their position without taking implicit bribes.

However, the most important currency in politics is votes. Without votes, politicians do not get influential. In the US, interest groups and institutions can help politicians get these votes by providing them with control of unlimited sums of other people's money for political advertisement. Incomplete information and malleability of preferences make voters receptive to political advertisement. This is the main reason that it costs a significant amount of money to persuade voters to think in a particular way. In the US, which places unusually few restrictions on political financing and the methods employed by candidates compared to most Western countries, money for advertising is particularly essential for a party or candidate to win an election. In effect, parties with platforms favoring cash-rich interest groups and institutions will have a better chance of winning, and either party will have an incentive to tilt their policies toward the preferences of such interest groups. In the 2005/06 election cycle, the 50 most generous donor industries in the US disbursed US$444 million to incumbents of the 109th Congress. Finance and health groups were among the most generous, as the high profits in these industries raised the stakes as well as spending power (Bombardini and Trebbi 2011).

Estimates of how much it costs a candidate to obtain an additional vote in the US range from US$100 to US$400, with more densely populated regions generally having the higher costs per vote due to higher advertising costs (Bombardini and Trebbi 2011). Unlike almost all other Western countries, there are no limits on how much may be spent on a candidate's election (indeed, many Western countries allocate a fixed sum of taxpayers' money to each candidate who qualifies for election, and no further monies may be spent by anybody beyond this amount on pain of disqualification and even criminal prosecution).

There is a pernicious feedback loop in this. The more an industry can elicit political favors which raise their profits, the more it can spend on eliciting still more favorable treatment from politicians. This feedback loop is clearly at work in the finance and health industries in the US, where profit rates are much higher than in other industries.

In recent years, a number of economists have examined the issue systematically and found that political connections and contributions are very important for companies and their management. One such study found that politically connected firms are significantly more likely to be bailed out by the government in case of financial distress even though they are in significantly worse financial shape than their non-connected peers at the time of the bailout. This implies that government protection distorts the flow of capital away from the most efficient companies (Faccio, Masulis and McConnell 2006).

Another study showed that political connections of company owners and managers are very common internationally. In Russia, for example, connected firms represent 87 percent of the market capitalization, even with a rather restrictive definition of political connectedness which includes only those firms of which a major shareholder or a top management official is a member of parliament, a minister, or a close relative of a top politician. In Britain, firms which are politically connected in a narrow sense make up a still staggering quota of 39 percent of market capitalization. In France, the respective number is 8 percent, in the US 5 percent, in Germany and Japan only 1 percent. If an officer or large shareholder of a corporation is entering politics, its share price and thus the value of the corporation increases significantly (Faccio 2006).

In light of the scandal around the US$50 billion investment fraud by Bernard Madoff, which the Securities and Exchange Commission (SEC) had not detected despite the numerous tips it had received, another study by Correia (2009) is particularly interesting. It reveals that more lenient treatment by regulatory agencies is an important channel through which political connections raise company value. An enforcement action by the SEC is often extremely costly for affected firms and their owners. Therefore if enforcement choices are sensitive to political pressure, firms with strong political connections should be less deterred by regulatory enforcement and exhibit lower accounting quality. Many of the firms involved in accounting scandals were known for their strong political connections. Enron, Global Crossing, Halliburton, Harken, Arthur Andersen. Fannie Mae and Freddie Mac had a lot in common with Bernie Madoff in this respect. Indeed, the study finds that the less accurate companies' accounts are, the more these companies spend on contributions and lobbying.

Taking into account that the financial industry has been extremely active in terms of lobbying and contributions in the years preceding the subprime crisis, the otherwise enigmatic lack of oversight exercised by the responsible authorities is less puzzling. There have been allegations that commissioners and politically appointed top officials of the SEC put pressure on SEC enforcement staff to avoid prosecution of politically connected firms and individuals. One SEC insider alleged that Pequot Capital Management traded on tips given by John Mack, the CEO of Morgan Stanley and a major political contributor. The Senate later concluded that the SEC had not devoted sufficient resources to the case and had been overly deferential in dealing with John Mack. SEC management had delayed Mack's testimony for over a year, until days after the statute of limitations expired, and had fired the whistleblower. No serious and credible investigation of his claims was ever conducted, according to the Senate. It is quite clear that the failure of the SEC to detect the huge Ponzi scheme of Bernard Madoff, a major contributor to federal candidates, parties and committees, was not an isolated case but part of a pattern (Correia 2009).

Conclusion: Strengthen and Protect the Political System from Itself

One school of thought concludes from this that it is best to have as small a government as possible and give it as little power as possible. This is the school of thought that inspired the US Constitution as laid down by the founding fathers after suffering decades of overbearing British rule. However, keeping the government small and weak disproportionately benefits the wealthy and economically powerful. It makes the government and the political system hostage to vested and powerful interests. Indeed, it makes the government hostage to itself, such as during the 2011 debt ceiling crisis when the US embarrassed itself by self-destructively playing chicken against itself.

It is far better to start modernizing the checks and balances within the US political system itself. The founding fathers designed the US system for an agrarian country with less than half a million citizens at a time when information took weeks or months to travel. They had no way of anticipating a country of more than 300 million citizens where information technology enables the automation of checks and balances. In this sense, the old-world European democratic structure, where there are few checks and balances on government (as the monarchy and the aristocracy historically exercised considerable countervailing power), has stood the test of time far better. In Europe, a newly elected government can achieve sweeping changes as they control a majority of votes and usually can rubberstamp new policy with no ability to filibuster or otherwise delay or modify implementation. For example, it is safe to say that the new British government of 2010 easily achieved more change in their first year than President Clinton did in two full presidential terms – the British system only permits the House of Lords to temporarily delay new legislation, and only the reigning monarch may reject it. Similarly, in Ireland the new government of 2011 had no constitutional impediments in enacting a large reduction in the size of government. Such freedom to enact change quickly is unthinkable under the US political system; while in Europe the losing parties can do little but carp from the sidelines, in the US they have the power to make life as difficult as possible for the winning party via procedural maneuvers and do just that. The result is a glacial pace to change, and increasingly stagnation.

For more effective government, a "constitutional reform committee" should be set up with the power to delete entire sections of procedural legislation – including articles in the Constitution and precedents set by the Supreme Court. The committee would have no power to create new legislation (as that is the role of the president and Congress), nor repeal anything not pertaining to the efficiency of the government. Their role would merely be to "clean out the cobwebs."

Such a "cobweb cleaning" committee is long overdue, but it would be naive to count on a more capable and efficient government to rein in the powers of the business elite. The enhanced powers of a captured government or bureaucracy can be used by the business elite to keep newcomers out, ossifying the economic structure in the process, and a more efficient government might well make capture by this business elite worse. The available economic research into the problem has found that political connections are more prevalent and more valuable if there are fewer legal restrictions on influencing politicians or bureaucrats and if the public exerts less control because political participation is low or because the media is not informing voters. Therefore the focus has to be on strengthening the political system to make it as difficult as possible to distort the outcome away from the ideal, in which government and opposition concentrate on doing what voters want. There is no easy alternative to working toward a transparent and accountable political system and an independent media that informs voters rather than manipulating them. Voters need the information to scrutinize individual political decisions to see if these unduly benefit particular interest groups.

Campaign contributions by wealthy individuals and companies perform the function that the *Dreiklassenwahlrecht* in Prussia or the restriction on voting rights to the wealthy fulfilled in the nineteenth century. They allow the wealthy to influence the rules of the economic game in their favor. This promotes a tendency toward ever-greater concentration of economic and political power. Therefore contributions to political parties and campaigns should not only be highly transparent, but also severely restricted to the point that only personal time and small sums of money can be legally contributed. Outside the US, political parties and campaigns are often financed almost exclusively from taxpayer money in a fair and transparent fashion, thus reducing the power of money over policymakers significantly.

Another important instrument to prevent the capture of the government by vested interests is the automatic publication of everything that happens to a policymaker; all their financial dealings and whom they meet with and when. Government and ruling parties should be required to keep interest groups at arm's length in the process of drafting laws. The widespread practice of enlisting their "know-how" for drafting complex laws regulating their industries is bad enough. Deliberately placing top members of the industry elite in charge of the government agency that regulates that industry is a disgrace in a democracy. The time-tested remedy since the Roman Empire has been investing in a professional and completely independent civil service to enact and police policy. This of course raises the problem of the civil service becoming a vested interest in itself, but the negatives in that proposition pale in comparison to intentionally placing foxes in charge of the hen coop.

Regarding the important role of the media in preserving democracy, it is not only dictatorships and weak third world democracies that have a lot left to do. The US used to require that news vendors not be openly political, that they try to present both sides of any newsworthy story, and these vendors were punished for repeating factual errors. This "Fairness Doctrine" ceased to be enforced in 1987 and was finally deleted in 2011 on the basis that it was too unwieldy. Yet practically every European country and most Latin American countries have exactly the same requirement of news vendors. Somehow these countries don't have insurmountable problems in enforcement, and the result is a press that is far less controlled by business and political interests. For example, the Murdoch empire owns FOX News in the US as well as Sky News in the UK. However, the UK very proactively enforces factuality, fairness and objectivity in news reporting, so Sky News is very different from FOX News. There is nothing preventing opinion in news reporting – as any muckraking British tabloid demonstrates. The difference lies in not being allowed to "dress up" news reporting with opinion as is permitted in the US. The result is that people in the UK are far more trusting of news vendors, and the feedback loop which reports to the people on what the politicians and business elite are up to is far stronger and more decisive in reigning in governmental capture and identifying corruption.

As imperfect as the democratic political process may be, and as much as it can be influenced by those with money and power, it is still a very powerful egalitarian device as it gives everyone one vote.

AFTERWORD

We would like to thank our families and friends for putting up with the many hours we spent hunched over a computer. We would also like to thank Janka Romero and Tej P. S. Sood at Anthem Press for their patience and help.

Economics is a fascinating field that we feel has been stunted by those who have misdirected it for other purposes. As the challenges of increasing basic resource scarcity grow ever greater as we progress into the twenty-first century, economics will have to mature as a field. Instead of hiding its biases behind the façade of a pseudoscience, it will need to become a social science in the best sense of the word if our civilization is to survive. It will need to be far more rigorous about how much is science (objective, mathematical modeling of truth), and how much is political economy and even moral philosophy dressed up as mathematical economics. This means being up-front about being political, about whose and which interests are served. Only people, like you, can demand that the discipline of economics demonstrate the rigor it claims for itself, and we hope that this book has furthered that process.

Thank you for purchasing this book. We hope you enjoyed reading it. If you did, please like it on Facebook and/or Google+, and do feel free to post a message to the book's wall.

Niall Douglas and Norbert Häring

REFERENCES

Acemoglu, Daron. 2001. "Good Jobs versus Bad Jobs." *Journal of Labour Economics* 19: 1–21.

Acemoglu, Daron, Davide Cantoni, Simon Johnson and James A. Robinson. 2009. "The Consequences of Radical Reform: The French Revolution." CEPR Discussion Paper 7245.

Acemoglu, Daron, Simon Johnson and James A. Robinson. 2005. "The Rise of Europe: Atlantic Trade, Institutional Change and Economic Growth." *American Economic Review* 95: 546–79.

Acemoglu, Daron and James A. Robinson. 2000. "Why Did the West Extend the Franchise? Democracy, Inequality, and Growth in Historical Perspective." *Quarterly Journal of Economics* 115: 1167–99.

———. 2008. "Persistence of Power, Elites and Institutions." *American Economic Review* 98: 267–93.

Acemoglu, Daron and Robert Shimer. 2000. "Productivity Gains from Unemployment Insurance." *European Economic Review* 44: 1195–1224.

Acharya, Viral V., Stewart C. Myers and Raghuram Rajan. 2009. "The Internal Governance of Firms." NBER Working Paper 15568.

Adler, Moshe. 2009. *Economics for the Rest of Us: Debunking the Science that Makes Life Dismal.* New York: New Press.

Adrian, Tobias and Hyun Song Shin. 2009. *The Shadow Banking System: Implications for Financial Regulation.* Federal Reserve Bank of New York Staff Report 382.

Aghion, Philippe and Benjamin F. Hermalin. 1990. "Legal Restrictions on Private Contracts Can Enhance Efficiency." *Journal of Law, Economics and Organization* 6: 381–409.

Aidt, Take S. and Peter S. Jensen. 2011. "Workers of the World, Unite! Franchise Extensions and the Threat of Revolution in Europe, 1820–1938." CESIfo Working Paper 3417.

Akerlof, George A. 1982. "Labor Contracts as Partial Gift Exchange." *Quarterly Journal of Economics* 97: 543–69.

Alchian, Armen A. and Harold Demsetz. 1972. "Production, Information Costs, and Economic Organization." *American Economic Review* 62: 777–95.

Alesina Alberto F., Yann Algan, Pierre Cahuc and Paola Giuliano. 2010. "Family Values and the Regulation of Labor." NBER Working Paper 15747.

Alloway, Tracy. 2010. "Mishkin's Very Own Icelandic Blow-up." Video interview. Alphaville weblog of the *Financial Times*, August 28. http://ftalphaville.ft.com/

blog/2010/08/25/325376/mishkins-very-own-icelandic-blow-up (accessed March 28, 2012).

Almodovar, António and José Luís Cardoso. 1998. *A History of Portuguese Economic Thought*. London: Routledge.

Alonso, William and Paul Starr. 1987. *The Politics of Numbers*. New York: Russell Sage Foundation.

Altaner, David. 2007. "Bear Stearns CEO Played Bridge, Golf, During Crisis, WSJ Says." Bloomberg, November 1.

Amadae, Sonja M. 2003. *Rationalizing Capitalist Democracy: The Cold War Origins of Rational Choice Liberalism*. Chicago: University of Chicago Press.

Anderson, Margaret L. 1981. *Windthorst: A Political Biography*. Oxford: Oxford University Press.

Anderson, S., J. Cavanagh, C. Collins, M. Lapham and S. Pizzigati. 2008. "Executive excess 2008: How average taxpayers subsidize runaway pay." *15th Annual CEO Compensation Survey*. Washington DC: Institute for Policy Studies.

Arnsperger, Christian and Yanis Varoufakis. 2006. "What is Neoclassical Economics?" *Post-Autistic Economics Review* 38, article 1.

Arrow, Kenneth J. 1951. *Social Choice and Individual Values*. New Haven: Yale University Press.

Arrow, Kenneth J. and Gerard Debreu. 1954. "Existence of an Equilibrium for a Competitive Economy." *Econometrica* 22: 265–90.

Arthur, Jeffrey B. 1994. "Effects of Human Resource Systems on Manufacturing Performance and Turnover." *Academy of Management Journal* 37: 670–87.

Ashenfelter, Orley and Štěpán Jurajda. 2010. "Cross-country Comparisons of Wage Rates: The McWage Index." Proceedings of the 2010 Conference of the European Association of Labour Economists.

Ashenfelter, Orley C., Kirk B. Doran and Bruce Schaller. 2010. "A Shred of Credible Evidence on the Long Run Elasticity of Labor Supply." NBER Working Paper 15746.

Associated Press. 2012. "Taiwan's Foxconn Raises Wages for Chinese Workers." February 18.

Augar, Philip. 2005. *The Greed Merchants: How the Investment Banks Played the Free Market Game*. New York: HarperCollins.

Autor, David H., John J. Donohue III and Stewart J. Schwab. 2006. "The Costs of Wrongful-Discharge Laws." *Review of Economics and Statistics* 88: 211–31.

Autor, David H., Richard Murnane and Frank Levy. 2002. "Upstairs Downstairs: Computers and Skills on Two Floors of a Large Bank." *Industrial and Labor Relations Review* 55: 432–47.

Barber, Brad M., Yi-Tsung-Jane Liu and Terrance Odean. 2009. "Just How Much Do Individual Investors Lose by Trading?" *Review of Financial Studies* 22: 609–32.

Barber, Brad M., Reuven Lehavy and Brett Trueman. 2007. "Comparing the Stock Recommendation Performance of Investment Banks and Independent Research Firms." *Journal of Financial Economics* 85: 490–517.

Barber, Brad M., Yi-Tsung Lee, Yu-Jane Liu and Terrance Odean. 2004. "Do Individual Day Traders Make Money?" University of California, Berkeley, working paper.

Bartels, Larry M., Hugh Heclo, Rodney E. Hero and Lawrence R. Jacobs. 2005. "Inequality and American Governance." In *Inequality and American Democracy:*

What We Know and What We Need to Learn, ed. Lawrence R. Jacobs and Theda Skocpol, 88–155. New York: Russell Sage Foundation.

Barth, Erling and Karl O. Moene. 2009. "The Equality Multiplier." NBER Working Paper 15076.

Bartling, Björn, Ernst Fehr and Klaus M. Schmidt. 2010. "Screening, Competition, and Job Design: Economic Origins of Good Jobs." CEPR Discussion Paper 7658.

Bebchuk, Lucian A. 2007. "The Myth of the Shareholder Franchise." *Virginia Law Review* 93: 675–732.

Bebchuk, Lucian A., Alma Cohen and Allen Ferrell. 2009. "What Matters in Corporate Governance." *Review of Financial Studies* 22: 783–827.

Bebchuk, Lucian A., Alma Cohen and Holger Spaman. 2010. "The Wages of Failure: Executive Compensation at Bear Stearns and Lehman 2000–2008." *Yale Journal of Regulation* 27: 257–82.

Bebchuk, Lucian, A. and Jesse M. Fried. 2003. "Executive Compensation as an Agency Problem." *Journal of Economic Perspectives* 17: 71–82.

———. 2004. *Pay Without Performance: The Unfulfilled Promise of Executive Compensation.* Cambridge, MA: Harvard University Press.

Bebchuk, Lucian A., Yanif Grinstein and Urs Peyer. 2010. "Lucky CEOs and Lucky Directors." *Journal of Finance* 65: 2363–2401.

———. Forthcoming. "Corporate Governance and the Timing of Option Grants." *Journal of Finance.*

Becht, Marco, Patrick Bolton and Ailsa Röell. 2007. "Corporate Governance and Control." In *Handbook of Law and Economics,* ed. A. M. Polinsky and S. Shavell. Amsterdam: North-Holland.

Becht, Marco, Julian Franks, Colin Mayer and Stefano Rossi. 2009. "Returns to Shareholder Activism: Evidence from a Clinical Study of the Hermes U.K. Focus Fund." *Review of Financial Studies* 22: 3093–3129.

Becker, Gary S. 1957/1971. *The Economics of Discrimination.* 2nd ed. Chicago: University of Chicago Press.

———. 1976. *The Economic Approach to Human Behavior.* Chicago: University of Chicago Press.

Bellante, Don. 2004. "Edward Chamberlin: Monopolisitic Competition and Pareto Optimality." *Journal of Business and Economics Research* 2: 17–28.

Benabou, Roland and Jean Tirole. 2006. "Belief in a Just World and Redistributive Politics." *Quarterly Journal of Economics* 121: 699–746.

Benmelech, Efraim, Eugene Kandel and Pietro Veronesi. 2010. "Stock-Based Compensation and CEO (Dis)Incentives." *Quarterly Journal of Economics* 125: 1769–1820.

Benmelech, Efraim and Toby Moskowitz. Forthcoming. "The Political Economy of Financial Regulation: Evidence from U.S. State Usury Laws in the 19th Century." *Journal of Finance.*

Bergstrom, Theodore C. 2002. "Evolution of Social Behavior: Individual and Group Selection." *Journal of Economic Perspectives* 16: 67–88.

———. 2003. "The Algebra of Assortative Encounters and the Evolution of Cooperation." *International Game Theory Review* 5: 1–18.

Berlin, Isaiah. 1958. *Two Concepts of Liberty.* Oxford: Clarendon Press.

Bernstein, Michael A. 2001. *A Perilous Progress: Economists and Public Purpose in Twentieth Century America*. Princeton: Princeton University Press.

Bewley, Truman F. 1995. "A Depressed Labor Market as Explained by Participants." *American Economic Review* 85: 250–54.

———. 1998. "Why Not Cut Pay?" *European Economic Review* 42: 459–90.

———. 2004. "Fairness, Reciprocity and Wage Rigidity." IZA Discussion Paper 1137.

Bhaktavatsalam, Sree Vidya. 2008. *Greenspan Helped Pimco Save Billions, Gross Says*. Bloomberg, April 21.

Bhardwaj, Geetesh, Gary B. Gorton and K. Geert Rouwenhorst. 2008. "Fooling Some of the People All of the Time: The Inefficient Performance and Persistence of Commodity Trading Advisors." NBER Working Paper 14424.

Bhaskar, V., Alan Manning and Ted To. 2002. "Oligopsony and Monopsonistic Competition in the Labor Markets." *Journal of Economic Perspectives* 16: 155–74.

Black, William. 2010. "Epidemics of 'Control Fraud' Lead to Recurrent, Intensifying Bubbles and Crises." Paper presented at the Murphy Conference on Corporate Law, Fordham Law School, March 12.

Blanchard, Olivier. 2006. "European Unemployment: The Evolution of Facts and Ideas." *Economic Policy* 21: 5–59.

Blinder, Alan S., Elies D. Canetti, David E. Lebow and Jeremy B. Rudd. 1998. *Asking About Prices*. New York: Russell Sage Foundation.

Bodnaruk, Andriy, Massimo Massa and Andrei Simonov. 2009. "Investment Banks as Insiders and the Market for Corporate Control." *Review of Financial Studies* 22: 4989–5026.

Bolton, Gary E. and Axel Ockenfels. 2000. "ERC – A Theory of Equity, Reciprocity and Competition." *American Economic Review* 90: 166–93.

Bombardini, Matilde and Francesco Trebbi. Forthcoming. "Votes or Money? Theory and Evidence from the US Congress." *Journal of Public Economics*.

Boot, Arnoud W. A., Radhakrishnan Gopalan and Anjan V. Thakor. 2006. "The Entrepreneur's Choice between Private and Public Ownership." *Journal of Finance* 61.2: 803–36.

Borokhovich, Kenneth A., Kelly R. Brunarski and Robert Parrino. 1997. "CEO Contracting and Antitakeover Amendments." *Journal of Finance* 52: 1495–1517.

Bourdieu, Pierre. 2005. *The Social Structures of the Economy*. Cambridge: Polity Press.

Bourguignon, François and Christian Morrison. 2002. "Inequality Among World Citizens: 1920–1992." *American Economic Review* 92.4: 727–44.

Boutin, Xavier, Giacinta Cestone, Chiara Fumagalli, Giovanni Pica and Nicolas Serrano-Velarde. 2009. "The Deep Pocket Effect of Internal Capital Markets." CEPR Discussion Paper 7184.

Bowles, Samuel. 2008. "Policies Designed for Self-Interested Citizens May Undermine 'The Moral Sentiments': Evidence from Economic Experiments." *Science* 320: 1605–9.

———. 2009. "Did Warfare Among Ancestral Hunter-Gatherers Affect the Evolution of Human Social Behaviors?" *Science* 324: 1293–8.

Bowles, Samuel and Herbert Gintis. 2006. "Social Preferences, Homo Economicus and Zoon Politicon." In *The Oxford Handbook of Contextual Political Analysis*, ed. Robert E. Goodin and Charles Tilly. Oxford: Oxford University Press.

_____. 2008. "Power." *New Palgrave Dictionary of Economics*. 2nd ed, ed. S. Durlauf and L. Blume. London: Macmillan.

Brandeis, Louis D. 1913. *Other People's Money*. The Louis Brandeis Collection. www. law/louisville.edu/library/collections/brandeis (accessed March 28, 2012).

British Broadcasting Corporation. 2002. *The Century of the Self*. http://archive.org/ details/the.century.of.the.self (accessed March 28, 2012).

_____. 2007. *The Trap: What Happened to Our Dream of Freedom*. http://archive.org/ details/AdamCurtis_TheTrap (accessed March 28, 2012).

Bruhn, Miriam and Inessa Love. 2009. "The Economic Impact of Banking the Unbanked: Evidence from Mexico." World Bank Policy Research Working Paper 4981.

Brunnermeier, Markus and Lasse H. Pedersen. 2005. "Predatory Trading." *Journal of Finance* 60: 1825–63.

Buchanan, James and Gordon Tullock. 1962. *The Calculus of Consent: Logical Foundations of Constitutional Democracy*. Ann Arbor: University of Michigan Press.

Burgess, Robin and Rohini Pande. 2005. "Can Rural Banks Reduce Poverty? Evidence from the Indian Social Banking Experiment." *American Economic Review* 95: 780–95.

Burns, Natasha and Simi Kedia. 2006. "The Impact of Performance-based Compensation on Misreporting." *Journal of Financial Economics* 79: 35–67.

Burton, Katherine and Saijel Kishan. 2011. "John Paulson Said to Have Made $5 Billion in 2010." Bloomberg, January 28.

Cadsby, Charles B. and Maynes, Elizabeth. 1998. "Choosing between a Socially Efficient and Free-Riding Equilibrium: Nurses versus Economics and Business Students." *Journal of Economic Behavior and Organization* 37: 183–92.

Cai, Fang. 2010. "Trader Exploitation of Order Flow Information during the LTCM Crisis." *Journal of Financial Research* 32: 261–84.

Cain, Daylian, George Loewenstein and Don Moore. 2005. "The Dirt on Coming Clean: Perverse Effects of Disclosing Conflicts of Interest." *Journal of Legal Studies* 34: 1–25.

Campbell, Carl M. III and Kunal S. Kamlani. 1997. "The Reasons for Wage Rigidity: Evidence from a Survey of Firms." *Quarterly Journal of Economics* 112: 759–89.

CapQM. 2009. "Kapitalanlagekosten der privaten Haushalte in Deutschland: Gegenwärtige Situation und Entwicklungsszenarien." Hamburg: CapQM.

Card, David and Alan B. Krueger. 1995. "Minimum Wages and Employment: A Case Study of the Fast-Food Industry in New Jersey and Pennsylvania." *American Economic Review* 84: 772–93.

_____. 2000. "Minimum Wages and Employment: A Case Study of the Fast-Food Industry in New Jersey and Pennsylvania: Reply." *American Economic Review* 90: 1397–1420.

Carlson, Mark and Galina Hale. 2006. "Rating Agencies and Sovereign Debt Roll-Over." *Topics in Macroeconomics* 6, article 8.

Carter, John. R. and Michael D. Irons. 1991. "Are Economists Different, and If So, Why?" *Journal of Economic Perspectives* 5: 171–7.

Chamberlain, Edward H. 1933. *Theory of Monopolistic Competition*. Cambridge, MA: Harvard University Press.

Chan, Swell. 2010. "Fifteen Economists Issue Crisis-Prevention Manual." *New York Times*, June 15.

Chau, Nancy. 2009. "Sweatshop Equilibrium." IZA Discussion Paper 4363.

Chen, Joseph, Samuel Hanson, Harrison Hong and Jeremy C. Stein. 2008. "Do Hedge Funds Profit from Mutual-Fund Distress?" NBER Working Paper 13786.

Chetty, Ray. 2008. "Moral Hazard vs. Liquidity and Optimal Unemployment Insurance." *Journal of Political Economy* 116: 173–234.

Citizens for Tax Justice. 2011. "Report: 280 Most Profitable U.S. Corporations Shelter Half Their Profits from Taxes; Thirty Companies Paid Less Than Zero in Taxes in the Last Three Years," November 3. http://www.ctj.org/corporatetaxdodgers/CorporateTaxDodgersPR.pdf (accessed March 28, 2012).

Clark, John Bates. 1899/2001. *The Distribution of Wealth: A Theory of Wages, Interest and Profits*. Boston: Adamant Media.

Cohen, Avi J. and G. C. Harcourt. 2003. "Whatever Happened to the Cambridge Capital Theory Controversies?" *Journal of Economic Perspectives* 17: 199–214.

Cohen, Lauren, Andrea Frazzini and Christopher Malloy. 2008. "Hiring Cheerleaders: Board Appointments of 'Independent' Directors." NBER Working Paper 14232.

Cohen, Lauren and Bruno Schmidt. 2009. "Attracting Flows by Attracting Big Clients: Conflicts of Interest and Mutual Fund Portfolio Choice." *Journal of Finance* 64: 1225–52.

Colander, David. 2007. "Edgeworth's Hedonimeter and the Quest to Measure Utility." *Journal of Economic Perspectives* 21: 215–25.

Cooter, Robert and Peter Rappoport. 1984. "Were the Ordinalists Wrong About Welfare Economics?" *Journal of Economic Literature* 22: 507–30.

Correia, Maria M. 2009. "Political Connections, SEC Enforcement and Accounting Quality." Working paper.

Coughlin, Peter. 1992. *Probabilistic Voting Theory*. Cambridge, MA: Cambridge University Press.

Cramer, James J. 2002. *Confessions of a Street Addict*. New York: Simon and Schuster.

Cuñat, Vincente, Mireia Gine and Maria Guadalupe. 2010. "The Vote is Cast: The Effect of Corporate Governance on Shareholder Value." NBER Working Paper 16574.

Curasi, Carolyn F. 1995. "Male Senior Citizens and their Shopping Preferences." *Journal of Consumer Marketing* 12: 123–133.

Das, Jishnu and Qui-Toan Do. 2009. "U.S. and Them: The Geography of Academic Research." World Bank Policy Research Paper 5152.

Datta, A. 2003. "Divestiture and its Implications for Innovation and Productivity Growth in US Telecommunications." *Southern Economic Journal* 69: 644–58.

Dawkins, Richard. 1976. *The Selfish Gene*. Oxford: Oxford University Press.

Deeds, David L. and Donna M. Decarolis. 1999. "The Impact of Stocks and Flows of Organizational Knowledge on Firm Performance: An Empirical Investigation of the Biotechnology Industry." *Strategic Management Journal* 20: 953–68.

Degeorge, Francois, Francois Derrien and Kent Womack. 2007. "Analyst Hype in IPOs. Explaining the Popularity of Book-Building." *Review of Financial Studies* 20: 1021–58.

Demirguc-Kunt, Asli and Ross Levine. 2009. "Finance and Inequality: Theory and Evidence." *Annual Review of Financial Economics* 1: 287–318.

Dichev, Ilia D. 2007. "What Are Stock Investors' Actual Historical Returns? Evidence from Dollar-Weighted Returns." *American Economic Review* 97: 386–401.

Dimson, Elroy, Paul R. Marsh and Mike Staunton. 2002. *Triumph of the Optimists: 101 Years of Global Investment Returns.* Princeton: Princeton University Press.

Dittmann, Ingolf, Ernst Maug and Christoph Schneider. 2010. "Bankers on the Boards of German Firms: What They Do, What They Are Worth, and Why They Are Still There." *Review of Finance* 14: 35–71.

Dixit, Avinash and Joseph Stiglitz. 1977. "Monopolistic Competition and Optimum Product Variety." *American Economic Review* 67: 297–308.

Docampo, Domingo. 2007. "International Comparisons in Higher Education Funding." *Higher Education in Europe* 32: 369–86.

Doellgast, Virginia and Ian Greer. 2007. "Vertical Disintegration and the Disorganization of German Industrial Relations." *British Journal of Industrial Relations* 45: 55–76.

Downs, Anthony. 1957. *An Economic Theory of Democracy.* New York: Harper.

Draca, Mirko, Stephen Machin and John Van Reenen. 2011. "Minimum Wages and Firm Profitability." *American Economic Journal: Applied Economics* 3: 129–51.

Dreilichman, Mauricio and Hans-Joachim Voth. 2009. "Lending to the Borrower from Hell: Debt and Default in the Age of Philip II, 1556–1598." CEPR Discussion Paper 7276.

Du Caju, Philip, François Rycx and Ilan Tojerow. 2009. "Inter-industry Wage Differentials – How Much Does Rent Sharing Matter?" ECB Working Paper 1103.

Dube, Arindrajit and Ethan Kaplan. 2010. "Does Outsourcing Reduce Wages in the Low-Wage-Service Occupations? Evidence from Janitors and Guards." *Industrial and Labor Relations Review*, January.

Dube, Arindrajit, William Lester and Michael Reich. 2010. "Minimum Wage Effects Across State Borders: Estimates Using Contiguous Counties." *Review of Economics and Statistics* 92: 945–64.

Duchin, Ran and Denis Sosyura. 2010. "TARP Investments: Financials and Politics." Ross School of Business Working Paper 1127.

Edlin, Aaron, Andrew Gelman and Noah Kaplan. 2007. "Voting as a Rational Choice: Why and How People Vote to Improve the Well-Being of Others." *Rationality and Society* 19: 293–314.

———. 2008. "Vote for Charity's Sake." *The Economists' Voice* 5.6. Available at: http://works.bepress.com/aaron_edlin/71 (accessed March 28, 2012).

Edmans, Alex. 2007. "Does the Stock Market Fully Value Intangibles? Employee Satisfaction and Equity Prices." Working paper.

———. 2011. "Does the Stock Market Fully Value Intangibles? Employee Satisfaction and Equity Prices." *Journal of Financial Economics* 101: 621–40.

Epple, K. and R. Schaefer. 1996. "The Transition from Monopoly to Competition: The Case of Housing Insurance in Baden-Württemberg." *European Economic Review* 40: 1123–31.

Eurostat. 2011. "Social Protection Statistics." Available at: http://epp.eurostat.ec.europa.eu/statistics_explained/index.php/Social_protection_statistics (accessed March 28, 2012).

Faccio, Mara. 2006. "Politically Connected Firms." *American Economic Review* 96: 369–86.

Faccio, Mara, Ronald W. Masulis and John J. McConnell. 2006. "Political Connections and Corporate Bailouts." *Journal of Finance* 61: 2597–2635.

Farber, Henry S. 2005. "What Do We Know About Job Loss in the United States: Evidence from the Displaced Workers Survey, 1984–2004." *Federal Reserve Bank of Chicago Regional Review*: 13–28.

Farhi, Emmanuel and Jean Tirole. 2009. "Collective Moral Hazard, Maturity Mismatch and Systemic Bailouts." NBER Working Paper 15138.

Farhi, Emmanuel and Iván Werning. 2008. "The Political Economy of Nonlinear Capital Taxation." Working paper.

Feenstra, Robert, Benjamin Mandel, Marshall B. Reisdorf and Matthew J. Slaughter. 2009. "Effects of Terms of Trade and Tariff Changes on the Measurement of U.S. Productivity Growth." NBER Working Paper 1592.

Fehr, Ernst, Lorenz Goette and Christian Zehnder. 2009. "A Behavioral Account of the Labor Market: The Role of Fairness Concerns." *Annual Review of Economics* 1: 355–84.

Felder, Stefan. 1996. "Fire Insurance in Germany: A Comparison of Price-Performance between State Monopolies and Competitive Regions." *European Economic Review* 40: 1133–1141.

Ferguson, Niall. 1998. *The House of Rothschild*, vols 1–2. New York: Penguin.

————. 2009. *The Ascent of Money*. New York: Penguin.

Fernandes, Nuno, Miguel A. Ferreira, Pedro Matos and Kevin J. Murphy. 2009. "The Pay Divide: Why Are U.S. Top Executives Paid More?" European Corporate Governance Institute Working Paper 255/2009.

Ferraro, Fabrizio, Jeffrey Pfeffer and Robert I. Sutton. 2005. "Economics Language and Assumptions: How Theories Can Become Self-Fulfilling." *Academy of Management Review* 30: 8–24.

Ferreira, Miguel A. and Pedro Matos. 2007. "When Banks Are Insiders: Evidence from the Global Syndicated Loan Market." Working paper.

Fisher, Irving. 1927. "A Statistical Method for Measuring 'Marginal Utility' and Testing the Justice of a Progressive Income Tax." In *Economic Essays Contributed in Honour of John Bates Clark*, ed. Jacob Hollander. New York: Macmillan.

————. 1936. *100% Money*. New York: Adelphi.

————. 1936/2009. *100 Money and the Public Debt*. Thai Sunset Publications.

FitzRoy, Felix and Kornelius Kraft. 2005. "Co-determination, Efficiency and Productivity." *British Journal of Industrial Relations* 43: 233–47.

Fonseca, Gonzalo L. 2009. "Vilfredo Pareto, 1848–1923." The History of Economic Thought website. http://homepage.newschool.edu/~het/profiles/pareto.htm (accessed February 27, 2011).

Foster, Julia, John Haltiwanger and Chad Syverson. 2010. "The Slow Growth of New Plants: Learning about Demand?" Working paper.

Frank, Robert H., Thomas D. Gilovich and Dennis T. Regan. 1993. "Does Studying Economics Inhibit Cooperation?" *Journal of Economic Perspectives* 7: 159–71.

Frankfurter Allgemeine Zeitung. 2008. "Dreistellige Millionenabfindungen sind in Amerika nicht unüblich." 1 November.

Freeman, Richard B. 2007. "Labor Market Institutions around the World." In *The Handbook of Industrial and Employment Relations*, ed. Nick Bacon, Paul Blyton, Jack Fiorito and Edmund Heery. New York: Russell Sage Foundation.

French, John R. P. and Bertram Raven. 1959. *The Bases of Social Power*. Ann Arbor Research Center for Group Dynamics, Institute for Social Research, University of Michigan.

Fried, Jesse. 1998. "Reducing the Profitability of Corporate Insider Trading Through Pre-trading Disclosure." *Southern California Law Review* 71: 303–92.

Frydman Carola and Dirk Jenter. 2010. "CEO Compensation." Rock Center for Corporate Governance Working Paper 77.

Galbraith, John Kenneth. 1987. *Economics in Perspective: A Critical History*. Boston: Houghton Mifflin.

Garvey, Gerald T. and Todd T. Milbourn. 2006. "Asymmetric Benchmarking in Compensation: Executives Are Rewarded for Good Luck but Not Penalized for Bad." *Journal of Financial Economics* 82: 197–225.

Gaspar, José-Miguel, Massimo Massa and Pedro Matos. 2006. "Favoritism in Mutual Fund Families? Evidence on Strategic Cross-Fund Subsidization." *Journal of Finance* 61: 73–104.

Georgiadis, Andreas and Alan Manning. 2007. "Spend It Like Beckham? Inequality and Redistribution in the UK, 1983–2004." CEP Discussion Paper 816.

Gill, Indermit S. and Martin Raiser. 2012. "Golden Growth: Restoring the Lustre of the European Economic Model." World Bank.

Gompers, Paul, Joy L. Ishii and Andrew Metrick. 2003. "Corporate Governance and Equity Prices." *Quarterly Journal of Economics* 118: 107–55.

Goolsbee, Austan and Chad Syverson. 2008. "How Do Incumbents Respond to the Threat of Entry? Evidence from the Major Airlines." *Quarterly Journal of Economics* 123: 1611–33.

Gorman, William M. 1955. "The Intransitivity of Certain Criteria Used in Welfare Economics." *Oxford Economic Papers* 7: 25–35.

Gottschalg, Oliver and Ludovic Phalippou. 2009. "The Performance of Private Equity Funds." *Review of Financial Studies* 22: 1747–76.

Gowan, Peter. 2009. "Crisis in the Heartland: Consequences of the New Wall Street System." *Real World Economics Review* 50: 101–17.

Grant, R. M. 1996. "Toward a Knowledge-Based Theory of the Firm." *Strategic Management Journal* 17: 109–22.

Greenlees, John S. and Robert B. McClelland. 2008. "Addressing Misconceptions about the Consumer Price Index." *Monthly Labor Review*, August 3–19.

Grocer, Stephen, Aaron Lucchetti and Liz Rappaport. 2010. "Wall Street Pay: A Record $144bn." *Wall Street Journal*, October 12.

Groeneveld, J. M. and A. Sjauw-Koen-Fa. 2009. "Cooperative Banks in the New Financial System." Rabobank Group Report for the Duisenberg Lecture. Annual Meeting of the IMF and World Bank, October, Istanbul.

Groeneveld, J. M. 2011. "Morality and Integrity in Cooperative Banking." *Ethical Perspectives*. 18.4: 515–40.

Habermeier, Karl F. and Andrei Kirilenko. 2001. "Securities Transaction Taxes and Financial Markets." International Monetary Fund.

Häring, Norbert. 1998. "Interjurisdictional Redistribution and Public Goods with Increasing Returns to Scale." *Public Choice* 95: 321–9.

———. 2010. "Der Statistik-Schmu der Amerikaner." *Handelsblatt*, June 4, 6.

Häring, Norbert and Olaf Storbeck. 2006. "Sind Mindestlöhne besser als ihr Ruf?" *Handelsblatt*, March 6.

Hallock, Kevin F. 2009. "Job Loss and the Fraying of the Implicit Employment Contract." *Journal of Economic Perspectives* 23: 69–93.

Harrison, Ann and Jason Scorse. 2010. "Multinationals and Anti-sweatshop Activism." *American Economic Review* 100: 247–73.

Hartwig, Jochen. 2006. "On Spurious Differences in Growth Performance and on the Misuse of National Accounts Data for Governance Purposes." *Review of International Political Economy* 13: 535–58.

———. 2008. "Productivity Growth in Service Industries: Are the Transatlantic Differences Measurement-Driven?" *Review of Income and Wealth* 54: 494–505.

Hatzell, Jay C. and Laura T. Starks. 2002. "Institutional Investors and Executive Compensation." *Journal of Political Economy* 98: 225–63.

Hauser, Frank, Andreas Schubert and Mona Aicher. 2005. "Unternehmenskultur, Arbeitsqualität und Mitarbeiterengagement in den Unternehmen in Deutschland." Research Project Final Report No. 18/05, Federal Ministry of Labour and Social Affairs. http://www.cbdata.de/hv-sales/HVConsult/Abschlu%C3%9FBericht.pdf (accessed May 14, 2012).

Hayes, Rachel M. and Scott Schaefer. 1999. "How Much Are Differences in Managerial Abilities Worth?" *Journal of Accounting and Economics* 27: 125–48.

Heckman, James. 2008. "Rifts Develop within MFI Committee." *Chicago Maroon*, October 17.

Heinrich, Joseph, Robert Boyd, Samuel Bowles, Colin Camerer, Ernst Fehr, Herbert Gintis and Richard McElreath. 2001. "Cooperation, Reciprocity and Punishment in Fifteen Small-Scale Societies." *American Economic Review* 91: 73–8.

Herbertsson, Tryggvi T. and Frederic Mishkin. 2006. *Financial Stability in Iceland.* Rejkyavik: Icelandic Chamber of Commerce.

Heron, Randall A. and Erik Lie. 2007. "Does Backdating Explain the Stock Price Pattern around Executive Stock Option Grants?" *Journal of Financial Economics* 83: 271–95.

———. 2009. "What Fraction of Stock Option Grants to Top Executives Have Been Backdated or Manipulated?" *Management Science* 55: 513–25.

Hicks, John. 1983. *Classics and Moderns: Collected Essays on Economic Theory*, vol. 3. Cambridge, MA: Harvard University Press.

Hicks, John and R. G. D. Allen. 1934. "A Reconsideration of the Theory of Value." *Economica* 1: 196–219.

Hill, Rod and Tony Myatt. 2010. *The Economics Anti-Textbook: A Critical Thinker's Guide to Microeconomics.* Blackpoint: Fernwood.

Holmes, Thomas J. and John Thornton Snider. 2011. "A Theory of Outsourcing and Wage Decline." *American Economic Journal: Macroeconomics* 3: 38–59.

Houseman, Susan. 2007. "Outsourcing, Offshoring, and Productivity Measurement in U.S. Manufacturing." *International Labor Review* 146: 61–80.

Huber, Joseph. 2007. "Der 100%-Ansatz als wegweisende Pionierleistung." Afterword to Irving Fisher, *100%-Money – 100%-Geld*. Kiel: Gauke.

Hwang, Byoung-Hyoun and Kim Seoyoung. 2009. "It Pays to Have Friends." *Journal of Financial Economics* 93: 138–58.

Igan, Deniz, Prachi Mishra and Thierry Tressel. 2009. "A Fistful of Dollars: Lobbying and the Financial Crisis." IMF Working Paper 09/287.

Ivashina, Victoria and Zheng Sun. Forthcoming. "Institutional Stock Trading on Loan Market Information." *Journal of Financial Economics*.

Jensen, Michael C. and Kevin J. Murphy. 1990. "Performance Pay and Top Management Incentives." *Journal of Political Economy* 98: 225–263.

_____. 1990. "CEO Incentives: It's Not How Much You Pay, But How." *Harvard Business Review* 68: 138–53.

Jensen, Michael C. and Kevin J. Murphy with Eric G. Wruck. 2004. "Remuneration: Where We've Been, How We Got to Here, What Are the Problems, and How to Fix Them." European Corporate Governance Institute Working Paper 44/2004.

Johnson, Simon. 2009. "The Quiet Coup." *Atlantic Monthly*, May.

Kaldor, Nicholas. 1939. "Welfare Propositions of Economics and Interpersonal Comparisons of Utility." *Economic Journal* 49: 549–52.

Kang, Qiang and Oscar Mitnik. 2009. "CEO Power and Compensation in Financially Distressed Firms." Working paper.

Kaplan, Herbert H. 2006. *Nathan Mayer Rothschild and the Creation of a Dynasty: The Critical Years, 1806–1816*. Stanford: Stanford University Press.

Kapur, Devesh. 2009. "Academics Have More to Declare Than Their Genius." *Financial Times*, June 24.

Kaufman, Bruce E. 2007. "The Impossibility of a Perfectly Competitive Labor Market." *Cambridge Journal of Economics* 31: 775–87.

_____. 2009. "Labor Law and Employment Regulation: Neoclassical and Institutional Perspectives." In *Elgar Encyclopaedia of Labor and Employment Law and Economics*, ed. Kenneth Dau-Schmidt. London: Edward Elgar.

Kay, Aaron C., S. Christian Wheeler, John A. Bargh and Lee Ross. 2004. "Material Priming: The Influence of Mundane Physical Objects on Situational Construal and Competitive Behavior Choice." *Organizational Behavior and Human Decision Processes* 95: 83–96.

Keen, Steve. 2001/2008. *Debunking Economics: The Naked Emperor of the Social Sciences*. Revised eBook version. London: Zed.

Keen, Steve and Russell Standish. 2006. "Profit Maximization, Industry Structure, and Competition: A Critique of Neoclassical Theory." *Physica A* 370: 81–5.

Keoun, Bradley. 2009a. "Weill to End Citi Consulting Job, Giving Up Millions in Perks." Bloomberg, January 29.

_____. 2009b. "Citi Cost-Cutters Skip Offices, Staff for Ex-CEOs Prince, Reed." Bloomberg, February 17.

King, Michael R. 2009. "Time to Buy or Just Buying Time? The Market Reaction to Bank Rescue Packages." BIS Working Paper 288.

Kirchgässner, Gebhard. 2007. "On the Efficiency of a Public Insurance Monopoly: The Case of Housing Insurance in Switzerland." In *Public Economics and Public*

Choice: Contributions in Honor of Charles B. Blankart, ed. P. Baake and R. Borck. Berlin: Springer.

Korpi, Walter and Joakim Palme. 1998. "The Paradox of Redistribution and Strategies of Equality: Welfare State Institutions, Inequality, and Poverty in the Western Countries." *American Sociological Review* 63 5: 661–87.

KPMG. 2010. "Competitive Alternatives 2010 Special Report: Focus on Tax." http://www.kpmg.com/Global/en/IssuesAndInsights/ArticlesPublications/Documents/Competitive-Alternatives-2010-Focus-on-Tax.pdf (accessed March 28, 2012).

Krueger, Alan B. and Alexandre Mas. 2004. "Strikes, Scabs and Tread Separations: Labor Strife and the Production of Defective Bridgestone/Firestone Tires." *Journal of Political Economy* 112: 253–89.

Kube, Sebastian, Michael André Maréchal and Clemens Puppe. 2008. "The Currency of Reciprocity." Working paper.

Kubik, Jeffrey D. and Harrison G. Hong. 2003. "Analysing the Analysts: Career Concerns and Biased Earnings Forecasts." *Journal of Finance* 58: 313–51.

Kuhnen, Camelia M. and Alexandra Niessen. 2009. "Is Executive Compensation Shaped by Public Attitudes?" Working paper.

Kuhnen, Camelia M. and Jeffrey Zwiebel. 2008. "Executive Pay, Hidden Compensation and Managerial Entrenchment." Working paper.

Laeven, Luc and Fabian Valencia. 2008. "Systemic Banking Crises: A New Database." IMF Working Paper 08/224.

Lattmann, Peter. 2007. "UnitedHealth CEO McGuire Gives Back $620 Million." *Wall Street Journal*, December 7.

Layard, Richard. 2006. *Happiness: Lessons from a New Science.* London: Penguin.

Lazear, Edward P. and Kathryn L. Shaw. 2007. "Personnel Economics: The Economist's View of Human Resources." *Journal of Economic Perspectives* 21: 91–114.

Levine, David I. 1991. "Just-Cause Employment Policies in the Presence of Worker Adverse Selection." *Journal of Labor Economics* 9: 294–305.

Levine, Ross. 2010. "An Autopsy of the U.S. Financial System." NBER Working Paper 15956.

Levy, Frank S. and Peter Temin. Forthcoming. "Inequality and Institutions in 20th Century America." In *Festschrift for Gavin Wright,* ed. Paul Rhode, Joshua Rosenbloom and David Weiman.

Liberman, Varda, Steven Samuels and Lee Ross. 2004. "The Name of the Game: Predictive Power of Reputation vs. Situational Labels in Determining Prisoner's Dilemma Game Moves." *Personality and Social Psychology Bulletin* 30: 1175–85.

Liu, Xiaoding and Jay R. Ritter. 2010. "The Economic Consequences of IPO Spinning." *Review of Financial Studies* 23: 2024–59.

Liu, Crocker and David Yermack. 2008. "Where Are the Shareholders' Mansions? CEOs' Home Purchases, Stock Sales, and Subsequent Company Performance." Working paper.

Maisch, Michael. 2010. "Kein Pardon für britische Insider." *Handelsblatt,* March 16.

Malmendier, Ulrike and Devin Shanthikumar. 2009. "Do Security Analysts Speak in Two Tongues?" NBER Working Paper 13570.

Mankiw, N. Gregory and Mark P. Taylor. 2006. *Economics.* London: Thomson Learning.

Maremont, Mark and Susanne Craig. 2008. "Trading in Deal Stock Triggers Look at Banks." *Wall Street Journal*, January 14.

Massa, Massimo and Zahid Rehman. 2008. "Information Flows within Financial Conglomerates: Evidence from the Banks-Mutual Funds Relationship." *Journal of Financial Economics* 89: 288–306.

Masulis, Ronald W., Cong Wang and Fei Xie. 2007. "Corporate Governance and Acquirer Returns." *Journal of Finance* 62: 1851–89.

Maxwell, Gerald and Ruth E. Ames, 1981. "Economists Free Ride, Does Anyone Else?" *Journal of Public Economics* 15: 295–310.

Mayew, William J. 2008. "Evidence of Management Discrimination among Analysts during Earnings Conference Calls." *Journal of Accounting Research* 46: 627–59.

McCool, Grant. 2009. "Code Theft Could Cost Goldman Millions, U.S. Says." Reuters, July 7.

McGuire, Patrick. 2009. "Bank Ties and Firm Performance in Japan: Some Evidence since FY 2002." BIS Working Paper 272.

McKeown, Timothy J. 2009. "How U.S. Decision-Makers Assessed Their Control of Multilateral Organizations, 1957–1982." *Review of International Organizations* 4: 269–91.

McKinnon, John D. and T. W. Farnam. 2009. "Hedge Fund Paid Summers $5.2 Million in Past Year." *Wall Street Journal*, April 5.

Metcalf, David. 2008. "Why Has the British Minimum Wage Had Little or No Impact on Employment?" *Journal of Industrial Relations* 50: 489–512.

Michaud, Pierre-Carl, Dina Goldman, Darius Lakdawalla, Adam Gailey and Yuhui Zheng. 2009. "International Differences in Longevity and Health and Their Economic Consequences." NBER Working Paper 15235.

Miller, Dale T. and Rebecca K. Ratner. 1998. "The Disparity between the Actual and Assumed Power of Self-Interest." *Journal of Personality & Social Psychology* 74: 53–62.

Minsky, Hyman. 1986. *Stabilizing an Unstable Economy*. New Haven: Yale University Press.

Morgan, Mary. 2001. "The Formation of 'Modern' Economics: Engineering and Ideology." London School of Economics Department of Economic History Working Paper 62/01.

Muller, Karl A. III, Monica Neamtiu and Edward J. Riedl. 2009. "Insider Trading Preceding Goodwill Impairments." Working paper.

Murphy, Kevin J. and Tatiana Sandino. 2010. "Executive Pay and 'Independent' Compensation Consultants." *Journal of Accounting and Economics* 49: 247–62.

Narayanan, M. P. and H. Nejat Seyhun. 2008. "The Dating Game: Do Managers Designate Option Grant Dates to Increase Their Compensation?" *Review of Financial Studies* 21: 1907–45.

Nettels, Curtis P. 1962. *The Emergence of a National Economy 1715–1815*. Armonk: M. E. Sharpe.

Neumark, David and William Waescher. 2000. "Minimum Wages and Employment: A Case Study of the Fast-Food Industry in New Jersey and Pennsylvania: Comment." *American Economic Review* 90: 1362–96.

Nguyen-Dang, Bang. 2008. "Does the Rolodex Matter? Corporate Elite's Small World and the Effectiveness of Boards of Directors." Working paper.

Nguyen-Dang, Bang and Kasper Meisner Nielsen. 2010. "What Death Can Tell: Are Executives Paid for Their Contributions to Firm Value?" Working paper.

OECD. 1994/2004/2007/2008. *OECD Employment Outlook*. Paris.

———. n.d. "Benefits and Wages: OECD Indicators." http://www.oecd.org/ document/3/0,3746,en_2649_33729_39617987_1_1_1_1,00.html. (accessed March 28, 2012).

Olson, Mancur. 1965. *The Logic of Collective Action: Public Goods and the Theory of Groups*. Cambridge, MA: Harvard University Press.

Oreopoulos, Philip, Andrew Heisz and Till von Wachter. 2006. "Short- and Long-Term Career Effects of Graduating in a Recession: Hysteresis and Heterogeneity in the Market for College Graduates." NBER Working Paper 12159.

Oyer, Paul. 2006. "Initial Labor Market Conditions and Long-Term Outcomes for Economists." *Journal of Economic Perspectives* 20: 143–6.

Pager, Devah, Bruce Western and Bart Bonikowski. 2009. "Discrimination in a Low-Wage Labor Market: A Field Experiment." IZA Discussion Paper 4469.

Pareto, Vilfredo. 1906/1971. *Manual of Political Economy*. New York: Augustus M. Kelley.

Parsley, David C. and Mara Faccio. 2009. "Sudden Deaths: Taking Stock of Geographic Ties." *Journal of Financial and Quantitative Analysis* 33: 683–718.

Partnoy, Frank. 1997/2009. *F.I.A.S.C.O.* 2nd ed. London: Profile.

———. 1999. "The Siskel and Ebert of Financial Markets? Two Thumbs Down for the Credit Rating Agencies." *Washington University Law Quarterly* 77: 619–723.

PBS. 2002. "Wall Street Email Trail Overview." http://www.pbs.org/now/politics/ wallstreet.html (accessed March 28, 2012).

Persky, Joseph. 2000. "The Neoclassical Advent: American Economics at the Dawn of the 20th Century." *Journal of Economic Perspectives* 14: 95–108.

Peukert, Helge. 2010. *Die große Finanzmarktkrise: Eine staatswissenschaftlich-finanzsoziologische Untersuchung*. Marburg: Metropolis.

Pew Center of the States. 2009. "One in 100: Behind Bars in America 2008." Washington DC: Pew Charitable Trusts.

Payscale. 2012. "Best Undergrad College Degrees by Salary." http://www.payscale.com/best-colleges/degrees.asp (accessed March 28, 2012).

Pfeffer, Jeffrey. 2007. "Human Resources from an Organizational Behavior Perspective: Some Paradoxes Explained." *Journal of Economic Perspectives* 21: 115–34.

Pfeffer, Jeffrey and Robert I. Sutton. 2006. *Hard Facts, Dangerous Half-Truths and Total Nonsense: Profiting From Evidence-Based Management*. New York: McGraw-Hill.

Phalippou, Ludovic. 2009. "Beware of Venturing into Private Equity." *Journal of Economic Perspectives* 23: 147–66.

Piketty, Thomas. 1997. "The Dynamics of the Wealth Distribution and the Interest Rate with Credit Rationing." *Review of Economic Studies* 64: 173–89.

Piketty, Thomas and Emmanuel Saez. 2006. "The Evolution of Top Incomes: A Historical and International Perspective." *American Economic Review* 96: 200–205.

Piore, Michael J. and Peter Doeringer. 1971. *Internal Labor Markets and Manpower Adjustment*. Lexington: Heath and Company.

Prasch, Robert E. 1999. "American Economists in the Progressive Era on the Minimum Wage." *Journal of Economic Perspectives* 13: 221–30.

Pulliam, Susan, Kate Kelly and Carrick Mollenkamp. 2010. "Hedge Funds Are Ganging up on Weaker Euro." *Wall Street Journal*, February 26.

Rajan, Raghuram and Rodney Ramcharan. 2008. "Landed Interests and Financial Underdevelopment." NBER Working Paper 14347.

Reinert, Erik S. 2007. *How Rich Countries Got Rich …and Why Poor Countries Stay Poor.* London: Constable.

Ritter, Jay R. 2008. "Forensic Finance." *Journal of Economic Perspectives* 22: 127–47.

Robbins, Lionel. 1935. *Essay on the Nature and Significance of Economic Science.* 2nd ed. London: Macmillan.

———. 1981. "Economics and Political Economy." *American Economic Review, Papers and Proceedings* 71: 1–10.

Robinson, Joan. 1933. *The Economics of Imperfect Competition.* London: Macmillan.

Rose, Nikolas. 1991. "Governing By Numbers: Figuring Out Democracy." *Accounting, Organizations and Society* 16.7: 673–92.

Rothbard, Murray N. 1985/2008. *The Mystery of Banking.* 2nd ed. Auburn: Ludwig von Mises Institute. http://mises.org/books/mysteryofbanking.pdf (accessed March 28, 2012).

Rupert, Peter, Elena Stancanelli and Etienne Wasmer. 2009. "Commuting, Wages and Bargaining Power." *Annales d'Economie et de Statistique* 95–6: 201–21.

Sachverständigenrat zur Begutachtung der gesamtwirtschaftlichen Entwicklung. 2004/2005/2006. *Jahresgutachten.* Wiesbaden.

Salas, Jesus M. 2010. "Entrenchment, Governance, and the Stock Price Reaction to Sudden Executive Deaths." *Journal of Banking and Finance* 34: 656–66.

Salerno, Joseph. 2008. "Foreword." In Murray N. Rothbard, *The Mystery of Banking.* 2nd ed. Auburn: Ludwig von Mises Institute.

Sanderson, Rachel. 2011. "Italian Banks Lobby to Tap into Surging Gold Prices." *Financial Times*, March 1.

Saunder, Francis S. 1999. *Who Paid the Piper? The CIA and the Cultural Cold War.* Cambridge: Granta.

Schmitt, John and Ben Zipperer. 2006. "Is the U.S. a Good Model for Reducing Social Exclusion in Europe?" *Post-autistic Economics Review* 40: 1–17.

Schmitt, Rick. 2009. "Prophet and Loss." *Stanford Magazine*, March/April. http://www.stanfordalumni.org/news/magazine/2009/marapr/features/born.html (accessed March 28, 2012).

Schmitz, James A. Jr. 2005. "What Determines Productivity? Lessons from the Dramatic Recovery of the U.S. and Canadian Iron Ore Industries Following Their Early 1980s Crisis." *Journal of Political Economy* 113: 582–625.

Schmitz, Patrick. 2004. "Job Protection Laws and Agency Problems under Asymmetric Information." *European Economic Review* 48: 1027–46.

Schularick, Moritz and Alan M. Taylor. 2009. "Credit Booms Gone Bust: Monetary Policy, Leverage Cycles and Financial Crises, 1870–2008." NBER Working Paper 15512.

Schumpeter, Joseph. 1943/2003. *Capitalism, Socialism and Democracy.* London: George Allen and Unwin.

Screpanti, Ernesto and Stefano Zamagni. 1993. *An Outline of the History of Economic Thought.* Oxford: Clarendon Press.

Scruggs, Lyle and James P. Allan. 2006. "The Material Consequences of Welfare States: Benefit Generosity and Absolute Poverty in 16 OECD Countries." *Comparative Political Studies* 39: 880–904.

Sender, Henry. 2009. "Galleon Hedge Fund Paid Wall Street Banks Lavish Fees for Secret Market Data." *Financial Times*, October 29.

Shapiro, Carl and Varian, Hal. 1999. *Information Rules: Strategic Guide to the Network Economy*. Harvard Business School Press.

SIGTARP. 2009. "Factors Affecting Efforts to Limit Payments to AIG Counterparties." Report of the Office of the Inspector General for the Troubled Asset Relief Program, 17 November. http://www.sigtarp.gov/reports/audit/2009/Factors_Affecting_Efforts_to_Limit_Payments_to_AIG_Counterparties.pdf (accessed March 28, 2012).

Simon, Zoltan. 2009. "Soros Fund Fined $2.2 Million by Hungarian Regulator." Bloomberg, March 27.

Smeeding, Timothy M. 2005. "Public Policy, Economic Inequality, and Poverty: The United States in Comparative Perspective." *Social Science Quarterly* 86: 955–83.

Smith, Adam. 1776/2007. *An Inquiry into the Nature and Causes of the Wealth of Nations*. Ed. Sálvio M. Soares. MetaLibri, 2007, v.1.0p. http://metalibri.wikidot.com/title:an-inquiry-into-the-nature-and-causes-of-the-wealth-of (accessed March 28, 2012).

Sonik, Sara and David Hemenway. 1998. "Is More Always Better? A Survey on Positional Concerns." *Journal of Economic Behavior and Organization* 37: 373–83.

Soros, George. 2008/2009. "The Crisis and What to Do About It." In *Crash – Why It Happened and What to Do About It*, ed. Edward Fullbrook, 71–7. http://www.paecon.net/CRASH-1.pdf (accessed March 28, 2012).

Sraffa, Piero. 1926. "The Laws of Returns under Competitive Conditions." *Economic Journal* 36: 535–50.

Steele, J. Michael. 2005. "Darrell Huff and Fifty Years of How to Lie with Statistics." *Statistical Science* 20.3: 205–9.

Stiglitz, Joseph E. 2001. "Information and the Change in the Paradigm of Economics." Nobel Prize Lecture, 8 December. http://classes.maxwell.syr.edu/ecn611/stiglitz-lecture.pdf (accessed March 28, 2012).

Stiglitz, Joseph E., Jean-Paul Fitoussi and Amartya Sen. 2009. "Report by the Commission on the Measurement of Economic Performance and Social Progress." Available from www.stiglitz-sen-fitoussi.fr.

Stone, Katherine V. W. 2011. "John R. Commons and the Origins of Legal Realism; or, the Other Tragedy of the Commons." In *Transformations in American Legal History*, vol. 2, ed. D. Hamilton and A. A. Brophy. Cambridge, MA: Harvard University Press.

Struve, Anja. 2005. "Berlin verspielt Kredit." *Die Welt*, September 27.

Syverson, Chad. 2004. "Market Structure and Productivity: A Concrete Example." *Journal of Political Economy* 112: 1181–1222.

_____. 2010. "What Determines Productivity?" NBER Working Paper 15712.

Tabbi, Matt. 2009. "The Great American Bubble Machine." *Rolling Stone*, July 9.

Towers Perrin. 2008. "Towers Perrin Global Workforce Study 2007–2008." http://www.towerswatson.com/global-workforce-study/reports (accessed March 15, 2012).

Tullock, Gordon. 1976. *The Vote Motive*. London: Institute for Economic Affairs.

UNICEF. 2007. "Child Poverty in Perspective: An Overview of Child Well-being in Rich Countries." Innocenti Report Card 7. http://www.unicef-irc.org/publications/pdf/rc7_eng.pdf (accessed March 28, 2012).

Vekshin, Alison. 2009. "Citigoup Chiefs to Defend Pay, Lending With U.S. Aid." Bloomberg, February 11.

Von Wachter, Till and Stefan Bender. 2006. "In the Right Place at the Wrong Time: The Role of Firms and Luck in Young Workers' Careers." American Economic Review 96: 1679–1705.

———. 2008. "Do Initial Conditions Persist Between Firms? An Analysis of Firm-Entry Cohort Effects and Job Losers Using Matched Employer-Employee Data." In The Analysis of Firms and Employees: Quantitative and Qualitative Approaches, ed. S. Bender, J. Lane, K. Shaw, F. Andersson and T. von Wachter. Chicago: University of Chicago Press.

Von Wieser, Friedrich. 1924. Theorie der gesellschaftlichen Wirtschaft. Tübingen: Verlag von J.C.B. Mohr (Paul Siebeck).

Ward, Michael. 2004. Quantifying the World: UN Ideas and Statistics, Bloomington: Indiana University Press.

Warwick Commission. 2009. "In Praise of Unlevel Playing Fields." Warwick University. http://www2.warwick.ac.uk/research/warwickcommission/news/147in_praise_of/ (accessed March 28, 2012).

Werner, Richard A. 2007. Neue Wirtschaftspolitik: Was Europa aus Japans Fehlern lernen kann. Munich: Vahlen.

Westphal, James D. and Michael B. Clement. 2008. "Sociopolitical Dynamics in Relations between Top Managers and Security Analysts: Favor Rendering, Reciprocity, and Analyst Stock Recommendations." Academy of Management Journal 51: 873–97.

Westphal, James D. and Poonam Khanna. 2003. "Keeping Directors in Line: Social Distancing as a Control Mechanism in the Corporate Elite." Administrative Science Quarterly 48: 361–98.

Westphal, James D. and Ithai Stern. 2006. "The Other Pathway to the Boardroom: Interpersonal Influence Behavior as a Substitute for Elite Credentials and Majority Status in Obtaining Board Appointments." Administrative Science Quarterly 51: 169–204.

Whigton, David and Ben White. 2007. "Merrill Lynch Allows O'Neal to Retire with a Package of $160m." Financial Times, October 31.

White, Lawrence J. 2010. "The Credit Rating Agencies." Journal of Economic Perspectives 24: 211–26.

Woolner, Anne. 2009. "Weill, Prince, O'Neal Are Gone Except for Perks." Bloomberg, February 18.

Xie, Ye. 2010. "Goldman Sachs Hands Clients Losses in 'Top Trades.'" Bloomberg, May 19.

World Health Organization. 2004. World Health Organization Disability-Adjusted Life Year statistics. Available from http://www.who.int/healthinfo/global_burden_disease/estimates_country/en/index.html

Yam, Joseph C. K. 2000. "Capital Flows, Hedge Funds and Market Failure: A Hong Kong Perspective." In Capital Flows and the International Financial System, ed. David Gruen and Luke Gower, 164–79. Adelaide: J.S. McMillan Printing Group.

Yermack, David. 1997. "Good Timing: CEO Stock Option Awards and Company News Announcements." *Journal of Finance* 52: 449–76.

_____. 2006. "Flights of Fancy: Corporate Jets, CEO Perquisites, and Inferior Shareholder Returns." *Journal of Financial Economics* 80: 211–42.

_____. 2006a. "Golden Handshakes: Separation Pay for Retired and Dismissed CEOs." *Journal of Accounting and Economics* 41: 237–56.

Zheng, Liu and Xiaming Zhou. 2009. "Executive Stock Options and the Manipulated Stock-Price Performance: Evidence from Retiring CEOs." Working paper.

Zingales, Luigi. 2009. "The Future of Securities Regulation." *Journal of Accounting Research* 47: 391–426.

INDEX